Success in Sight: Visioning

D0878072

■ SMART STRATEGIES SERIES ■

Success in Sight: Visioning

Edited by

Andrew P. Kakabadse

Frédéric Nortier

and

Nello-Bernard Abramovici

INTERNATIONAL THOMSON BUSINESS PRESS
I(T)P® An International Thomson Publishing Company

London • Bonn • Boston • Johannesburg • Madrid • Melbourne • Mexico City • New York • Paris
• Singapore • Tokyo • Toronto • Albany, NY • Belmont, CA • Cincinnati, OH • Detroit, MI

HD57.7
.S833
1998

Success In Sight: Visioning

Copyright © 1998 International Thomson Publishing

 A division of International Thomson Publishing Inc.
The ITP logo is a trademark under licence

All rights reserved. No part of this work which is copyright may be reproduced or used in any form or by any means – graphic, electronic, or mechanical, including photocopying, recording, taping or information storage and retrieval systems – without the written permission of the Publisher, except in accordance with the provisions of the Copyright Designs and Patents Act 1988.

Whilst the Publisher has taken all reasonable care in the preparation of this book the Publisher makes no representation, express or implied, with regard to the accuracy of the information contained in this book and cannot accept any legal responsibility or liability for any errors or omissions from the book or the consequences thereof.

Products and services that are referred to in this book may be either trademarks and/or registered trademarks of their respective owners. The Publisher/s and Author/s make no claim to these trademarks.

British Library Cataloguing-in-Publication Data
A catalogue record for this book is available from the British Library

First published 1998 by International Thomson Business Press

Typeset by MHL Typesetting Limited, Coventry
Printed in the UK by TJ International, Padstow, Cornwall

ISBN 1-86152-160-X

International Thomson Business Press
Berkshire House
168–173 High Holborn
London WC1V 7AA
UK

http://www.itbp.com

Contents

List of contributors

Andrew P. Kakabadse *BSc, MA, PhD, AAPSW, CPsychol, FBPS, FIAM, FRSA, MBPS*

Professor of International Management Development
Chairman of the Human Resources Network
Director of the Cranfield Centre for International Management Development
Vice Chancellor, International Academy of Management
Visiting Professor, Hangzhou University, China
Fellow of the International Academy of Management
Fellow of the British Psychological Society
Member of the Advisory Board of Sunningdale Civil Service College

Andrew P. Kakabadse worked in the health and social services field, and from there undertook various consultancy assignments concerned with local government reorganization and on large capital projects in developing countries. He is currently consultant to numerous organizations ranging from banks, motor manufacturers, high-tech companies, oil companies, police and other public sector organizations, and numerous multinational corporations. He has consulted and lectured in the UK, Europe, USA, South East Asia, Gulf States and Australia.

His current areas of interest focus on improving the performance of top executives and top executive teams, excellence in consultancy practice, and the politics of decision making. He is also the director of the Cranfield Centre for International Management Development and chairman of the Human Resources Network.

He has published 18 books, 12 monographs and 104 articles, including the best-selling books *Politics of Management*, *Working in Organisations* and *The Wealth Creators*. He holds positions on the boards of a number of companies and is external examiner to several universities. He is joint editor of the *Journal of Management Development*, is the previous editor of the *Journal of Managerial Psychology* and associate editor of the

Leadership and Organisation Development Journal. He has also been adviser to a Channel 4 Business Series.

Frédéric Nortier

Frédéric Nortier, with a Masters Degree in Economics from University Louis Pasteur, Strasbourg, France, and an MBA from Université Laval, Quebec, Canada, is fluent in French, English and German and a practising neuro-linguistic programme consultant. He is currently senior consultant with ARJ SA, Lyon, France and has been with the firm for over seven years. He has consulted with a wide number of organizations in the areas of visioning, top executive coaching, leadership development, team building and transitional management. He has published a number of articles, including a recent article on managing transitions in the *Journal of Management Development* and was previously head of the management training department of Association Interprofessionnel de la Formation Continue Calvados, Cannes, France.

Nello Bernard Abramovici

Nello Bernard Abramovici was educated at the University of Lyon and is fluent in French, English and German. He is chief executive officer of Groupe ARJ and has been with his present organization for 16 years. He consults with a wide number of clients in the areas of leadership, top executive coaching, senior team building, strategic HR development, managing change and growing international businesses. He is a certified trainer in Euro-linguistic programming and holds membership on a number of professional bodies. He is an accomplished writer and, as Professor, holds positions at the Ecole Supérieure de Commerce de Lyon. He has been managing director of a retail company and has been both senior consultant and regional managing director of PA Consultants, France.

Philip Davies

Philip Davies is a Lecturer in Strategic Management at Cranfield School of Management in England. He studied Modern History at Exeter College, Oxford and holds an MBA from Cranfield. Prior to joining Cranfield he was a serving officer in the British Army, specializing in strategic intelligence. He is researching the relationship between the social networks of senior executives and strategy processes. He also acts as a strategy consultant and co-directs the strategic consulting programme on the MBA programme.

Mike Jeans

Mike Jeans led the development, over two years, of KPMG's global change management approach based upon academic research coupled with the experience of KPMG field consultants. He has been a practising consultant for over 25 years. He is also a non-executive director of Ross Group Plc, and an independent business adviser to the Planning Inspectorate.

Mike Jeans holds a BA from the University of Bristol, and is a Chartered Accountant, Chartered Management Accountant, Certified Management Consultant, and a member of the Institute of Management Services. In 1996 he was awarded an Honorary MBA from Cranfield University.

Nada Korac-Kakabadse *BSc, MPA, PhD, Grad Dip Mgt Services*

Nada Korac-Kakabadse is currently a senior research fellow in the Information Systems Department at the Cranfield School of Management where, together with the management development research team, she undertook a comprehensive study of leadership at senior service level, Federal Government of Australia.

Previously, she was employed as a senior information technology officer with the Australian Public Service's Department of Employment, Education and Training. In the role of innovation director, Nada led a research and development team which attracted a multimillion dollar budget which affected the work of 16,500 employees and their 300,000 service providers.

Her other activities in government have included liaison across other agencies and chairing and participating in a number of committees, and coaching others in improving job performance.

Her work with the international organization, Alfa-Leval and with the Canadian Federal Government, Department of External Affairs and Trade, in management positions, provided her with opportunities of working within a variety of cultures in Europe, the Middle East, Canada and North Africa.

Her research interests include: the strategic use of information systems; management best practice, organizational design; strategic decision support systems; and vulnerability.

She has published two books, one monograph and numerous articles.

Andrew Myers *BSc (Hons)*

Andrew Myers currently works as an independent consultant, specializing in attitude, behaviour, opinion and culture surveys.

After completing a degree in Geography and Statistics, he went on to spend several years at Cranfield School of Management as a researcher. At Cranfield, he was involved in a number of research projects, specializing in survey design, to include preliminary research, questionnaire design and sampling. He was also involved in the analysis and write-up of the research, some of which was subsequently published in academic and practitioner articles.

Stephen P. Colloff

Stephen Colloff is a Visiting Fellow at Cranfield School of Management where his research interests are in the differences top business leaders make in renewing companies. In previous jobs as vice-president of personnel for ICL International, and then as director of personnel development for British Railways Board, he has had direct involvement in change and renewal.

Lola I. Okazaki-Ward *BA MPhil, Fil, PGGE*

Lola Okazaki-Ward has a BA from Nottingham and an MPhil from Sheffield, and is research fellow at Cranfield School of Management specializing in Japanese management at board level since 1992. Having worked in a European subsidiary of a Japanese company for two years as its European Liaison Officer in the mid-1980s, she began researching on management education and training in Japan whilst at Warwick University. She carried on with this research at Stirling University, and finally published a book on the subject in 1993. At Cranfield, she has been working with Andrew Kakabadse on the management behaviour of Japanese business leaders and co-authored a book, *Japanese Business Leaders*, in 1996. She is currently researching on the issues of corporate governance in Japan.

A.L. Buley *MA DPhil*

Tony Buley has spent most of his career as a senior executive and consultant responsible for education and development policies and programmes in progressive blue-chip companies such as Unilever, ICL, GKN and most recently Bass PLC where he was the Group's adviser and executive head of Organisation and Management Development. He is now an independent consultant and writer and a Director of MLI Ltd, advising clients on the design of integrated learning strategies as a key component of overall business strategy.

List of figures

List of tables

Introduction

At a reunion dinner, a CEO of a well-known company and a good friend from the past we had not seen for quite a while, entered into deep conversation about the challenges of leading change.

'It really is not easy (i.e. leading change) and what's more you not only have to be resilient, but also have to win hearts and minds and also make sure that the people you have won over stay with you,' he commented. He continued, 'the way I started winning people's attention and enthusiasm for change in my last company, was unusual. The way I got my team to go with me, who really were not very cohesive, was through painting. In order to move forward as a company, we had to have a vision we shared. For me to hold the vision would have split the team further. So what we did was paint our vision. We sat together and painted. Everybody thought we were crazy, but what happened was that we put our ideas and feelings onto canvas and then explained to our colleagues what the pictures meant. Soon we were enthralled and the more we painted, the more we became hooked, the more we listened, the more we appreciated, the more we shared.'

'Did any of you paint prior to this?' he was asked. 'No,' he replied, 'we hired a professional art teacher to help us use water colours and oils, but most of all to help us translate what we thought and experienced onto canvas.'

He described how relationships became more trusting as each senior manager entered into even greater detailed explanation of their work of art. As trust was enhanced, dialogue became more robust. As colleagues spoke more openly, deeply hidden, but known issues, emerged.

'We really got to a point where we could really see where to go, how to get there, supported by a clear statement of purpose, mission and values. We were so proud of our progress and work, that we devoted one office as an art gallery, open to all staff and management. The very best paintings, however, were exhibited throughout the company. You know how we then progressed as a business, with such positive results that attracted wide public acclaim.'

However, his story was not over. 'As you know, things have not worked out so well in my present company. I tried the same approach and was just publicly laughed at, in fact humiliated. Embarking on a journey of fundamental shifts in company culture, structure and direction with this painting thing almost destroyed my credibility. I really had to backtrack. In fact, despite improvements which most recognize are down to me, I've still not made the impact I should. I wonder if I ever will?'

Interesting man, our friend: risk taker, wealthy socialite, well spoken, widely read and opinionated. His comments of an individual vision needing to be shared by senior colleagues and communicated through the organization and the fact that what may work in one organization does not guarantee success in another, echoes the sentiments of so many top managers we have met. The process of visioning is highly likely to draw to the surface contrasting sentiments, ranging from the particulars of an individual to the reactions and deeply shared feelings of people in groups. The peculiarities of any one organization requires such a distinct approach, that it is possible that little or no learning can be transferred to another.

The range of views, sentiments and experiences expressed by our CEO friend are captured and discussed in the contributions to this book. This ten-chapter text of edited papers begins in Chapter 1, with an overview of the current learning of the topics of vision, visioning and leadership. A literature review examination of the concept of vision from Moses to the present day offers insights as to how leaders can raise themselves to the vision they desire, a point which beckons the necessity for an examination of the visioning process. Chapter 1 highlights that modern-day writers, as well as those throughout the ages, emphasize that attention to the process of visioning is crucial to the effective pursuit of a vision. It is emphasized just how much attention needs to be given to the need to attain a 'visioning culture', whereby promoting positive values and attitudes in the top team, and paying attention to and being responsive to the nurturing of key stakeholders, are vital considerations. In effect, attaining high-quality dialogue, crucial to effective visioning, promotes visions that count.

Promoting that high-quality dialogue cannot be achieved unless attention is given to understanding leadership, concludes Chapter 1, and in so doing, provides the bridge into Chapter 2, which examines the nature of leadership from a historical perspective. Fundamental to

Chapter 2, is the addressing of the question of whether leaders are born or made and a dip into history and philosophy highlights that 'leaders are made', a strongly held opinion of historians, philosophers, psychologists and social commentators.

On the basis that the weight of evidence emphasizes that visions emerge through man's discourse with his or her fellow, and that all are blessed with the potential to envisage and pursue their dream, if they so desire, Chapter 3 provides a practical guide of how to embark on a vision process, bearing in mind the intricacies of particular contexts in organizations. The learning points emphasized in Chapter 3, backed by 'real-life' case examples, offer a step-by-step guide through the processes of visioning to the ultimate goal of emerging with a vision which the staff and management in the organization can identify with and be excited by.

Whereas Chapter 3 begins by highlighting the damage that can ensue in not positively pursuing a vision, Chapter 4 discusses how clearly thought through visions can be rejected. In effect, Chapter 4 emphasizes the necessity for attention to *process*, namely, how people go about doing their work, rather than *content*, namely, their work and their goals. Delightfully entitled, The Cassandra Complex, from the mythologies of ancient Greece, whereby Apollo gave Cassandra the gift to foretell but also the curse of never being believed, Chapter 4 emphasizes that an understanding and management of networks, is vital to the process of buy-in. Similar to other papers in this book, practical limits to appreciating the nature of and effectively working within different networks, are provided.

On a more practical basis, Chapter 5 discusses work developed at KPMG, one of the big six audit/consultancy practices, to generate practically visions that work. Based on work undertaken within the area of forecasting the need for more fundamental change through the adoption of the Sigmoid Curve analysis, Chapter 5 emphasizes the approach adopted by one of the world's major consultancies to visioning and change management. Chapter 5 concludes by highlighting that so much depends on the culture of the organization, and in so doing indicates how to work effectively within different cultures.

Taking this lead, the next three chapters adopt a pragmatic case study approach to culture and working issues through different cultures. The study of National Health Service (NHS) Trusts, highlighted in Chapter 6, examines the culture and leadership nature of health service organizations in the UK. Further, Chapters 7 and 8, discuss case study examples of how particular leaders have turned around dying organizations or grown competent organizations to become world leaders. The case of Lord Shepherd's renewal of an already successful organization, Grand Metropolitan, is backed by the interesting analysis of the turnaround of the ailing Toray Industries.

Having examined how visioning has been made to work, Chapter 9 emphasizes how learning during the process of visioning is a critical consideration. Depending on why a vision has been embarked upon and the nature of the vision being pursued, the learning process of how to turn a desire into reality, is considered in Chapter 9.

Finally, Chapter 10, supporting the points made in the previous chapters, provides also a note of caution as to the limits of visioning. The authors identify the traps top managers can fall into, once having embarked on a journey of pursuing a vision. The key points made in this chapter truly capture the underlying themes of this book, namely the power that is inherent in well-directed sentiment, the need to pay attention to process and how visions that succeed have, ultimately, to be pragmatic in nature.

Andrew P. Kakabadse
Frédéric Nortier
Nello-Bernard Abramovici

CHAPTER ONE

Vision, visionary leadership and the visioning process: an overview

Nada Korac-Kakabadse and Andrew P. Kakabadse

Introduction

Generating a vision for an organization is held to be important, because from that platform the enterprise is helped to model strategic plans and provide a kind of touchstone for goal setting (Allen, 1995). An effective vision is considered to be one which defines ways into the future, and is even more worthy if it allows for a flexibility of means to attain the vision. Increasingly, organizations are making visioning an integral part of their strategic planning process. Many successful examples of visioning can be found in the electronics industry which is shifting its priorities, communicating its view of the future and influencing other industries and society at large. For example, space exploration, such as the Apollo series, from October 1968 through to July 1975, with a landing on the moon, the Galileo mission to Jupiter, and the Voyager 1 and 2 missions, were only possible because scientists had the ability and technology to predict, with accuracy, the position of the moon and other planets at some future date, and in the last-mentioned case, some years ahead. Taking advantage of a rare geometric arrangement of the outer planets, namely Jupiter, Saturn, Uranus and Neptune, which occurs about every 175 years, this foresight allowed Voyager to swing from one planet to the next without the need for large on-board propulsion systems.

Notwithstanding that the current management literature overwhelmingly suggests that organizations cannot see far ahead without having a clear, well-established and mutually agreed vision, it could be argued that executives always had visions for their organizations, but whether these visions were shared is another matter. What has become apparent in the last decade is that even the most successful organizations were amazed at their own lack of agreement concerning the corporate vision. Research shows (Kakabadse, 1991; Kakabadse and Korac-Kakabadse, 1996; Kakabadse et al., 1996) that top managers may not be sufficiently aware that they are running in different directions. Some top executives seem to have their vision, a desired end, confused with goals and objectives and the manner by which to get there (Allen, 1995). Others, owing to the nature of structural and interpersonal relations within the enterprise, exhibit a split of vision, resulting in each part of the organization pursuing somewhat different visions, and ultimately different goals (Kakabadse, 1991).

This chapter posits that for organizations to be effective, their top management needs better to understand the visioning process, and equally importantly, to develop its leadership in effective visioning, vision communication and sharing, as well as following through an implementation. A clarification of various visioning concepts, supported by an overview of current visionary leadership literature, is presented. Some real-life examples are also provided as illustrations of successful visioning. Further, the visioning process is reviewed and six key elements of vision are identified and addressed, followed by an overview of two vision-communication strategies – selling the vision, and buying into the vision. In conclusion, a common thread between the theoretical and practical perspectives is identified.

Exploring the concept of vision

One view of vision is that it is about possibilities, desired futures, and expresses optimism and hope and, in so doing, it has been defined as a 'pre-analytic cognitive act' (Schumpeter, 1954: 41) or as 'the sense or feeling of an individual a priori to the constraint of a theory' or agenda (Sowell, 1987: 14). Vision constitutes partly the sensing, by an individual, of what an organization or system should look like and/or how it works, and partly how this working organization is to be taken into the future. As such, visions are based on a web of beliefs, both supported and mediated by each individual's personal values and beliefs, with the ever-present possibility of different players promoting alternative visions. It has been forcefully argued (Sowell, 1987), that visions play an important role in both developing initial insights and relying on influencing the ultimate choices that are made by individuals from the alternative options that evolve.

Biblical and historical leaders all appeared to have and, thereby, followed a vision. Moses had a vision that he would lead his people out of bondage. Alexander the Great had a vision for expanding Macedonia through Asia Minor. Mahatma Gandhi had the dream of an independent India, whilst Martin Luther King, Jr., an admirer of Gandhi's philosophy, had a 'dream' (vision) of an America in which there were equal rights for all peoples. Nelson Mandela, like Moses and Martin Luther King, had a vision of delivering his people from the bondage of apartheid into a South Africa driven by equal rights.

Early research into the ability to think into the future was conducted by Jaques (1968) who focused upon the concept of time, in the sense of identifying the period of time during which a person could be left alone to determine his/her level of performance in his/her job without direct intervention from a supervisor, and equating that period of time with that individual's capability. Paskins (1985) confirmed Jaques' (1968) early work and suggested that managers higher up in the hierarchy had wider planning horizons availed to them by virtue of the role they held, than had those managers at lower levels (Paskins, 1997). The work of Jaques (1968) and Paskins (1985) raises an interesting question, namely, whether people with an innate ability to think into the future are more likely to be successful, or that seeming success is driven by role opportunities, in that people higher up in an organization have the opportunity and freedom to pursue their discretionary decisions over wider/broader planning horizons. Even Moses, it is written, had 40 years of freedom to pursue his vision, which endured many challenges.

Switching from time-related discretion to prescription, Nietsche used the metaphor of viewing the overall reality through different windows (Kaufman, 1950: 610), whilst other scholars define ultimate reality itself as a perspective (Ortega y Gasset, 1961: 45). The perspective viewpoint proposes that every choice involves a certain way of looking at, and thereby imposing an order on, that which is perceived (Ortega y Gasset, 1961) and as such enacts reality (Weick, 1969). For example, every social interaction can be perceived either in purely conflictual or purely idealistic visions, or any combination of these two extremes. Each individual will have his or her own perceptions of an interaction. These visions are, indeed, alternative 'windows' to the world – an expression often quoted by Margaret Thatcher in her public appearances. However, the process by which individuals choose from such windows of opportunity remains predominantly mysterious and individualistic, as vision implicitly involves matters of structure, authority and resources, all of which involve power, status and personal ambitions (Senge, 1990a; 1990b).

Sowell (1987) defines two extremes of vision, which he terms 'constrained' and 'unconstrained'. He argues that there exists a fundamental conflict between these two polarities. Sowell's (1987) 'unconstrained' vision is based on the work of Godwin's (1976) *Enquiry Concerning Political Justice,* where the essence of individual virtue is seen to be the intention to benefit others. The underlying assumption is that man is fully capable of placing the interest of others before his personal desires, and of acting consistently with respect to this priority, even though personal desire occasionally may dominate (Sowell, 1987). The 'unconstrained' interpretation of vision, advanced by Rousseau (1967) and adopted by the French during the Revolution, which ended in persecution, and in the dictatorship of Napoleon Bonaparte, has evolved into a perspective referred to as 'constructivist rationalism' (Eggertsson, 1995) with its roots in the writings of Condorcet (1785), Arrow (1951; 1967; 1983), Rousseau (1953), Galbraith (1967), Marx (1975; 1976), Godwin (1976), and Descartes (1991). 'Constrained' vision refers to the modification of a vision through mechanisms which individuals choose to experience or are coerced to experience through human action and/or institutions (Buchman, 1975). Institutions either evolve without conscious design or are shaped and formed by boundedly rational individuals which, Condorcet (1785) argues, narrows and corrupts human nature. Individuals act, whether separately or in combination, in ways bounded by assumptions or values derived from the past. 'Constrained' vision has evolved into a perspective referred to as 'methodological individualism' (Eggertsson, 1995), based on the work of Smith (1776; 1790), Hayek (1937; 1945), Buchman (1954; 1975), Hume (1967), and Locke (1971).

Peter Murray (1997) argues along the lines of Condorcet (1785), namely, that human nature is not constrained inherently, but rather tends to be narrowed through the education system and other socialization processes. He argues that vision is a creative process and a pre-analytical state. However, because of the Platonic dialectic analysis influence inherent in Western education (the Platonic 'curse'), actors are trained to construct vision only through an analysis and design process. That is, by analysing a current situation and defining current problems and identifying possible solutions, rather than by designing a vision which comprises a situation that has eliminated current problems.

Murray's (1997) argument is that Western training prevents creative or 'unconstrained' visioning, and thus focuses on visioning by analysis and design, where vision evolves through the process of *noxiants* elimination, and decisions are made to discard undesirable courses of action. Thus, each decision that receives an outcome of 'yes' may well imply a series of 'no's. In effect, the avoidance-of-noxiants (anything undesirable/unwholesome) approach may underpin much of the visioning process (Murray, 1997). The study of biblical and historical characters (even those of a pre-Platonic era) supports Murray's (1997) views, as they reveal that great visions were created by the elimination of undesired elements of realities. It is not only Alexander the Great, who was particularly influenced by Platonic thoughts that constructed his vision based on the desire not to be overtaken by others thus expanding his territory by invading others, but also others such as Mahatma Gandhi, Martin Luther King, Jr. and Nelson Mandela who all appear to exhibit design by avoidance of noxiants. Even the admirable visions of Moses were constructed only after he understood his origins and context, and the desire for elimination of the noxiants. Morgan (1986) suggests that principles of avoiding noxiants to define space or action in an evolving manner can be found in a range of events spanning from the Ten Commandments to contemporary legal systems. Senge (1990b), also sees vision as an ongoing process of noxiant elimination and modifications. However, Murray (1997) argues that artists can overcome the socially constricted bias for analysis and design and can express 'unconstrained' vision in their views and works.

For Senge (1990b) vision is about a 'creative tension', which emerges from seeing clearly where one wishes to be, one's 'vision', and facing the truth about one's 'current reality'. The gap between the two generates a natural tension (Senge, 1990b). In order to be motivating, a vision needs to challenge organizational actors, as a vision which is easily attainable is unlikely to motivate (Covey, 1990). Learning how to use this creative tension and the energy it produces can help individuals, groups and organizations move steadily/reliably towards their vision (Senge, 1990b).

For some, vision is that perfect state that might never be reached, but which one never stops trying to achieve (Latham, 1995). For example, the inventor of the giant electronic network for Planet Earth, the World Wide Web (WWW), Tim Berners-Lee, had a vision of the networked Web as an organic expanse of collaboration between families, workplace, groups, schools, towns, companies, the nation, the planet; making things work smoothly at all these levels as well as between them, like a neural connection between the 'individual brain' and the 'social brain' (Wright, 1997), perhaps an 'unconstrained' vision. Although Berners-Lee has not yet achieved his dream, and has compromised his original design of 'browser-editor' (search and edit facility) to 'browser' (search) only, in order to bring technical harmony to the Web, he is still working on his vision. As the software evolves to higher capabilities and standards, the WWW will start to follow the technological lines Berners-Lee originally envisioned (Wright, 1997).

Distinguishing vision and mission

Although an organization's vision and mission are similar and are often difficult to distinguish, they differ in subtle ways. The basic difference between mission and vision is that 'a mission speaks for the purpose of the organization and a vision describes what the organization will look like in achieving its mission' (Rhinesmith, 1993: 91). Vision is a 'shape' of the future that an individual or group desires. Mission includes the broad objectives of the organization, considerably subsuming long-term vision (Rhinesmith, 1993: 91). In addition to a set of goals, vision also comprises a set of ambitions that once internalized by actors, creates a powerful intrinsic motivation to work in that direction (Javidon, 1991). Thus, a vision expresses optimism and hope about possibilities and desired futures (Rhinesmith, 1993). In a way, vision acts as a clearing agent in that, in a world of tensions driven by conflicting interpretations, it clears openings for opportunity (Heidegger, 1977). Khan (1995: 23) positions that 'vision is a basic structure of the future that allows one the flexibility of means to build around it.' His definition of vision is that of an 'act of power of imagination, a mode of seeing or conceiving, an unusual discernment or foresight' (Khan 1995: 23). Once the vision and mission and the resulting functions are envisaged, it is possible to consider an appropriate organizational shape and structure that will facilitate the achievement of the vision (Jaques and Clement, 1995). Forging a vision is an ongoing process, not a one- or two-step quick fix, but requires a willingness to consider all alternatives, to share the information needed to develop it, and to commit to following through on the plan of action that best serves the longer-term interests of the organization (Murphy and Snell, 1993).

Visionary leadership

Martin Luther King, Jr. once observed that 'people cannot become devoted to Christianity until they find Christ, to democracy until they find Lincoln and Jefferson and Roosevelt, to Communism until they find Marx and Lenin' (Martin Luther King, Jr. quoted in Bennett, 1964: 127). A similar perspective is that 'people are often led to causes and often become committed to great ideas through a person who personifies those ideas' (Bennett, 1964: 127). The Martin Luther King, Jr. message is that for vision to be effective, it needs a champion. A motivating vision, or one that produces 'creative tension' (Senge, 1990a; 1990b), by its nature implies business or organizational innovation, which often departs in a significant way from past practice, requiring quite different organizational capabilities. The presence of a champion in promoting innovation, an individual who makes 'a decisive contribution to the innovation by actively and enthusiastically promoting its progress through the critical organizational stages' (Achilladelis et al., 1971: 14), is well documented in the innovation literature (Schön, 1963; Achilladelis et al., 1971; Rothwell et al., 1974). In a seminal article on radical military innovations, Schön (1963) identifies the role of a champion. He concludes that in order to overcome the indifference and resistance that major innovation provokes, a champion is required to identify the idea as his or her own, to promote the idea actively and vigorously through informal networks, and to risk his or her position and prestige to ensure the innovation's success. According to Schön (1963: 84) 'the new idea either finds a champion or dies'.

A multitude of field and case studies have found strong support for Schön's (1963) contention that innovation success is closely linked with the presence of a forceful advocate (Roberts, 1968; Achilladelis et al., 1971; Rothwell et al., 1974; Burgelman, 1983; Ettlie et al., 1984; Howell and Higgins, 1990). This literature highlights the capacity of champions to inspire and enthuse others with their vision of the potential of an innovation, to persist in promoting their vision despite strong opposition, to show extraordinary confidence in themselves and their vision, and to gain the commitment of others to support the innovation. In Schön's (1963: 84) words 'it is the character of champions ... that they identify with the idea as their own, and with its promotion as a cause, to a degree that goes far beyond the requirements of their job'. These champion-driven behaviours are similar to the qualities of transformational leaders. That is, those leaders who inspire their followers to transcend their own self-interest for a higher collective purpose (Burns, 1978). From the trans-formational leadership literature perspective that links transformational leadership to the innovation process (Oberg, 1972; House, 1977; Bass, 1985; Conger and Kanungo, 1987), it can be concluded that in order to promote innovation in an organization, it is likely that champions will exhibit transformational leadership behaviour, and by the same token, that transformational leaders will also be visionary leaders. For visions to be effective, leaders have to live the vision by making all their actions and behaviours consistent with it, and by creating a sense of urgency and passion for its attainment (Nanus, 1992). That is, the vision becomes an integral part of a leader (Nanus, 1992). Sashkin (1997: 147) argues that defining 'a philosophy or vision is the most abstract aspect of organizational leadership, calling for a high degree of cognitive capability', because in addition to the use of cognitive abilities, the development of a vision or value-based philosophy also requires effective application of behavioural competencies (Sashkin, 1997).

The necessity for leaders to have a vision was recognized in ancient, and now in contemporary, leadership literature, especially in the transformational and spiritual stream (Tichy and Devanna, 1986; Kouzes and Posner, 1987; Kets de Vries, 1989; Senge, 1990a; 1990b; Fairholm, 1991; Hunt, 1991; Nanus, 1992; Bennis, 1993; Block, 1993; Conger, 1993; Rhinesmith, 1993; 1995; Gross, 1996). For ancient philosophers, vision and wisdom were prerequisites for the leadership of a well-governed city. Plato (1952), for example, argued that the possession of the 'wisdom' of an 'intellectual vision', informing the principles of government as it informs the principles of human conduct in general, distinguishes leaders from followers. The Aristotelian leader needs to have a healthy vision of self which can be forged only through a combination of knowledge (epistémé) and practical wisdom (phronésis) (Aristotle, 1985).

Contemporary scholars re-assert this line of thought. Bass (1985; 1990), for example, postulates that transformational leaders, besides other qualities, require an ability to articulate vision. Whilst Conger (1989a; 1989b) asserts that one of the first requirements for transforming the organization is through the expression of a shared vision of what the future may be, Kouzes and Posner (1987) state that leaders need to display a vision, which means that leaders must be forward looking and have a clear sense of the direction they wish their organization to take. DePree's (1993) servant–leader task is to create a vision, agree tough goals in partnership with employees, and then help people become winners in the performance game. Similarly, Covey's (1989; 1990) consultative approach to leadership attempts to develop implicit visions, with the interest of key stakeholders in mind. By nature, implicit vision seeks a win-win solution driven by leaders who display a clear sense of direction (Covey, 1989; 1990), while Jeannot (1989: 35) defines leaders as 'self-possessed individuals, possessed of humanity, principles, vision and the craft to make them real'.

Essentially, within the visionary leadership framework, it is held that leaders believe they can have a major impact on the organization by empowering organizational members to realize the leader's long-range vision (Hunt, 1991). Besides appropriate abilities, skills and opportunities, visionary leaders are motivated by consenting to be leaders. They are socially oriented (directed towards others rather than self) and feel competent and efficient in exerting their power and assuming a leadership role (Sashkin and Burke, 1990). For example, Franklin Delano Roosevelt, through his concept of the New Deal, empowered not only himself but also his administration and the American people to fight the

Great Depression (Kets de Vries, 1989). Turning vision into reality requires exemplary behaviour. In essence, visionary leadership behaviour consists of focusing attention on the vision, personally communicating the vision, demonstrating trustworthiness, displaying respect, and taking risks (Hunt, 1991). In pursuit of their vision, visionary leaders also develop new organizational cultures. Through the process of vision and culture building, visionary leaders transform organizations and strengthen and re-establish organization legitimacy and effectiveness (Hunt, 1991). For example, when Frances Hesselbein introduced her vision for re-orienting the Girl Scouts from the traditional interests of household skills to activities reflecting new opportunities for women in science and business, she had initially to work within the established culture (Bennis, 1989). However, through the introduction of new symbols, such as modernized merit badges, through the updating of uniforms, and through the *Girl Scout Handbook,* and training, she managed not only to achieve her vision, but also to change traditional culture, and to transform an old-fashioned organization into an example of contemporary organization known as 'web' management (Bennis, 1989). Likewise, Betty Ford reframed the attitudes about addiction in mainstream American culture (Gross, 1996).

Visionary leadership is transformational by nature, and as such, quite different from planning, which is a managerial or transactional process (Kotter, 1990). The best-practice style of a visionary leader brings with it different salient leader capabilities and perhaps even different levels of cognitive complexity. A set of exploratory studies from the Organizational Vision Project Team (1990) derived three vision clusters based on the database of business school deans and CEOs: reactive leaders (relatively low in risk, flexibility and bottom-line orientation), lone managers (keep visions close to self, little formal expression, communication, or acceptance by others, difficult to describe vision), and strategic actors (action-oriented, inspirational, integrated with others' visions, long-term, strategic, responsive to competition). While some visionary leaders may be incremental in their approach, like Lee Iaccoca, who built his vision interactionally, with both a product and an organizational need, with his focus targeted at the government, union and customers (Westley and Mintzberg, 1988), others may be holistic like Edwin Land who built his vision in a discontinuous but holistic and introspective manner, with the focus on independent consumers and the scientific community (Westley and Mintzberg, 1989). Others are equally radical in their approach, like John Brown Engineering and Construction's CEO, David Moorhouse, who in a span of five years (1990–1995) transformed his organization, repositioning it from number 25 to number

1 in the marketplace, with operations in more than 30 countries (Moorhouse in Shell's video, 1996).

Visioning

Visioning, within an organizational setting, is a process by which leaders can articulate the future direction they wish to pursue. Visioning is a multiphased process which is used to assist organizations to create new realities and meet challenges by utilizing approaches that integrate executive strategy and expectations on the macro level with operational restraints and realities of managers at the micro level (Rhinesmith, 1993). This process results in top-down driven and/or bottom-up consensus measures, but focuses on the future of the organization and its role in society. Forming a vision is a complex procedure involving a sophisticated process of discerning and equally sophisticated negotiations with all key stakeholders who need to be involved in achieving the vision (Rhinesmith, 1993: 91). In the words of David Moorhouse, upon communicating vision or whatever one wishes to do, 'it is a mistake to think that others will wave the flag and support it wholeheartedly. What you want to do has to be sold to others in organizations', which requires sophisticated negotiation and equally strong focus (Moorhouse in Shell's video, 1996).

An effective visioning process is an emotional, intellectual, (ir)rational, behavioural and existential process (Senge, 1990b). It requires both divergent (right-brained) and convergent (left-brained) thinking (Leonard and Straus, 1997). It is a process involving introspection and even regression, during which time the key players may or may not put aside a reason, and may or may not look beyond the past and present to the future (Senge, 1990b). Senge (1990b) argues that visioning is an ongoing process, which creates, modifies and renews a vision. Although the majority of visions are initiated by one person and then negotiated through and with others, a number of organizations practise a team approach to visioning, substantially dependent upon quality of dialogue (Kakabadse, 1991). Team members must be able to discuss contrasting views to explore the different strands of a vision and its potential significance for them and their organization. They should be convinced by their own reasoning, and appreciate the opportunities the vision holds, and not feel forced to accept a particular viewpoint because of the power held by the vision initiator.

Javidon (1991) argues that visioning depends upon understanding existing organizational realties (culture, history, formative context) and developing a clear sense of direction for the organization, driven as much by a leader's deeply held personal values and ideas. Being a creative process, visioning may require discarding anything that will interfere with the visioning process (Simpson, 1990). Techniques such as remembering and letting go of past experiences have been reported as helpful for executives to feel free to vision, as well as other visioning techniques (sensory awareness, guided imagery) (Simpson, 1990), or bringing an artist to a team to assist in alternative ways of thinking, and in creative or unconstrained visioning. Once the vision has been created (exclusively by the leader or in consultation with the team), then and only then, the creator(s) should re-examine the present, as they need to have a clear non-judgemental awareness of their current situation before they feel confident to commence turning their vision into a reality, or testing out their ideas (Bennis and Nanus, 1985; Kouzes and Posner, 1987; Conger, 1990). Many have argued that the refinement and development of a successfully implemented vision will probably have involved informal consultation and reality testing with key stakeholders (Senge, 1990a; Tichy and Sherman, 1993).

The outcome of visioning is not merely the realization of a vision, a statement of mission, a philosophy or a strategic objective, but rather an attempt to articulate what is the desired future for the organization (Belgard et al., 1988). The outcome may be linked to an organizational dream that stretches the imagination and motivates people to rethink what is possible (Belgard et al., 1988). In order to make it real or more tangible for others, vision creator(s) need to add to their vision a sensitivity and criteria of time, place and person, so that others can identify with the vision. Many (Bennis and Nanus, 1985; Kouzes and Posner, 1987; Conger, 1990; Covey, 1990) hold that visioning will contribute significantly to improved decision making, better planning, more effective communications and enhanced conflict-resolution, in the never-ending effort to hold together the many systems and initiatives present within any organization at any one time, regardless of purpose or mission. Visioning can be, and has been, used as an enabler to re-engineer, consolidate, divest, acquire, and change market focus and direction.

Key elements of visioning

Effective visioning requires introducing a structural and systematic process, and a lot of hard work. Michelangelo, for example, commented on his creativity 'if people knew how hard I worked to gain my mastery, they would not be impressed at all with what I do' (Bissell, 1988). Similarly, the German Chancellor, Helmut Kohl, in achieving the vision of unifying East and West Germany, did not simply seize the opportunity presented by a disintegrating Soviet Union, but had to work very hard in negotiating the vision with both sides and make it acceptable to all stakeholders (Naisbitt, 1994; Tjosvold and Tjosvold, 1995). To activate the visioning process, at a minimum, there is a need for establishing a visioning culture in the organization, a need for gaining access to relevant information, for understanding the desires of others, for nurturing the ability to create vision, for promoting quality communication and for displaying an awareness of the time necessary to forge and implement a vision. From the literature review, six elements of the visioning process emerge as critical factors for effective visioning, namely, the creation of a visioning culture, the identification and nurture of key stakeholders, an understanding of information and values, an understanding of the desires in creating a vision, the nurture of quality communication, and an understanding of the time perspective.

Creating a visioning culture

Before a top executive or executive team launches into a visioning exercise, it is important to set a foundation for a visioning culture, where the expression and sharing of ideas is not sneered at. People need to learn to collaborate and to develop a collective sense of responsibility for the direction and performance of the organization. The essential visioning challenge is to create a culture that is built on trust and rewards creativity and diversity. Being creative and responding to change and uncertainty requires a willingness to accept that all decisions and actions will not necessarily be correct. Punishing decisions which turn out to be mistaken, discourages the kind of innovation that is necessary to deal with new situations in which uncertainty is present (Toffler, 1990; Kelly, 1994). Mistakes and imperfections play an important part in creating long-term sustainability and keeping organizations moving forward (Kelly, 1994). Unfortunately, in many organizations, especially in those that keep 'lean and mean' as the way of dealing with the uncertainty of the modern world, making mistakes is regarded as something to be avoided, because it wastes precious resources, whereas in the long term, not allowing mistakes and learning from them is probably more costly because it stifles creativity (Korac-Kakabadse and Kouzmin, 1996). Jungk and Mullert (1987) suggest that creativity requires a preparedness to: think the otherwise unthinkable; be enterprising and inquisitive; be nonconformist and flexible; be open-minded to the irrational and off-beat; take a chance on being wrong or failing; shun cynical, know-all and perfectionist attitudes; and to stand up for cranky ideas.

Furthermore, people approach innovation and change in their lives in a variety of ways, such as through envisaging a new state where they want to be, modifying current states through an incremental approach, experimenting with different ideas or sensations, or simply exploring (Miller, 1995). None of these approaches is superior to the other, for they simply reflect the individual's philosophies to change and innovation exploring (Miller, 1995). Each individual's capacity to generate and implement good ideas and solutions demands from him/her and from teams, abilities in communicating and approaching tasks in different ways (Miller, 1995).

As top executives are responsible for building up their organization, where people are continually expanding their capabilities to shape their futures, executives, in turn, will need to understand themselves, their people, and potential sources of conflict, all of which require reflection, listening, and giving people the freedom and the power they need for continuous innovation and reality testing (Covey, 1990). To achieve this, organizations need to adopt what DePree (1993) calls 'lavish communication', which occurs only in organizational cultures that promote truth and does not suppress or limit the distribution of information. Organizational cultures are powerful forces because they can determine people's attitudes which, in turn, determine how well a business performs. That is, organizational culture provides a *genius loci*, or 'spirit of place', in terms of 'orientation', which is about knowing where one is in relation to one's context, and also in terms of 'identification' which is about knowing how one is able to relate to certain actions (Schulz, 1980). The *genius loci* provides individuals with the dimension of experience of safety and belonging, openness and honesty, love and appreciation, social and cultural rules, sexuality, freedom and responsibility, support, control and power, and membership (Schulz, 1980).

Fundamental to an effective visioning culture, is social structure, based on trust and personal engagement (Kiesler et al., 1984), which requires a *quality dialogue* and increased face-to-face interaction (Kakabadse, 1991). Thus, building cultures which promote a high degree of quality involvement in visioning is dependent upon the development of a quality dialogue and trust. Once a quality dialogue has evolved between key stakeholders, the individuals can openly discuss sensitive issues, and in this way a culture of visioning starts to unfold as team members learn how to work with creative tension (Senge, 1990b). When individuals, groups and organizations learn how to work with creative tension and use its energy, they move towards the shaping of a vision (Senge, 1990a). The skills required are those of negotiating various paradoxes, such as those of different beliefs, positions, perspectives, or of unequal access to information (Senge, 1990b). The visioning culture should encourage the individual expression of personal desires, honest and open communication, and the soliciting of support. In the appropriate culture, visioning is conveyed as an ongoing process, blending extrinsic and intrinsic visions, and distinguishing positive from negative visions (Senge, 1990a).

In the early stages of building a visioning culture, which on average takes three to five years, the holding environment can be a temporary 'place' in which executives create conditions for diverse groups to talk to one another about the challenges facing them, to frame and debate issues, and to clarify the assumptions behind competing perspectives and values (Senge, 1990b). Building a credible executive team, communicating with increasingly fragmented organizations, defining new measures of performance and product or service qualities, all take time (Kakabadse, 1991). One of the most difficult missions of leadership is getting people on the executive team to listen to and learn from one another (Kakabadse, 1991). Once held in debate, people can learn their way to collective solutions, when they understand one another's assumptions, likes, dislikes, fears and doubts. Obstacles and distractions need to be identified when they occur, so that people can go forward and be focused (Kakabadse, 1991). The process of sharing values and basic beliefs as a group is an important part of creating a visioning culture. People have to discover the value of consulting with one another, and recognize the benefits of working together in the problem-finding and solving process. The executive team needs to maintain those values that must endure, and challenge those that need to change. If executive teams cannot deal with divisive issues, they will not be able to agree on the future of the organization or on an appropriate vision (Kakabadse, 1991).

Visions are expected to unite people and groups. However, there must be some basic unity in their relationship before work towards a vision can succeed. Basic relationships develop within the organizational culture. To achieve a robust organizational culture, executives must have the emotional capacity to tolerate uncertainty, frustration, paradoxes and pain (Kakabadse, 1991). Because many situations involve uncertainty, it is necessary for an individual to be open to different perspectives based on varying values, positions and views. That is, each individual needs to appreciate diversity. However, to accept the existence of differences, and even conflict, between different perspectives, and to attempt to work with tensions and encourage debate, is not easy, as varying forms of justification are used to support each different view as the one true path. Accepting the validity of different perspectives often challenges many of one's own perceptions. For example, the simple notion of right versus wrong may need to be replaced by a realization that there exist more complex interrelationships than simply right and wrong, depending on how each issue is approached and how other contextual factors influence these relationships. The ability to recognize and appreciate diversity provides for a valuable resource in the management of human affairs. Diversity also means complexity, but as Monbiot (1995: 13) argues, although 'living with complexity is a messy, difficult business, which requires constant responsiveness, creativity and goodwill', a learning approach in other words, 'simplicity is very much harder', because it limits the perspectives available.

Identification and nurture of key stakeholders

Every organization has a spread of constituents or stakeholders, whose needs, if ignored, can lead to substantial negative consequences. A stakeholder is someone who has the power to exert an influence on the organization, or who is strongly influenced by the organization in some significant way (Tjosvold and Tjosvold, 1995). A key stakeholder is one who wields considerable influence on the direction and operation of the organization. Stakeholders may be individuals, a group of individuals, an organization or institutions. Each stakeholder has a unique involvement with the organization in terms of differing interests, priorities and expectations. To understand the role of the key stakeholders and to involve them in a visioning process, it is necessary to identify all stakeholders (internal and external to the organization) and identify which of them has the greatest influence on the organization (Tjosvold and Tjosvold, 1995). Considering that every organization has multiple stakeholders, it is often helpful to list separately all internal and external stakeholders. External stakeholders are usually major clients, major competitors, key suppliers, lenders, and those communities within which the organization operates. Similar attention needs to be given to the identification of internal stakeholders (Kakabadse, 1991).

Understanding information and values

Visioning requires access to relevant information, such as the present state of the organization, the current values, and by predicting the future environment through developing a broad description of that environment (Schwarz, 1991). Information plays a critical role, particularly in evaluating action and closely monitoring development in those areas which are likely to have a significant impact on the organization, which is not always obvious, as new knowledge often develops at the fringes (Schwarz, 1991). Executive teams crafting a vision need to have access to the technical expertise and the tools they need to calculate the benefits of a merger or restructuring, to understand future trends and discontinuities, identify opportunities, map existing competencies, and identify the steering mechanisms to support their strategic directions (Kakabadse and Korac-Kakabadse, 1998). Many of these tools and techniques are readily available both within the organizations themselves and from a variety of consulting firms, and although useful, they are not sufficient for visioning, as everyone in the organization has special access to information that comes from his/her particular vantage point. For example, people who sense early changes in the marketplace are often at the periphery, but the organization can thrive if it can bring that information to bear on the process of strategic decision making.

Not everyone adopts the same approach to the visioning process. Some individuals start visioning by using the past, the present or the future as a starting point, depending on the person's time-frame pattern. Often, it is necessary to use information about identified stakeholders and attempt to view the future through their eyes (Tjosvold and Tjosvold, 1995). To discount someone's perspective, owing to bad timing, lack of clarity or seeming unreasonableness, is to lose potentially valuable information. If an individual or team is to envisage the organization's future over the next 10, 20 or 25 years, the individual or team needs to imagine what the future environment is to look like (Hunt, 1991). Whatever the timespan for the vision, access to information about future trends in that timespan, or any other information that the members of the visioning team consider essential, is important to attain. Customers, suppliers, marketing agents, and investors need to be consulted and their positions, interests and suggestions solicited (Tjosvold and Tjosvold, 1995). Such sources highlight an organization's strengths and weaknesses, and its opportunities and threats. The ideas and suggestions of employees and other stakeholders provide useful information that is required for the refinement of the vision. Failure to search for new information and to continually assess its importance as it emerges, restricts the value of the information available by preventing the identification of potential problems in their formative stage, and their recognition when they have become established and possibly more serious. An anthropological study of engineers, conducted by Downey (1988), postulates that social influence can derive from the human hunger for information. This finding is in line with Feldman and March's (1981) study of organizations which concludes that individuals in organizations see information as having symbolic power. Symbolic value enhances the status of information and of information sources, inspiring greater confidence in the emerging vision or final decision (Feldman and March, 1981). Thus, the symbolic value placed on information and the promise of reduction in uncertainty, means that the individual who offers such information gains a considerable measure of influence in decisions (Feldman and March, 1981). The individual or organization that gives the appearance of having the ability to supply information, becomes able to secure an influential relationship and to drive future actions.

However, the values of each executive guide the selection of information for a vision in a variety of ways. Values influence the search for information and the questions one asks concerning alternative avenues (Greene, 1990; Hunt, 1991). Values guide the choice of information and how it is evaluated (Nanus, 1992). Information and values are the raw materials required for constructing the platform on which the visionary structure is built (Nanus, 1992).

Understanding desires and creating vision

Since no organization, no matter how large or versatile, can be all things to all people, understanding people's different desires is important in constructing a vision (Nanus, 1992). An important step in the creative visioning process involves the construction of the vision, actively creating the idea of a vision on behalf of the community and its culture for all the people involved with that community. Creating a vision is that magic moment when all the elements carried come together – information, conceptual models, experience, values, judgement and intuition (Nanus, 1992). It is that point at which left-brain thinking (analytical, logical, sequential in approach, data-oriented) and right-brain thinking (holistic/image-oriented, intuitive, non-linear in approach, value-based,) unite, as individuals attempt to synthesize a possible vision for their organization (Nanus, 1992; Leonard and Straus, 1997). This highly creative process often starts by brainstorming a list of the most attractive possible visions for the organization, with no holding back, no premature criticism, no concern about feasibility or acceptability, only a simple listing of dreams (Greene, 1990; Nanus, 1992). That is, visioning requires brainstorming and action planning (Leonard and Straus, 1997). Some organizations apply a 'holistic' approach to hiring people, where vision and creativity are required. Nissan Design, for example, 'hires designers in virtual pairs. That is, when they hire a designer who glories in the freedom of pure colour and rhythm, they will next hire a very rational, Bauhaus-trained designer who favours analysis and focuses on function' (Leonard and Straus, 1997: 118).

In the creative visioning process, the initial visions may be developed without respect for circumstances, be they financial, commercial, competitive, personnel or market conditions. Initial visions are dreams that come from within the hearts and minds of the visioning team (Nanus, 1992). The vision is what the individual or team desires to create, what an individual or team desires to bring to reality (Nanus, 1992). Each individual must comprehend what it is that they see and know, and then put these together in a manner that makes sense not only to the originator(s), but also to others. It is not enough to create a vision statement, the visioning team must work at making it a reality (Greene, 1990). For example, the breathtaking growth of the World Wide Web is a lesson for all vision setters. The 1980s vision of its creator, Berners-Lee, of 'memory substitute' software, 'Enquire', that can browse through databases by clicking on the word leading to other documents for further elaboration, 'hypertext', has grown to a commercially successful enterprise with over 15 million Internet hosts around the globe (Wright, 1997). Creating a vision can vary from being a brainstorming to an evolutionary process in the life of an individual (Greene, 1990).

Whilst one has to do some deliberate thinking to come up with ideas, the ideas do not have to be new or original. Old ideas can be put to new uses. By looking at issues from a different perspective 'new ideas' can emerge. The concern to guard against is the pride in one's own inventions or achievements. Although some pride is healthy, an excess of it can be a serious disadvantage, as it blinds one to the benefits of learning from others. A not-invented-here mentality/outlook is a severe handicap to a flexible approach to visioning, as some lessons are learned in the most unexpected places. For example, the vision of German reunification had been in existence for more than four decades. However, Chancellor Helmut Kohl made that vision his own and thereafter worked hard to make it happen (Naisbitt, 1994). In the process, he had to make his vision acceptable to all stakeholders inside and outside the two Germanys, and had to take a series of decisions that radically altered their socio-economic and political landscapes (Tjosvold and Tjosvold, 1995).

Nurturing quality communication

Quality of communication is crucial to the visioning process. Considering that organizational visioning is an activity most often undertaken by the top team of an organization, each top team member may have a different philosophy to approaching the visioning process, such as envisaging, incremental, experimental or exploring philosophies (Miller, 1995). Thus, there is always a need for influencing and negotiating individual differences through quality of dialogue (Kakabadse, 1991). Fundamental to relationship building and organizational learning is *dialogue*: a process of inner reflection, through the sharing of experience, enabling one to gain an understanding of one's own and relevant others' practice (Kakabadse, 1991). Only those who reflect on their experience can develop competence to deal with new situations. Through this exchange between participation and observation, between action and reflection, knowledge grows, as does the need to develop the quality, depth and breadth of dialogue which serves as a foundation for building relationships (Kouzmin et al., 1996).

Face-to-face dialogue plays an essential role in establishing and maintaining the kind of multidimensional and robust relationships necessary for effective interaction and coordinated action, especially in situations of uncertainty, ambiguity and risk (Trevino et al., 1987; Allen and Hauptman, 1990; Nohria and Eccles, 1992; Kouzmin et al., 1996). Even if disagreement or fissure occurs during dialogue, within the context of face-to-face communication it is easier to repair situations and resecure relationships because of dialogue's capacity for rapid feedback and multiple cues (Trevino et al., 1987; Allen and Hauptman, 1990; Nohria and Eccles, 1992; Kouzmin et al., 1996). Additional cues of commitment, building teamwork, manifesting trust, an acknowledgement of expert power, and informality add to the importance of dialogue (Nohria and Eccles, 1992). A willingness to listen is needed, as is respect for other people's point of view. Thus, a relationship of trust, making for frank dialogue between leaders and followers, is a precondition for success in preventing regressive behaviour in a visioning team (Kakabadse, 1991).

An international study of management competencies indicates that when the quality of dialogue is high and the relationship amongst senior management is positive, issues and concerns facing organizations tend to be more openly addressed (Kakabadse, 1991). In organizations where relationships are tense and the quality of dialogue restricted, certain issues and problems tend not to be raised, because to do so would generate unacceptable levels of discomfort amongst some, if not all, of the members of the senior executive (Kakabadse, 1991). In this context, dialogue encompasses *knowledge transfer* driven by the content of conversations concerning the present and the future vision of the organization; the quality of relationships amongst executives and employees; external developments which may affect the organization; and the views and responses of individuals and groups within the organization (Kakabadse, 1991).

The linguist, Tannen (Coughling, 1990: A9), claims that language is not only used to communicate ideas in the most efficient way, but is also used to negotiate social relationships and, as such, the meanings of words are quite secondary in dialogue. In his concept of purposive rational/ instrumental action and communicative action, Habermas (1984) puts forward similar arguments. From their ethno-methodological study of giving testimony, Molotch and Boden (1985) also conclude that dialogue is used to play out power relationships. Thus, in addition to quality dialogue, accurately reading context and understanding the perspective and personal orientation of individual team members are equally important.

Understanding time perspective

An early comment aimed at thinking about the future was made by the great philosopher, St Augustine (1988: 48), in the third century, when he stated that

> it is abundantly clear that neither the future nor the past exist, and that strictly speaking, it is not strictly correct to say that there are three times, past, present and future. It may be correct to say that there are three times; a present of things past; a present of things present; and a present of future things.

For St Augustine (1988), different times exist in the minds of people, but cannot be seen anywhere else, as the present of past things is the memory; the present of things present is direct perception; and the present of future things is expectation. St Augustine's statement challenges a particular view of time as linear, as we live in the present, which is continually moving away from the past towards, but never reaching, the future. The past stretches out behind us, and can be selectively recorded as history, whilst the future has yet to happen (Coveney and Highfield, 1990). However, some non-Western cultures hold different assumptions and thus have different views of time, namely, that all time exists, but it is revealed to us only in the present (Hawkins, 1983). Certain nuclear physicists have taken a similar view. Einstein, for example, observed that 'the distinction between the past, present and future is only an illusion' (Coveney and Highfield, 1990: 38). Einstein showed that, if quantum mechanics describes events, then the past is as uncertain as the future. After all, the past can exist only within the mind, in the form of memory, in the same way as the future (Coveney and Highfield, 1990). To explain the difference between the perception of theoretical physics and our everyday experience, Hawking (1994) distinguishes between imaginary time and real time. In imaginary time, there is no distinction between forwards and backwards, whereas in real time there is (Hawking, 1994).

Time is a complex concept. Time is not linear or segmented, but is continuous and interconnected. Time connects the past with the present and with the future. People can be preoccupied with any of the three time perspectives. In some cases, the past can remain too long in an organization (Kelly, 1994). Some organizations cannot let go of the past, especially if the shared memory is one of success, and the current reality, grim. For example, the British civil service has undergone substantial reforms, emerging with a strong agency structure, with 70 per cent of civil servants working in agencies (Mountfield, 1997). However, because of deeply held traditional values of objectivity, impartiality and equity, agencies are finding it difficult to adopt new values of flexibility, responsiveness and leadership, leaving senior executives, managers and employees to operate within a paradox (Kakabadse and Korac-Kakabadse, 1998).

Fundamentally, time plays a role in the reaching of judgements (Carter et al., 1962). Today's judgements may look wiser or less wise with tomorrow's benefit of hindsight; thus the need for vision renewal. An image of a future that is a simple extrapolation of one's 'present and of one's past' is inappropriate in a contemporary world. Tradition can pose problems to organizations adapting to change (May, 1997). Tradition and established ways of doing things, on the one hand, are powerful and valuable forces, which provide a focus for human interaction and stability (May, 1997). On the other hand, change questions the pertinence of tradition and poses the dilemma of how and when it is disadvantageous to retain established customs. To remain effective, it is necessary to balance the need for retaining links with the past along with the need to develop continually evolving responses to new concerns, making such a balance a dynamic concept (Kelly, 1994; May, 1997).

Furthermore, time may also have different values attached to it by different team members. For example, although many culturally different milieus have common meanings of time such as mornings, midday, evening, night, they often view time differently. Most western cultures have a preoccupation with time; to be late for an appointment is regarded as rude, thus unethical (Hawkins, 1983; Korac-Kakabadse and Knyght, 1995). Setting a deadline is quite acceptable and is indicative of the urgency of an activity, or its relative importance (Jaques, 1968; Paskins, 1985), and thus is considered ethical behaviour. However, time takes on different meanings in other parts of the world. In many parts of Africa or the Pacific Islands, time is viewed as flexible, not rigid or segmented; people and friendships matter more than time (Hawkins, 1983). If an individual, pressed for time, rushes throughout a meeting, agenda or negotiation, he/she will generally be suspected of cheating, and thus of pursuing unethical behaviour (Hawkins, 1983: 50–51).

The differing time perception of the British and Americans was noted by Handy (1989) at the start of his book, *The Age of Unreason*, when he wrote, 'Europeans I suggest, look backwards ... Americans look forward, and want to change'. Handy's (1989) comment is supported in Tom Cottle's work, reported by Trompenaars (1993) in his book, *Riding the Waves of Culture*. Cottle evaluated that people in different societies held different values of the past, the present and the future. The USA was found to be heavily future-oriented, whilst people in the UK showed a more equal balance between the three timespans. It also appears that the French use the past as the context for understanding the present (Cottle quoted in Trompenaars, 1993). Decisions draw attention to the time perspectives that people hold. Decisions imply that any one person is considering more than one future, because if only one future exists, then there is little need to make decisions (Carter et al., 1962).

The visioning process needs to negotiate a common under-standing of time amongst the members of a team. Time spent on communication, on checking out, and on discussion between team members, is time invested in the future, and the first step towards evolving a common vision. Only from a shared time perspective can a vision be shared effectively. A timespan of the vision should be agreed by the key stakeholders. Hunt's (1991) research suggests that substantial variations exist between top managers, with a sizeable number of his sampled executives reporting visions of ten years or longer, with a few visions extending beyond 20 years. Similarly, Jacobs and Jaques' (1990) research of three- and four-star Army generals, found that 15 per cent of the three-star generals and 50 per cent of a smaller sample of four-star generals reported visions of 20 years or more. Cohesion concerning time is fundamental to introducing reform, as engineering the steps to pursue for implementation would be impossible without such a foundation.

Selling the vision

Having agreed upon the vision within the visioning team, it is necessary to communicate that vision to all stakeholders. The process of vision communication or 'cognitive politics', utilizes the 'conscious or unconscious use of distorted language, the intent of which is to induce people to interpret reality' (Ramos, 1981: 76) in terms that produce the direct and/or indirect benefits to the agents of such distortion. That is, a vision requires translation from words to images meaningful to others, with a vivid description of what will be achieved. Vision needs to be communicated in a way that motivates and empowers others (Covey, 1989; 1990; Kelley, 1992). This communication needs to be done in a way that excites and attracts the members of the group, so that they will want to do what needs to be done to progress from vision to reality. 'Selling' the vision requires passion, emotion and conviction (Greenleaf, 1977; 1983; Covey, 1989; 1990) or skills of persuasion.

Articulation of a vision that motivates and empowers provides for a powerful social glue of citizenship (Schulz, 1980). The five attributes that emerge in the literature as necessary for the successful communication of a vision that will induce commitment from people, are: clarity of the message (need to be clear about the vision statements and values from which these derive); complementary (how and to what extent the vision will benefit the people to whom it is imparted); use of language (use of meaningful metaphors that unite stakeholders in a way that allows the listeners to see the vision as if it were real); credibility (leaders' personal commitment to the vision must be visible); and leading by example (leaders should set an example to others by behaving in ways which are consistent with their stated values – 'walking the vision') (Iaccoca and Novak, 1984; Tichy and Devanna, 1986; Kouzes and Posner, 1987; Westley and Mintzberg, 1989; Manz and Sims, 1990, 1991; Conger, 1990; Kakabadse, 1991; 1993; Senge, 1992; Kelley, 1992; Tichy and Sherman, 1993).

Effective leaders and their communication of vision, in a way, emanates a theatre performance (Kets de Vries, 1989). They tell or embody stories that speak to other people (Gardner, 1995, Bennis, 1996). They possess great oratorical skills and know how to make use of humour, irony and the colloquial (Kets de Vries, 1989; Senge, 1992). They know how to talk directly to their followers' unconscious, employing figurative language such as similes and metaphors to facilitate identification by their followers (Gardner, 1995). In such a dialogue, simplification, stark contrast, and extremes become the rule; dramatization and histrionics are essential (Kets de Vries, 1989). Gardner (1995) argues that the thread that links together Margaret Mead, Pope John XXIII, Mahatma Gandhi,

Martin Luther King, Jr., Jean Monnet and Alfred P. Sloane, Jr., is their ability to tell a simple story.

Effective leaders use simple language, which makes their message come across easily (Kets de Vries, 1989; Covey, 1990; Gardner, 1995; Bennis, 1996). Some outstanding examples of skills in conjuring up dramatic images through metaphors and stories and in conveying the teller's own enthusiasm and passion for the vision to a diverse audience, capturing their imagination and inducing excitement, include Abraham Lincoln's Gettysburg address, John F. Kennedy's (1961) inaugural speech and his Berlin Wall address, and Martin Luther King's 'I have a Dream' speeches (Kets de Vries, 1989).

The significance of communicating visions, emphasised in transformational leadership theses, is that it expresses the moral experience of the leaders and serves to support their vision or ideology by establishing their authority and identity as well as inspiring follower commitment. In this sense, vision or ideology supports socio-economic norms through emergent institutionalized arrangements linking organizational heroes (leaders) with other actors (Zaleznik, 1977; Bennis, 1984; Kets de Vries, 1989; Gardner, 1995). The institutionalisation of a leader's ideology or vision is critical for organizational transformation, as exemplified by historical leaders such as Lincoln, Marx, Lenin, Roosevelt, Gandhi and Mandela, all ideological leaders linked to particular modes of radical reform (Kets de Vries, 1989).

Buying into the vision

In contrast to selling the vision, buying into communication is based on shared vision and ownership, and the inner motivation or passion which stems from the opportunity of involvement in enterprise achievements, for their own sakes rather than being reward-driven (Manz and Sims, 1990, 1991; Conger, 1990; Senge, 1992; Kakabadse and Korac-Kakabadse, 1996). Because key stakeholders in the vision-creation and implementation process become advocates for the future of their organizations in a variety of settings, such as boards of directors, government, unions, regulatory agencies and clients, they need to believe in the vision and feel strong ownership. Thus, key stakeholders need to buy into the vision and promote it as their own (Manz and Sims, 1990; 1991). Hence, buy-in communication needs to facilitate the expression of individuals' perspectives, where individual concerns are discussed and understood by the top team. Top team members need to display that they are able to accept the perspective of others and to analyse issues from those perspectives. Consequently, each team member is helped to feel more understood and participative and thus the perspective taker, in turn, becomes more open-minded and aware. Perspective-taking stimulates intellectual development and moral reasoning; people become aware of the goals and aspirations of others, and sensitive to a range of feelings (Covey, 1990). The commitment of stakeholders to a vision which is mutually negotiated and understood, is motivating.

Although there are myriads of books on the effective communication of the vision, Aristotle's (1946) classical essay, *Rhetoric*, written in the third century BC, concerning how to persuade anyone to do anything, stands out. *Rhetoric* is filled with concepts and much practical guidance. It provides rules for the refutation of the listener's objections, as well as offering sensible guidance about style, such as when to avoid strong words, how to use smiles, and how to use humour. For Aristotle (1946), rhetoric exists to affect decision making and thereby asserts that there exist three elements to persuasive speech. First, there is the need to project the speaker's personal character, or *ethos*, in a way which will make his/her speech credible. Second, the speaker must stir the emotions of the listeners in a favourable manner, namely evoke *pathos*. Thirdly, the speaker must prove the truth of his/her premise by resort to persuasive argument, through appealing to reason, or *logos*. According to Aristotle (1946) the most common error generally committed by leaders attempting to affect another person's decisions and actions flows from the apparent belief that it is sufficient to make one's argument demonstrative and worthy of belief, by appeals to *logos*. Aristotle (1946) asserts that this approach is not enough and is likely to end in failure. In addition to *logos*, the speaker must make his own character credible, *ethos*, and also put the listener into the right frame of mind, *pathos* (Aristotle, 1946).

Concluding thoughts

From a developmental and spiritual perspective, scholars have argued that leaders should provide others with various opportunities to develop and maintain their sense of self-control, competence and purpose, and hence, empowerment (Kouzes and Posner, 1987; Conger, 1989a; 1989b; Covey, 1990; Kakabadse, 1991; Senge, 1992). Thus, the need for buying into the vision approach, so that stakeholders can feel ownership, is imperative. People who feel insulated or excluded often adopt an attitude of being tough and close-minded, as they devalue those they hold accountable for their exclusion, and hold them in contempt (Conger, 1989a; 1989b; Senge, 1992).

Other scholars, like Nadler and Tushman (1990), highlight that not all people can be motivated through passion to be involved in enterprise achievements for their own sake rather than for reward. Thus, there is a need for selling vision to some stakeholders through 'instrumental leadership', which relies on the more traditional method of motivation through rewards (Nadler and Tushman, 1990). A number of mechanisms for ensuring that the organization achieves its vision are present in various forms, such as financial, resources, targets, rewards, supervision, technical, professional, cultural (Johnson and Scholes, 1993).

Beckhard and Harris (1977), for instance, suggest that all changes should be explicitly specified, as well as how the new organization should look (organizational structure, reward system, personal policies, authority and task-responsibility distribution, managerial style and roles, performance review system, and performance outcomes), so that the end picture can serve as a descriptive guide for determining the change strategy. However, explicit details of a vision are more likely to be achievable for an incremental vision than for a transformational one.

Talking about his own experience, John Brown's CEO, David Moorhouse, advises, 'do not expect that everyone will buy into into your ideas. There will be always those who will not want to come on board' (Moorhouse in Shell's video, 1996). He argues that there will always be people who cannot be motivated to join in, and that these persons will need to be moved aside into less critical positions. However, David Moorhouse (in Shell's video, 1996) believes that 'most dangers are from those who know the jargon and talk the same language, giving the impression that they are into it, but in reality are not; they cause the damage'. The publicly compliant, but privately defiant behaviour of key stakeholders is at its most damaging when trying to promote and implement vision. Moorhouse (in Shell's video, 1996) also suggests that there is the need for a certain toughness in pushing through vision, as well as a need for learning from others.

Notwithstanding that there exist a number of theoretical and practical perspectives, the emergent consensus for successful visioning is that of effective leadership. Only those organizations with effective leadership can expect to achieve an effective visioning process. It is the leadership team that must not only create a vision, but also communicate that vision in a way that excites and attracts others so that 'they will want to do what needs to be done to go from vision to reality' (Greene, 1990: 84). Whilst it will take time, sophisticated negotiations, resources and a lot of hard work to bring a vision to reality, without vision, organizations will not go forward.

References

Achilladelis, B., Jarvis, P. and Robertson, A. (1971), *A Study of Success and Failure in Industrial Innovation*, University of Sussex Press, Sussex.

Allen, R. (1995), 'On a Clear Day You Can Have a Vision: A Visioning Model for Everyone', *Leadership and Organization Development Journal*, Vol. 16, No. 4, pp. 39–44.

Allen, T.J. and Hauptman, O. (1990), 'The Substitution of Communication Technologies For Organizational Structure in Research and Development', in Fulk, J. and Steinfield, C., (eds.), *Organizations and Communication Technology*, Sage, Beverly Hills, pp. 187–201.

Aristotle (1946), *Rhetoric*, Oxford University Press, Oxford.

Aristotle (1985), *The Nicomachean Ethics*, Translated by Irwin, T., Hackett, Indianapolis.

Arrow, K.J. (1951), *Social Choice and Individual Values*, John Wiley, New York.

Arrow, K.J. (1967), 'Values and Collective Decision Making' in Laslett, P. and Runciman, W.G., (eds.), *Philosophy, Politics and Society*, Basil Blackwell, Oxford.

Arrow, K.J. (1983), *Social Choice and Justice*, Belknap Press of Harvard University Press, Cambridge, MA.

Bass, B.M. (1985), *Leadership and Performance Beyond Expectations*, Free Press, New York.

Bass, B.M. (1990), *Bass and Stogdill's Handbook of Leadership: Theory Research and Management Applications*, 3rd Edition, Free Press, New York.

Beckhard, R. and Harris, R.T. (1977), *Organizational Transitions: Managing Complex Change*, Addison-Wesley, Reading.

Belgard, W., Fisher, K.K. and Rauner, S. (1988), 'Vision, Opportunity, and Tenacity: Three Information Processes that Influence Formal Transformation', in Kilman, R. and Covin, T.J., (eds.), *Corporate Transformation*, Jossey-Bass, San Francisco.

Bennett, L. (1964), *What Manner of Man*, Johnson, Chicago.

Bennis, W. (1984), 'Where Have All the Leaders Gone?', in Rosenbasck, W.E. and Taylor, R.L., (eds.), *Contemporary Issues in Leadership*, Westview Press, Boulder, pp. 42–60.

Bennis, W. (1989), *On Becoming Leader*, Addison-Wesley, New York.

Bennis, W. (1993), *An Invented Life: Reflections on Leadership and Change*, Addison-Wesley, Reading.

Bennis, W. (1996), 'The Leader as a Story-teller', *Harvard Business Review*, Vol. 74, No. 1, January–February, pp. 154–167.

Bennis, W. and Nanus, B. (1985), *Leaders: The Strategies for Taking Charge*, Harper and Row, New York.

Bissell, B. (1988), 'The Manager's Balancing Act', *Management World*, Vol. 17, No. 3, pp. 39–40.

Block, P. (1993), *Stewardship: Choosing Service Over Self-interest*, Berrett-Koehler, New York.

Buchman, J.M. (1954), 'Individual Choice in Voting and the Market', *Journal of Political Economy*, Vol. LXII, pp. 334–343.

Buchman, J.M. (1975), *The Limits of Liberty: Between Anarchy and Leviathan*, University Press, Chicago.

Burgelman, R.A. (1983), 'A Process Model of Internal Corporate Venturing in the Diversified Major Firm', *Administrative Science Quarterly*, Vol. 28, No. 2, pp. 223–244.

Burns, J.M. (1978), *Leadership*, Harper and Row, New York.

Carter, C.F., Meridith, G.P. and Shackle, G.L.S. (1962), *Uncertainty and Business Decisions*, Liverpool University Press, Liverpool.

Condorcet, M. de. (1785), *Essai sur L'Application de L'Analyse à la Probabilité des Decisions Rendues à la Pluralité des Voix*, Paris.

Conger, J.A. (1989a), 'Inspiring Others: The Language of Leadership', *Academy of Management Executives*, Vol. 5, No. 1, pp. 31–45.

Conger, J.A. (1989b), *The Charismatic Leader: Behind the Mystique of Exceptional Leadership*, Jossey-Bass, San Francisco.

Conger, J.A. (1990), 'The Dark Side of Leadership', *Organisational Dynamics*, Vol. 19, No. 2, Autumn, pp. 44–55.

Conger, J.A. (1993), 'The Brave New World of Leadership Training', *Organisational Dynamics*, Vol. 21, No. 3, Winter, pp. 46–58.

Conger, J.A. and Kanungo, R.N. (1987), 'Toward a Behavioural Theory of Charismatic Leadership in Organisational Settings', *Academy of Management Review*, Vol. 12, No. 4, pp. 637–647.

Coughling, E.K. (1990), 'Linguist: Listening Between the Words Marks Different Styles of Everyday Talk', *The Chronicle of Higher Education*, 3 October, pp. A6; A8; A9.

Coveney, P. and Highfield, R. (1990), *The Arrow of Time: A Voyage Through Science to Solve Time's Greatest Mystery*, W.H. Allen, London.

Covey, S.R. (1989), *The Seven Habits of Highly Effective Leaders*, Simon and Schuster, New York.

Covey, S.R. (1990), *Principle Centred Leadership*, Summit, New York.

DePree, M. (1993), *Leadership Jazz*, Dell, New York.

Descartes, R. (1991), *The Philosophical Writings of Descartes*, Third Edition, Edited and translated by Cottingham, J., Stoothoff, R., Murdoch, D. and Kenny, A., Cambridge University Press, Cambridge.

Downey, G.L. (1988), 'Structure and Practice in the Cultural Identities of Science: Negotiating Nuclear Waste in New Mexico', *Anthropological Quarterly*, Vol. 61, No. 1, pp. 26–38.

Eggertsson, T. (1995), 'Economic Perspectives on Property Rights and the Economic Institutions', in Foss, P. (ed.), *Economic Approaches to Organisation and Institutions: An Introduction*, Dartmouth, Aldershot, pp. 47–104.

Ettlie, J.E., Bridges, W.P. and O'Keefe, R.D. (1984), 'Organisation Strategy and Structural Differences for Radical Versus Incremental Innovation', *Management Science*, Vol. 30, No. 4, pp. 582–695.

Fairholm, G.W. (1991), *Values Leadership: Towards a New Philosophy of Leadership*, Praeger, London.

Feldman, M.S. and March, J.G. (1981), 'Information in Organizations as Signal and Symbol', *Administrative Science Quarterly*, Vol. 26, No. 2, June, pp. 171–186.

Galbraith, J.K. (1967), *The New Industrial State*, Hamish Hamilton, London.

Gardner, H. (1995), *Leading Minds: An Anatomy of Leadership*, Basic Books, New York.

Godwin, W. (1976), *An Enquiry Concerning Political Justice*, Edited by Kramnick, I., Penguin, Harmondsworth.

Greene, R.J. (1990), 'A Vision for Greene, New York', *The Journal for Quality and Participation*, July-August, pp. 82–85.

Greenleaf, R.K. (1977), *Servant Leadership*, Paulist Press, New York.

Greenleaf, R.K. (1983), *Servant Leadership: A Journey into the Nature of Legitimate Power and Greatness*, Paulist Press, New York.

Gross, T. (1996), *The Last Word on Power: Executive Re-Invention for Leaders Who Must Make the Impossible Happen*, Doubleday, New York.

Habermas, J. (1984), *The Theory of Communicative Action – Volume 1: Reason and the Rationalization of Society*, Translated by McCarthy, T., Beacon Press, Boston.

Handy, C. (1989), *The Age of Unreason*, Century Hutchinson, London.

Hawking, S.W. (1994), *A Brief History of Time: From the Big Bang to Black Holes*, Bantam Press, London.

Hawkins, S. (1983), 'How to Understand Your Partner's Cultural Baggage', *International Management, European Edition*, September, pp. 48–51.

Hayek, F.A. (1937), 'Economics and Knowledge in Society', *Economics*, Vol. IV, pp. 33–54.

Hayek, F.A. (1945), 'The Use of Knowledge in Economics', *American Economic Review*, Vol. 35, pp. 519–530.

Heidegger, M. (1977), 'The Turning', in Lovitt, W. (translation), *The Question Concerning Technology and Other Essays*, Harper and Row, New York, p. 43.

Hodgson, T. (1988), 'Stimulating Self-Development' in Pedler, M., Burgoyne, J. and Boydell, T., (eds.), *Applying Self-Development in Organizations*, Prentice-Hall, New York.

House, R.J. (1977), 'A 1976 Theory of Charismatic Leadership', in Hunt, J.G. and Larson, L.L. (eds.), *Leadership: The Cutting Edge*, Southern Illinois University Press, Carbondale, pp. 76–94.

Howell, J.M. and Higgins, C.A. (1990), 'Champions of Technological Innovation', *Administrative Science Quarterly*, Vol. 35, pp. 317–343.

Hume, D. (1967), *A Treatise of Human Nature*, Edited by Selby-Bigge, L.A., Clarendon Press, Oxford.

Hunt, J.G. (1991), *Leadership: A New Synthesis*, Sage, London.

Iaccoca, L. and Novak, W. (1984), *Iaccoca: An Autobiography*, Bantam Books, New York.

Jacobs, T.O. and Jaques, E. (1990), 'Military Executive Leadership', in Clark, K.E. and Clark, M.B. (eds.), *Measures of Leadership*, Leadership Library of America, West Orange, pp. 281–295.

Jaques, E. (1968), *Time Span Handbook*, Heinemann Educational, London.

Jaques, E. and Clement, S.D. (1995), *Executive Leadership: A Practical Guide to Managing Complexity*, Blackwell, Cambridge.

Javidon, M. (1991), 'Leading a High-Commitment, High-Performance Organisation', *Long Range Planning*, Vol. 24, No. 2, pp. 28–36.

Jeannot, T.M. (1989), 'Moral Leadership and Practical Wisdom', *International*

Journal of Social Economies, Vol. 16, No. 6, pp. 14–38.

Johnson, G. and Scholes, K. (1993), *Exploring Corporate Strategy: Text and Cases,* 3rd Edition, Prentice-Hall, New York.

Jungk, R. and Mullert, N. (1987), *Futures Workshops: How to Create Desirable Futures,* Institute for Social Inventions, London.

Kakabadse, A.P. (1991), *The Wealth Creators: Top People, Top Teams and Executive Best Practice,* Kogan Page, London.

Kakabadse, A. P. (1993), 'Success Levers for Europe: The Cranfield Executive Competencies Survey', *Journal of Management Development,* Vol. 13, No. 1, pp. 75–96.

Kakabadse, A.P. and Korac-Kakabadse, N. (1996), The Kakabadse Report, 'Leadership in Government: Study of the Australian Public Service', Report Submitted to the Commonwealth Government, Canberra, Australia, Cranfield School of Management.

Kakabadse, A.P. and Korac-Kakabadse, N. (1998), *Essence of Leadership,* International Thomson, London.

Kakabadse, A.P., Korac-Kakabadse, N. and Myers, A. (1996), 'Leadership and the Public Sector: An Internationally Comparative Benchmarking Analysis', *Journal of Public Administration,* Vol. 16, No. 4, October, pp. 377–396.

Kaufman, W. (1950), *Nietzsche,* Princeton University Press, Princeton.

Kelley, R. (1992), *The Power of Followership,* Doubleday, New York.

Kelly, K. (1994), *Out of Control: The New Biology of Machines,* Fourth Estate, London.

Kennedy, J.F. (1961), *Inaugural Address,* 20 January, White House, Washington.

Kets de Vries, M.F.R. (1989), *Prisoners of Leadership,* John Wiley and Sons, New York.

Khan, T.R. (1995), 'Seeing Where You Want To Go', *Electric Perspectives,* Vol. 20, No. 1, January–February, pp. 23–28.

Kiesler, S., Siegel, J. and McGuire, T. (1984), 'Social Psychological Aspects of Computer-mediated Communication', *American Psychologist,* Vol. 39, No. 10, pp. 1123–1134.

Korac-Kakabadse, N. and Knyght, P.R. (1995), 'Inequality of Discourse and the Problem of Access to Justice', Paper presented at Australian and New Zealand Academy of Management (ANZAM) Conference, James Cook University, Townsville, 3–6 December.

Korac-Kakabadse, N. and Kouzmin, A. (1996), 'Innovation Strategies for the Adoption of New IT in Government: An Australian Experience', *Journal of Public Administration,* Vol. 16, No. 4, October, pp. 317–330.

Kotter, J.P. (1990), *A Force for Change: How Leadership Differs from Management,* Free Press, New York.

Kouzes, J.M. and Posner, B.Z. (1987), *The Leadership Challenge: How to Get Extraordinary Things Done in Organizations,* Jossey-Bass, San Francisco.

Kouzmin, A., Korac-Kakabadse, N. and Jarman, A. (1996), 'Economic Rationalism, Risk and Institutional Vulnerability', *Risk, Decision and Policy,* Vol. 1, No. 2, December, pp. 229–256.

Latham, J.R. (1995), 'Visioning: The Concept, Trilogy and Process', *Quality Progress,* Vol. 28, No. 4, April, pp. 65–68.

Leonard, D. and Straus, S. (1997), 'Putting Your Company's Whole Brain to Work', *Harvard Business Review,* Vol. 75, No. 4, July–August, pp. 111–121.

Locke, J. (1971), *Social Contract*, Oxford University Press, London.

Manz, C.C. and Sims, H.P., Jr. (1990), *Super-leadership: Leading Others to Lead Themselves*, Prentice-Hall, Berkeley.

Manz, C.C. and Sims, H.P., Jr. (1991), 'Super-leadership: Beyond the Myth of Heroic Leadership', *Organizational Dynamics*, Vol. 19, Summer, pp. 18–35.

Marx, K. (1975), *Early Writings*, Penguin, Harmondsworth.

Marx, K. (1976), *Capital*, Penguin, Harmondsworth.

May, G.H. (1997), 'The Sisyphus Factor or a Leering Approach to the Future', *Futures*, Vol. 29, No. 3, pp. 229–241.

Miller, W.C. (1995), 'Is Innovation Built into your Improvement Processes?', *Journal of Quality and Participation*, Vol. 18, No. 1, January–February, pp. 46–48.

Molotch, H.L. and Boden, D. (1985), 'Talking Social Structure: Discourse, Domination and the Watergate Hearings', *American Sociological Review*, Vol. 50, No. 2, June, pp. 273–288.

Monbiot, G. (1995), 'Global Villagers Speak with Forked Tongues', *The Guardian*, 24 August, p. 13.

Moorhouse, D. (1996), 'John Brown Engineering and Construction', Shell's Video.

Morgan, G. (1986), *Images of Organization*, Sage, Beverly Hills.

Mountfield, R. (1997), 'Organizational Reform Within Government: Accountability and Policy Management', *Public Administration and Development*, Vol. 17, No. 1, pp. 71–76.

Murphy, E.C. and Snell, M. (1993), *The Genius of Sitting Bull*, Prentice-Hall, Englewood Cliffs.

Murray, P. (1997), *A Discussion with Peter Murray on Pondering Over Vision*, Cranfield University, 4 December, Cranfield.

Nadler, D.A. and Tushman, M.L. (1990), 'Beyond the Charismatic Leader: Leadership and Organizational Change', *California Management Review*, Vol. 32, No. 2, Winter, pp. 77–97.

Naisbitt, J. (1994), *Global Paradox: The Bigger the World Economy, the More Powerful its Smallest Player*, William, Morrow and Co. Inc., New York.

Nanus, B. (1992), *Visionary Leadership*, Jossey-Bass, San Francisco.

Nohria, N. and Eccles, R.G. (1992), 'Face-to-Face: Making Network Organizations Work', in Nohria, N. and Eccles, R.G., (eds.), *Networks and Organizations: Structure, Form and Action*, Harvard Business School Press, Boston, pp. 288–308.

Oberg, W. (1972), 'Charisma, Commitment and Contemporary Organization Theory', *M.S.U. Business Topics*, Vol. 20, No. 1, pp. 18–32.

Organizational Vision Project Team (1990), 'Organizational Vision; Theory, Research and Practice' (members: Larwood, Kriger, Falbe and Miesing) Symposium Presentation at the National Meeting of the Academy of Management, San Francisco, August.

Ortega y Gasset, J. (1961), *Meditations on Quixote*, Norton, New York.

Paskins, D. (1985), 'Planning Horizons and Their Measurement Within the Organisational Strata', PhD Thesis, Brunel University, England.

Paskins, D. (1997), 'Thinking Futures – How to Survive and Thrive in a Fast Changing (Business) World', *Futures*, Vol. 29, No. 3, pp. 257–266.

Plato (1952), *The Statesman*, Routledge and Kegan Paul, London.

Ramos, A.G. (1981), *The New Science of Organization: A Reconceptualization of the Wealth of Nations*, University of Toronto Press, Toronto.

Rhinesmith, S.H. (1993), *A Manager's Guide to Globalization: Six Keys to Success in a Changing World,* The American Society for Training and Development, Irwin, New York.

Rhinesmith, S.H. (1995), 'Open the Door to a Global Mindset', *Training and Development,* May, pp. 35–43.

Roberts, E.B. (1968), 'A Basic Study of Innovators: How to Keep and Capitalize on Their Talents', *Research Management,* Vol. 11, pp. 249–266.

Rothwell, R., Freeman, C., Horsley, A., Jarvis, V.T.P., Robertson, A.B. and Townsend, J. (1974), 'SAPPHO Update Project SAPPHO Phase II', *Research Policy,* Vol. 3, pp. 258–291.

Rousseau, J.J. (1953), *Confessions,* Translated by Foxley, B., Dutton, New York.

Rousseau, J.J. (1967), *Du Contract Social ou Principes du Droit Politique (Social Contract, and the Principles of the Law)* in *Oeuvres Complète (Complete Works),* Vol. 2, Editions du Seuil, Paris, pp. 518–525.

Saint Augustine (1988), *Confessions,* Translated by Pine-Coffin, R.S., Penguin Classics, London.

Sashkin, M. (1997), 'Strategy Leadership Competencies', in Phillips, R.L. and Hunt, J.G., *Strategic Leadership,* Quorum Books, London, pp. 139–160.

Sashkin, M and Burke, W.W. (1990), 'Understanding and Assessing Organizational Leadership', in Clark, K.E. and Clark, M.B. (eds.), *Leadership Library of America, Measures of Leadership,* West Orange, pp. 297–326.

Schön, D.A. (1963), 'Champions for Radical New Inventions', *Harvard Business Review,* Vol. 41, No. 2, March–April, pp. 77–86.

Schulz, N. (1980), *Genius Loci,* Academy Edition, London.

Schumpeter, J. (1954), *Capitalism, Socialism and Democracy,* Harper, New York.

Schwarz, P. (1991), *The Art of the Long View: Scenario Planning – Protecting Your Company Against an Uncertain World,* Century Business, London.

Senge, P.M. (1990a), 'The Leader's New Work', *Executive Excellence,* Vol. 11, No. 11, November, pp. 8–9.

Senge, P.M. (1990b), 'The Leader's New Work: Building Learning Organizations', *Sloan Management Review,* Vol. 32, No. 1, Fall, pp. 7–23.

Senge, P.M. (1992), *The Fifth Discipline: The Art and Practice of the Learning Organization,* Random House, Sydney.

Simpson, J. (1990), 'Visioning: More than Meets the Eye', *Training and Development Journal,* Vol. 44, No. 9, September, pp. 70–72.

Smith, A. (1776), *The Wealth of Nations,* Thomas Nelson, Edinburgh.

Smith, A. (1790). *The Theory of Moral Sentiments,* Edited by Raphael, D.D. and Macfie, A., Clarendon Press, Oxford.

Sowell, T., (1987), *A Conflict of Visions: Ideological Origins of Political Struggles,* William, Morrow and Co. Inc., New York.

Tichy, N.M. and Devanna, M.A. (1986), *The Transformational Leader,* John Wiley, New York.

Tichy, N.M. and Sherman, S. (1993), *Control Your Destiny or Someone Else Will: How Jack Welch is Making General Electric the World's Most Competitive Corporation,* Doubleday, New York.

Tjosvold, D. and Tjosvold, M.M. (1995), *Psychology for Leaders,* John Wiley, New York.

Toffler, A. (1990), *Powershift: Knowledge, Wealth and Violence at the Edge of the 21st Century,* Bantam Press, New York.

Trevino, L.K., Lengel, R.H. and Daft, R.L. (1987), 'Media Symbolism, Media

Richness and Media Choice in Organizations: A Symbolic Interactions Perspective', *Communication Research*, Vol. 14, No. 5, pp. 553–574.

Trompenaars, F. (1993), *Riding the Waves of Culture*, Brealy Publishing, London.

Weick, K.E. (1969), *The Social Psychology of Organization*, Addison-Wesley, Reading.

Westley, F.R. and Mintzberg, H. (1988), 'Profiles of Strategic Visions: Levesque and Iaccoca', in Conger, J.A. and Kanungo, R.N. (eds.), *Charismatic Leadership*, Jossey-Bass, San Francisco, pp. 161–212.

Westley, F.R. and Mintzberg, H. (1989), 'Visionary Leadership and Strategic Management', *Strategic Management Journal*, Vol. 10, No. 1, pp. 17–32.

Wright, R. (1997), 'The Man who Invented the Web', *Time*, Vol. 149, No. 20, May 19, pp. 52–55.

Zaleznik, A. (1977), 'Managers and Leaders: Are They Different?', *Harvard Business Review*, Vol. 55, No. 3, May-June, p. 67–74.

CHAPTER TWO

History of leadership

Andrew P. Kakabadse and Nada Korac-Kakabadse

Preoccupation with leadership

Little doubt exists that leadership is one of the oldest and most potent forces of organized life. From Mother Theresa to Idi Amin, the influence of the good and the infamous of the past and the present, are witness to this statement. Yet despite the fact that so many words have been written about it, leadership still remains one of the least understood subjects. Some writers define leadership as a personal relationship between the individual and the group (Jeannot, 1989), others in terms of the sharing of common goals and values (Semler, 1993), and some see leadership as that behaviour, which is not so much in the control of the individual, but driven by multiple forces in their environment (Kouzes and Posner, 1987). Little is acknowledged beyond these three basic ideas.

The view of leaders as definers of common goals and philosophies, accounting for contextual factors through the display of particular personal characteristics, historically provides for the most common interpretation of leadership. Powerful warriors and chiefs, priests and priestesses seductive in the projection of guilt, generals and kings, led their followers through the persuasion that they as leaders received inspiration and wisdom. Any society, as witnessed in Bosnia, today, that has experienced catastrophic change and faces both physical and spiritual uncertainty, turns its attention to community and to the leadership that can provide hope and direction from present predicaments. Leadership, as much as community, has been a focal perspective in thinking through the centuries in literature, philosophy and religion alike, and in broader writings on society.

As early as 386 BC, Plato (1952; 1956a; 1956b) initiated one of the first leadership training centres in the world, an institute he called the Academy, in an attempt to create a new type of statesman, a person who would be able to withstand the pressures of office. Plato seemed to be aware of the 'dark side' of leaders and developed a draconian curriculum to inhibit undesired sentiments and ambition from coming to the fore. Analyses of certain historical leaders, such as the biblical King Saul, Rome's Caligula, Russia's Ivan the Terrible, and today's Saddam Hussein, and Serbia's Milosovic and business leaders who resort to pathological behaviour upon reaching the top, provide ample examples of the satanic side of leadership that Plato wanted to guard against. For Plato, (1957) the possession of a 'wisdom', the 'one truth' of an 'intellectual vision', providing the pathway to effective government as it assists in the appropriate conduct of human affairs, distinguishes leaders from followers.

Plato's concern with community, authority, leadership, hierarchy, ethics, morality, depravity, and the sacred, was profound. Plato's ideas, intertwined with Aristotle can be found in modified form, in the writings of the Roman moral philosophers in the first century BC, four centuries later in the works of the Christian philosophers, searching for that which is *'holy in this life'* and, by implication, man's proper place in a natural order that ultimately lay at the feet of God. After the Middle Ages, Plato's ideas were championed once more, adding muscle to the search for a natural order, in which all knew their place, but in so being experienced enlightenment, not restriction. Thus, for more than 2,000 years, the moral philosophy of leadership has concerned itself with ideal and appropriate behaviour, with the distinction between good and evil, and with the difference between real and apparent good. The great moral philosophers, Plato (1952), Aristotle (1985), Aquinas (1963), Pascal (1990), Locke (1971) , offered sound, common-sense advice about the goals all men ought to seek, and how to achieve these goals.

Throughout, the twin themes of inspiring what to do and communicating how to get there are profound in the writings of Western culture. Plato's *Republic,* for example, contains much useful information on how modern leaders may inspire trust and confidence, provide psychological support, and obtain the best performance possible from followers. Niccolo Machiavelli's *The Discourse* (1950), and *The Prince* (1958), both written in 1513, were produced as manuals for administration. The importance and manner of communicating objectives to followers may be found in King Archidamus' address to his lieutenants, or to exemplify the 'dark side', in Hitler's rallies to the military and common folk alike and in Mussolini's powerful and dramatic pronouncements.

Hence, the essence of leadership has been a concern with how social groups organize and conduct work, as they encounter the challenges of constant change, invasion, new technology, transformed workplaces and new standards of, and expectations for, life and work. Throughout history, the very essence of leadership has been concerned with nurturing, developing, destroying and rebuilding.

However, the modern-day manager has altered this scene. Increasing social and organizational complexity has firmly replaced the leader, conferring presence and omnipotence on managers who exhibit a classical, rhetorical education. The transition from leadership based on charisma, to one based on control – from fascination to logic – is the history of the rise of management to pre-eminence in social and organized settings in this century. In order to establish how that rise has taken place, and where leadership is today, we enter into an exploration of leadership throughout the centuries.

Roots of leadership

The following quotation from the Bible sets the scene for the development of leadership: 'Choose from the people at large some capable and God-fearing men, trustworthy and incorruptible, and appoint them as leaders of the people; leaders of thousands, hundreds, fifties, tens' (Exodus 18:21). What is landmarked is the prime driver of leadership, the desire to unify man.

Hunting, the central pastime of primitive societies, provided the forerunner to a more conventionally understood form of leadership, the leader on the battlefield. Once leadership was interwoven with war, the age of the hero ascended. In primitive societies' battlefields, however, there were no heroes, as primitive warrior behaviour required that all perform identically, namely, as heroes. 'Insofar as there was exceptional behaviour on the field of battle' in primitive societies, 'it was that of the elders', who mediated between disputing parties when, 'the level of violence exceeded the accepted norm'.[1] So, negotiation and the settlement of claims led to the emergence of elders, the pre-heroic leaders, or those who cajoled, persuaded and pushed from the back, than, those who determindly, pulled and drove through from the front.

The maturing of pre-heroic or hunting-based leadership, to that of leadership on the battlefield, laid the foundation for the heroic leader, the distinguished warrior, the one who took that additional risk to be seen to lead and win. As fighting on the battlefield moved to taking over the land and the domain of others, the heroic leader came to the fore, outstanding, dramatic, envied and feared (Keegan, 1988).

Through hunting and war became established two prime aspects of leadership; on the one hand the thinking, negotiating, working through paradox and reformulating meanings, namely the more passive, leading-from-the-back style of leadership, noted for its insights accumulated from life's rich experiences; and contrastingly on the other, the upfront, direct, break-down-barriers approach, requiring zest, strength, courage and charisma. The former is typified by the wisdom and self-development school, and the latter the belief in being born to lead school of thought, giving rise to the preoccupation with the search for the great man/woman. A historical, brief, guided tour through both schools of thought is provided, supported by a view as to their impact on late 20th-century thinking.

Wisdom and the self-development school

Socrates' philosopher leader

Socrates' fundamental question, 'What ought one do?' (Plato's recording) promotes a powerful ethical dilemma for contemporary leaders as it may have done to philosophers in ancient times. The power of this question lies in the fact that the answer demands an account from individuals as to why they choose one good over another. Socrates' question requires a person to articulate what they consider to be a 'good' for which Socrates recognized there is no one truth. Indeed, Socrates details the origins of his humility and the fact that he has no prerogative on any one or other truth. After visiting and conversing with a wise man, he, Socrates, went away thinking 'I am wiser than this man: neither of us knows anything that is really worth knowing, but he thinks that he has knowledge when he has not, while I have no knowledge, nor do I think that I have'.[2]

The Socratic 'ignorance' paradox serves as the basis for an understanding of the deeper natures of leaders who will not say, 'cannot' and whose striving is supported by an aspiration towards achieving wisdom. As Socrates claims, 'an unexamined life is not worth living. Therefore it is incumbent on the philosopher to subject him or herself to the practice of an endless humility; the practice of opening oneself to the limitedness of one's own perspective.'[3]

The Socratic message is one of a continual intellectual and emotional movement, with the ultimate aim of freeing oneself from the presumption of knowing. Thus leadership, as an exercise of Socratic humility, leaves nothing untouched and is an exercise in the willingness to aspire to wisdom, the essence of Socratic teaching. The Socratic message found in the Platonic dialogue *Theetetus*, suggests that a leadership role is an awakening, which is precisely the birth of all learning.

> I am so far like the midwife that I cannot myself give birth to wisdom; and the common reproach is true, that though I question the other, I can myself bring nothing to light because there is no wisdom in me. The reason is this: heaven constrains me to serve as a midwife, but has debarred me from giving birth.[4]

The leader–follower relationship, in the Socratic sense, is one which empowers the followers, and where both members of the relationship stretch each other to new meanings and interpretations concerning their issues at hand.

Plato's philosopher–king model of leadership is based on Socratic teaching. Writing in the fourth century BC, in Athens, Plato (1956b; 1957) describes how the philosopher-king rules the state with an authority derived from his knowledge of the, 'One Truth'. For Plato, the possession of 'wisdom' (an intellectual vision), earmarking the desired principles of government, so that the enlightened leader can overcome the convolutions of human conduct, distinguishes leaders from followers. In his *Republic*, Plato claims that until 'political greatness and wisdom meet in one' and 'those commoner natures who pursue either to the exclusion of the other, are compelled to stand aside, cities will never have rest from their evils – no, nor the human race'.[5]

Plato's desire for the 'One Truth' is, in fact, a defence against those who would rule the state according to whim and fancy, driven to satisfy their own needs, emerging as arbitrary and capricious. Thus, what distinguishes contemporary leaders from followers in the Platonic sense, is the possession, by the former, of a degree of critical perspective, which can be enhanced in the latter. The developer-leader, for example, can develop only insofar as he or she possesses a higher level of capability than the developing-follower. Followers are thus followers, only insomuch as they are hooked to the status quo and unable to visualize an ever widening series of perspectives. If and when they break out of their perceptual 'strait-jackets', they are no longer followers. The very essence of Socratic development, which consists of learning through mutuality, allows and promotes the movement of followers into leader roles.

Aristotle and moral philosophy

Aristotle established a difference between the exercise of power and the exercise of leadership, and that difference was morality. Moral leadership, according to Aristotle, has a profound impact on those led, for the leader is able to withstand everyday pressures and promote moral development for those in his or her charge through pursuing reasoned, explicit and clear values.

Aristotle outlines that transformational leadership needs to be tempered by a certain kind of wisdom which Aristotle terms 'practical wisdom'. Aristotle distinguishes practical wisdom *(phronésis)* from scientific knowledge *(epistémé)* on three counts. First, scientific knowledge is concerned with an objectivity that is long lasting, whereas practical wisdom is about people's daily lives and concerns. Second, scientific knowledge is knowledge of the universal truths, whereas practical wisdom address the peculiarities of human existence. Third, scientific knowledge is contemplative, whereas practical wisdom is concerned with action.

Aristotle does not suggest that scientific knowledge is irrelevant to leadership or that general principles are unimportant to the practically wise person, but that knowledge of preconstructed or abstract procedures is not the same as consideration, deliberation and concern for one's fellows. As Aristotle views the content of practical wisdom as being in perpetual motion, he considers it misguided to expect that scientific formalism determines the nature of wisdom.

For Aristotle, practical wisdom is more like a craft than a science, and in order to study practical wisdom fruitfully, people need to have experienced living, gained some maturity and assumed some responsibility as householders and members of their civic communities. Abstract formulae generated in a theoretical vacuum cannot substitute for deliberating finally about what promotes living well. He notes:

> the fact that whereas young people do become accomplished in geometry and mathematics, and wise within these limits, practically wise young people do not seem to be found. The reason is that practical wisdom is concerned with particulars as well as universals, and particulars become known from experience, but a young person lacks experience, since some length of time is needed to produce it.[6]

Aristotle argues that a 'youth is not a suitable student of political science', of which leadership is a branch, 'as they have not yet learnt to deliberate and cannot possess *søphrosuné* (moderation, temperance, self-control) that practical wisdom demands'.[7]

The search for practical wisdom denotes a continuous ongoing experience and as such, there exist no leaders without frailty and imperfection. According to Aristotle, the will to action marks a leader from followers, not inherent greatness, for that is a camouflage masking deep vulnerabilities. In essence, the Aristotelian message of learning from action, a movement so popular today, emphasizes how sorrow promotes understanding, how rebuke enhances insights, how doubt engenders reflection and how those who dare emerge as precise in decision.

The Aristotelian message is well acceded to today. The prolific and insightful American writer on leadership, Warren Bennis (1993), asserts that leaders need to know themselves. They must take specific actions to learn about themselves through their experience, as there is no greater teacher about self than the grasping of responsibility. It is in that taking of responsibility that people are developed through the choices they make.

It is in the making of choices that Socrates, Plato and Aristotle promote a virtue approach, which emphasizes the will, intentions and character of the individual. The virtuous leader acts according to inner conviction and strength, irrespective of the consequences of his/her action and its impact on relationships, whether they be based on kinship, professional or friendship ties. This focus on the individual as the pillar of ethics, has advantage in that the onus of accountability is clearly allocated. This view, however, has the disadvantage of being rigid, and presuming wrongly that all that is needed to achieve an ethical society is for its members to act according to subjective notions of virtue.

Machiavelli's 'prince' (strong ruler) leader

Still remaining within the developmental school of leadership, but less concerned with virtue and values and more with practical actions, the Renaissance philosopher, Niccolo Machiavelli (1950), focuses on how leaders ought to behave. Machiavelli asserts that it appears more proper to pursue the trail of truth, than an ideal, 'for how we live is so far removed from how we ought to live, that he who abounds what is done for what ought to be done, will rather learn to bring about his own ruin than his preservation'.[8]

Machiavelli's analysis of history asserts that if political anarchy is to be avoided, then concerns of rights and morality come second place to the struggle and establishment of power. Given the nature of circumstances, the leader must be prepared to employ whichever means he considers fit in order that he defend and promote the welfare of the state. Through so arguing, Machiavelli asserts that all human beings are motivated by power. In the case of conflict amongst individuals, the one who succeeds at the game of power becomes the leader. In his *Discourse*, Machiavelli concludes that the only way to establish any kind of order is to establish 'superior power' which is of sufficient force to curb the excessive ambitions and corruptive elements of others who wield power.

Whilst Socrates gives leadership philosophy and values, Niccolo Machiavelli gives leadership a pragmatic boost. Machiavelli's contribution to the leadership debate is in understanding the balance between principle and opportunism, which in his view provides the best guide for actions for a prince in the medieval Italian city states. His prescription extends not only to relations with other city states, but also to the most effective style with which to relate to advisers and to one's subjects. Effective leadership, in Machiavelli's view, is a matter of maintaining an adequate flow of accurate information on the issues to be decided, whilst at the same time commanding sufficient respect to enable actions to be taken.

Spirituality, Taoism and Buddhism

With a growing need to find comfort and meaning in the overburdened, stress-driven, insecure workplace of the 1990s, the leadership literature has shifted towards a leadership philosophy which is unashamedly spiritual, and is finding a home in the secular world of corporations. Spirituality in leadership is conceived by many as an awareness within individuals of the value of their inner selves within a threatening outer world. A number of writers, such as Steven Covey (1990), unequivocally cite that the essence of leadership stems from the leader's soul rather than from his or her behaviour. This movement of sensitivity towards life embraces an active and dynamic interest in people and a far broader global consciousness. The acceptance of the 'whole person' in the workplace, and an action learning approach that is holistic in its nature, have been compared to Taoism and Bhuddism (Ross, 1980; Hesse, 1995).

What is less commonly known is how old are the references to Taoism and Bhuddism in the West. Many Taoist notions were introduced into Western thought through the work of the ancient Greek, Heraclitus, of Ephesus, the pre-Socratic philosopher, and have influenced generations of social theorists in what is now known as a dialectical view of reality. For example, Taoism and Bhuddism had a strong influence on the work of Hegel (1971), the 19th-century German philosopher who did much to advance dialectical methods, which in turn deeply influenced the work of the social theorist, Karl Marx.

Taoisim can be seen as, 'a religious and philosophical concept that is all-pervading, a self existent eternal unity, the source from which all created things emanate and to which they all return'.[9] Taoism is a description of nature (Tao means way), in turn shaped by the dynamic interplay of Yin and Yang. Yin and Yang, which originally denote the dark and sunny sides of a hill, emphasise how the Tao is shaped by a flow of complementary yet opposite forces. In other words, to have one side also means the other exists. In this way, the Tao reconciles such contrasts as sociality with individuality, order with spontaneity, unity with diversity. Of considerable importance to Taoist philosophy is the way in which human life is an integral part of the world process, and therefore of nature. The Taoist holds that any situation can be understood in terms of Yin and Yang, and that many human situations can be balanced and improved by influencing the relationship between those opposite elements.

Another profound and subtle concept is Wu-Wei or non-action, which should not be confused with doing nothing. 'It is rather a knowledge of the principles, structures and trends of human and natural affairs, so that one uses the least amount of energy in dealing with people and life'.[10] In pragmatic leadership terms, this could be seen as innate wisdom. Wu-Wei is a concept that captures natural spontaneity, an acceptance of life, events and a will to allow processes to follow their own natural course. For a leader, the Wu-Wei principle implies a reliance on capable managers, whilst avoiding the adoption of an authoritarian, top-down stance.

The Taoist approach to leadership embraces the philosophy of Wu-Wei and, therefore, seeks to maintain a balance between thought and action, between self and environment. Wu-Wei is a search for synergy, it is about patience, accepting life as it unfolds and of being involved and not isolating oneself from challenging circumstances. As such, Wu-Wei implies a harmony between actions, situations and self. The Taoist approach to leadership seeks balance and integration, in contrast to Western philosophy where action is linked to the optimisation of resources in order to fulfil objectives.

Integrating Taoism as a philosophical basis to leadership, means that leading cannot be *ad hoc*; that is, the leader cannot be isolated from the community he/she is serving, and the impetus is to provide for bottom-up processes and commitment (Mair, 1990).

From a comparable philosophical base comes Bhuddism (Watts, 1992). Central to Buddhist philosophy is compassion. Compassion arises from understanding, that all of life is in some way interconnected, and that separation from people is an illusion. Buddha, upon his enlightenment, returned to his former companions and shared the four noble truths,[11]

■ Suffering is inherent in existence.

■ Suffering and dissatisfaction arise from our grasping and our sense of separateness (created by the ego).

■ We can let go of our grasping and sense of separation.

■ The release from ego and greed can occur through following the Buddhist eightfold path.

Through his teachings and practice, Buddha encouraged his followers not to engage in intellectual, philosophical or theoretical debates, as he felt this side-tracked individuals from their path to wisdom and compassion. The teachings of Buddha do not promote a philosophy, but rather an almost psycho-therapeutic approach of how to get rid of deeply rooted and unhelpful attitudes. Through Buddhism, the goal towards which the individual tends is wholeness or integration, a condition in which all the different elements of the psyche, both conscious and unconscious, are moulded.

The Taoist and Buddist themes of spiritualism, journeying and wholeness have influenced certain writers in the areas of social psychology and personality. Abraham Maslow (1968) argues that in order to understand the fully matured person (authentic, self-actualizing, individuated, productive, healthy), he/she should not be seen in environment-centred terms, namely, 'possessing the ability to master the environment and being capable, adequate, effective, competent in relation to it',[12] but rather the mature person should be recognized by his/her independence of the environment, by being able to stand against it, to fight it, to neglect it, to turn their back on it, or to refuse it. He stresses detachment, independence, the self-governing character of people and their requirement to look within for their guiding values and rules.

The message is that spiritual leadership finds solutions in contemplation. Fundamental to spiritual leadership is to approach situations with an attitude of discernment rather than one of intervention, of acceptance rather than control, of letting go rather than holding on, of humility rather than arrogance. The Taoist principles are that the wise leader does not push to make things happen, but allows processes to unfold. The enlightened leader exhibits service not selfishness; holds a moderate ego, and demonstrates wisdom. This leader speaks simply and honestly, and intervenes only to shed light and promote harmony. Such a leader sets time for silent reflection; so that he/she and others should not lose sight of the single principle of how everything works. Through so being the leader knows when to listen, when to act, and when to withdraw.

The philosopher/trainers

Socratic and spiritualist teachings have had a profound impact on management trainers, management consultants, organization development specialists and broader client-driven specialists. In fact, in the USA, a strong movement has emerged amongst those specialists who have been striving to establish a place for self-development philosophy in management and leadership theory.

Peter Senge (1992) identifies the need for *metanoia* (transcendence of mind), a shift of mind, if organizations are to make the transformation into learning organizations. Senge asserts

When you ask people about what it is like being part of a great team, what is most striking is the meaningfulness of the experience. People talk about being a part of something larger than themselves, of being connected, of being generative. It becomes quite clear that, for many, their experience, as part of their lives, is looking for a way to recapture that spirit.[13]

Senge's (1992) representation of leadership in the *Fifth Discipline*, focuses on stewardship and facilitation, and not on the heroic transformational leader of the 'excellence' literature driven by Tom Peters and Bob Waterman (1982).

Stephen Covey (1990) also exhorts managers to some form of metanoia by advocating the resurrection of philosophical principles as the basis for leadership. Covey, in Socratic spirit, posits that an individual's character is the principal determinant of their personal effectiveness. Covey's seven habits which explain how highly effective people become so, are derived from a set of principles that include integrity, humility and fidelity. The seventh habit, 'sharpening the saw', includes spiritual renewal, which Covey defines as the continual clarification of values and commitment to others.

With spirituality and humility in mind, Semler (1993), in his book, *Maverick*, describes how he went through the process of letting go in order to transform his company, Semco, into what has been described as the world's most unusual organization. Similar sentiment has been expressed by the two authors, Arnold and Plas (1993), in their book *The Human Touch*. In Socratic style they declare, 'Those of us who run businesses today, need to raise our clenched fists, slowly extend our fingers, and let go of our organisations.'[14]

The modern Western leadership literature of the late 1980s and 1990s suggests a philosophical turn to Socratic and spiritual contemplation. There exists a strong philosophical push to have managers and leaders approach situations with an attitude of acceptance rather than control; of listening rather than doing; and of concern rather than superiority.

Born to lead school

Nietzsche's *Ubermensch* leader

By the late 19th century, the philosophy of leadership turned towards a prescriptive rather than a descriptive philosophical analysis. Friedrich Nietzsche's (1969) *Ubermensch* (superman) is a leader by his unique ability to transform, as the result of his exceptional human nature. As the embodiment of his extraordinary qualities, the *Ubermensch* leads by creating ever-new values to replace the ones destroyed in his 'overcoming' of the previous ethical, religious and political order. The leader, in Nietzschean terms, heralds nothing short of an ongoing, radical transformation of society, whereby domination of all those around provides for the guiding philosophy.

The Nietzschean superman, therefore, is not to be characterized by the possession of any determinate set of leadership attributes. The *Ubermensch* is superhuman, an essence not of this world. The Nietzschean *Ubermensch* is the image of the ideal leader, surpassing the 'merely human' and thereby challenging Christian morality, which dominated Nietzsche's age. The *Ubermensch* concept provides a fundamentally contrasting philosophical perspective on leadership from the ancient Greeks onwards. Humility is superseded by strength, whilst sense of being within a community is overturned by the will to conquer.

Biographers and biographical historians

The quick flirtation with history and philosophy highlights one fact, that history is on the side of the developmental school of leadership. Terms such as values, self-discovery, essence of self, abound more in the leadership philosophy literature than do concepts of born to be great, of genetic superiority, or of superhuman people. How is it then that the 'great leader school of leadership' has emerged with such popularity as of the great philosophers, Nietzsche is the one who goes against the grain? Is the belief that people are born to greatness nothing more than a signal of frailty in those who aspire towards achieving greatness, but who are emotionally unwilling to encounter the pain and stretching experience of command?

Glorification attribution, as much due to feelings of inadequacy, may hold true, but there exists another significant influence which glorifies leaders, not on a comparative analytical basis as has been the wont of the 20th century, but on a singular basis, namely the analysis of the one great person, as epitomized by biographers and historians. The influence of the biographers and biographical historians has been profound in promoting the image of the great leader.

In conducting an analysis of the impact of biographers, a collection of works has been randomly selected, in order to explore how the biographer and historian have acclaimed the object of their attention:

> Although he died in 1975, Eamon de Valera, generally known as Dev. or the Long Fellow, casts a long shadow that still falls over Irish life. Quite simply, the history of Ireland for much of the twentieth century is the history of de Valera ... His intangible influences can still be found in the divisions between the leading Irish political parties ..., in the attitudes towards Northern Ireland Church–State relationships, the role of women in Irish society, the Irish language and the whole concept of an Irish nation, ... Was he a Lincoln or Machiavelli? A saint or charlatan? A man of peace or one who incited young men to hatred and violence? Was he a revolutionary or a conservative? An unscrupulous manipulator or nice guy? The truth is that in a sense, the answer to all these questions is 'Yes'. (Tim Pat Coogan (1993) on De Valera)

> Few have exercised more power, personal and political, than Mao Zedong and Deng Xiaoping, true huangi-ti ... The great Chinese dynastic scholar, Zhong Zhi says of Mao 'He founded the first peasant dynasty in six hundred years.' In Chinese history, a capable minister or victorious general has often won the Mandate of Heaven. Deng Xiaoping fits the concept perfectly. Both men earned the title of huang-ti, despite the fact that both considered themselves Marxists. Both were Sons of Heaven, rulers by a kind of divine right. (Morrison E. Salisbury (1992) on Mao and Deng, the rulers of China for a substantial part of the 20th century)

> No Prime Minister of modern times has sought to change Britain and its place in the world as radically as she did. Her government, she says, was about the application of a philosophy, not the implementation of an administrative programme. She sets out here with forcefulness and conviction the reasons for her beliefs and how

she sought to turn them into action. (Foreword to Margaret Thatcher's (1993): *The Downing Street Years*)

... unmasks a woman who was calculating in the extreme in her pursuit of power from an early age ... It provides a picture of a singularly complex woman – a superb public performer and formidable strategist, yet prone in large measure to social vanity, materialism and vengefulness. And in effect, it puts into perspective the whole American electoral system, showing how it is possible for someone of modest accomplishment, but startling ambition, to create her husband's career and thus become without question the most powerful woman in the world. (Foreword to *Nancy Reagan*, by Kitty Kelley (1991))

A former Assistant Attorney General under President Johnson, Mitchell Ragovin, thought Hoover's life had been 'a passion play of good and evil, and when there was good, it was hollow'. That a man with a crippled psyche, capable of great evil, became the trusted symbol of all that was safe and good, is a paradox of our time ... epitomised the American dream, while renowned psychiatrists considered he would have been well suited for high office in Nazi Germany. (Anthony Summers (1993) on J. Edgar Hoover)

He had many admirers, but has been criticised by both liberal intellectuals and conservative activists who considered him a Dr Strangelove-figure, a manipulator who seemed dangerously devoid of moral principles ... Kissinger's character – brilliant, conspiratorial, furtive, prone to rivalry – related to the *Realpolitick* of the times, ... Kissinger's instinct for power was crucial in creating a new global balance that helped America cope with the aftermath of Vietnam. (Walter Isaacson (1992) on Henry Kissinger)

Charles cannot be called a great king or a great man; except when aroused, he was too lazy, cynical or opportunist. Yet he came near to being a genius, was a brilliant politician, a wit, a shrewd philosopher of life and a brave, highly intelligent and charming man ... For though indisputably naughty – indeed very naughty – he was amusing, appreciative and generous, he was lewd, he was brave and he was a gentleman; and what, except fidelity, can a lady want more? (Arthur Bryant (1955) on King Charles II of England)

Stalin had the reputation of being one of the harshest and wilful of the leaders ... Intellectually and morally he was no match for most of the leaders of the revolution, but in the struggle for succession, it was purposefulness, political will and cunning that counted ... Stalin, moreover, was a great actor ... the modest leader, the fighter for the purity of party ideals and later the leader and father of the people, great commander, theorist, connoisseur of arts, prophet ... Stalin cast his huge baneful shadow over our lives ... (Dmitri Volkogonov (1991) on Stalin)

Stalin's successors live in such grotesque horror of Trotsky's shade because they are so afraid of coming to grips with the issues with which he, so much ahead of his time, did come to grips ... I do indeed consider Trotsky as one of the most outstanding revolutionary leaders of all times, outstanding as fighter, thinker and martyr. (Isaac Deutscher (1959) on Trotsky)

Remembered today as 'Supermac', Britain's most urbane and unflappable statesman, Macmillan, for much of his life, was an insecure and deeply unhappy man ... A leading architect of the Tory revival after 1945 ... Macmillan emerged as the most powerful politician of the post war Conservative Party ... Few men could have been more constituted of paradoxes than Harold Macmillan; it was what gave him his charm and mischief ... (Alistair Horne (1988) on Harold Macmillan)

Ten biographers and historians, analysing and concluding on the lives of people who have profoundly influenced the lives of others; males and females, who in their own right can be considered as renowned leaders. Whatever may be the reality of these subjects' lives, the biographers and historians have been instrumental in the promulgation of an alternative consciousness, the cult of the great personality. The biographers and historians have used four simple but exceptionally powerful techniques to promote a glittering image of a great person, namely, contrast of capabilities, the thirst for power, social intelligence and the biographers' own interest.

Contrast of capabilities

Alistair Horne captures contrast in his description of Macmillan as a 'paradox' – unflappable yet insecure; similarly with Tim Pat Coogan, through the opposites of saint or charlatan, for De Valera; likewise with Kitty Kelley's analysis of the formidable strategist, yet vengeful, for Nancy Reagan; again, by Walter Isaacson, the contrast of brilliant but prone to rivalry, for Kissinger; Arthur Bryant's lazy and cynical, or, genius and brilliant politician, for King Charles II; and Anthony Summer's passion play of good and evil, for Hoover. Contrast denotes a particular mystique; contrast equally conjures images of exceptional talent. How can any one person be so different and yet still achieve broad acclaim? The reader is gripped and the scene is set for intriguing enquiry. Outstanding people appear mysterious. They are said to be driven by inner forces and secrets which few others are likely to experience, and by so doing, fall into a category of being unique. The mystique is heightened by the descriptions of violent swings of mood, by displays of capability, or exceptional oratory, and yet of underlying despair. The image given is that such a broad stretching sweep of emotions is for the selected few, as most individuals could not sustain such deep, inner passions within the more normal, humdrum existence of community and family life. Bombarded with such prose, it is no surprise to find that a poorly questioned quest has arisen to discover the secret of leadership, especially for those who hope to escape from the trivialities of followership.

Drive for power

A second mystique is the overwhelming attraction to power, to dominance and to control. Statements such as 'the history of Ireland is the history of De Valera'; 'political will and cunning', for Stalin; 'instinct for power', for Kissinger; 'sought to change Britain', for Margaret Thatcher, highlight an overwhelming sense of purpose and mission, for country, for passion, for ideals, or for self. Thus are characterized the writings of biographers, who take a human being and mould them to that of a cult figure. The image presented, which may or may not be accurate, is of someone with a superhuman drive, with which certain individuals have been blessed or tainted. The drive for power overcomes other deficiencies, such as humble background, poor education, or just a lower level of intelligence, as was highlighted in the cases of Nancy Reagan and Joseph Stalin. The view given is that the 'street' skills of life can compensate for a lack of development in other areas. The question raised is where such force of life can be found; the raising of which further strengthening the view that ideal and idolatry in leadership must exist.

Intelligence and social intelligence

Two concepts which are often intertwined by biographers, are the rational skills of analysis and intelligence, and the capability to read multiple contexts simultaneously (social intelligence), and with their twinning and emerging insight, knowing how to proceed. Trotsky as both thinker and fighter; Kissinger as both brilliant, and manipulative, and the philosophical platform and intellect to drive change of Margaret Thatcher, emphasize that being clever is simply not sufficient. The cerebral tools of analysis are part of a broader kitbag of influence which involves recognizing what to do and when to back off, of knowing how to negotiate, but with foresight and cleverly packed argument. The 'real' experience that most tend to have is of one or the other, of being mentally quick, or of knowing how to influence. 'He or she may be clever, but doesn't really have much commonsense', is expressed with common regularity. However, to package both in the same person, coupled with the mystery invoked by distance (most people have never met Margaret Thatcher or Trotsky), adds to the curiosity to search for those hidden qualities which will promulgate the 'ordinary' person to power, responsibility and greatness.

Biographers' self-interest

His success at Jaguar cars is the nearest thing to an Arthurian Knightly quest that modern industrial society is capable of producing. (Walter Goldsmith and Barry Ritchie (1987) on Sir John Egan, whilst at Jaguar cars)

Walters is not a charismatic leader in the Montgomery mould . . . His brain works very fast and he has the ability to go straight to the heart of a subject. He listens to what others have to say, but usually seems to know in advance what that is going to be. (Walter Goldsmith and Barry Ritchie (1987) on Sir Peter Walters, Chairman, Chief Executive of British Petroleum)

The same use of contrasts, mixture of analytical skills, social intelligence and drive are used by biographers to describe business leaders. It should be noted that it is in the biographer's interests that their subjects curry attention. Without the distraction of comparison with others, the subject in question may be attributed with strengths which exude uniqueness and exclusivity.

Whatever the rightness or wrongness of such thinking, the emerging mystery of the character of the great leader, has provided the force to source further exploration in order to unravel the secrets of what it takes to be great!

Contemplating leaders

The twin themes of the ideal character make-up of leaders, and the pathways of development unique to each life traveller, have dominated transformational leadership thinking. This double-sided analysis assists in providing a historical appreciation of how leadership as a concept has evolved. However, in order better to appreciate individual leaders, a more sophisticated level of analysis is necessary, which can provide a view as to how wisdom and the art of communication can be well or badly used, and how leaders can also use and misuse charismatic greatness. Understanding leadership has to be coupled with appreciating the unique nature of each individual who happens to be a leader.

The military historian, John Keegan (1988), provides an interesting framework by which to analyse leaders. He places leaders in one of four categories, namely heroic leaders, anti-heroic leaders, unheroic leaders and the false heroic leaders. The heroic leaders epitomise dashing bravery, and display strength, skill and charisma on and off the battlefield. Heroic leaders are supposedly quicker, smarter and sharper than their contemporaries, displaying the characteristics of a leader born with all the attributes of high office and command.

The anti-heroic leader supposedly displays a mental agility and a sharpness similar to those of the heroic leader, but without the phenomenal flair and charismatic attraction. The anti-heroic leader could be symbolised as a cold fish, stern, an organizer, and communicator through the written word, but not the orator that excites. Nevertheless, the individual possesses, or they and others believe they possess, the qualities benefiting command.

The unheroic leader is captioned by the, 'local boy makes good' syndrome; the leader who has weathered and learned from life's challenges, and has ensured that he/she has maintained a perspective of continuous development. The unheroic nature of such leaders is that they see themselves as part of the throng from which they came. Within unheroic leadership, there is no need to display ego, because to have self-accomplished, and to have made the best of the potential of others, are both sufficient ends in themselves. The unheroic leader attempts to marry the dialectic of leading with being democratic, whilst holding the view that he/she is no better than any one else. Unheroic leaders are unlikely to exude charisma, but are likely to have charisma attributed to them.

The false leader, similar to the unheroic leader, may have emerged from humble beginnings, but in reality is ego driven and controls situations to satisfy his/her ends. False leaders are unlikely to harbour any inhibitions in their use of terror and cruelty. Their view of themselves and the portrayal of what they are, are likely to contrast sharply with the reality of others' experience of them. The ego-driven impetus for recognition and adulation is one reason why they need to control and cajole. They truly believe they are great, or should be seen as such, and if not, feel hard done by. The second, is an unwillingness or inability to trust. The false hero may display a deep suspicion and paranoia, and in extreme cases may resort to psychopathic behaviour.

The four typologies of John Keegan fit well with the two sides of transformational leadership. The heroic leader epitomises the great man/ woman model. The anti-hero falls into the downside of the great person school of thought. The unheroic leader depicts the image of the individual who pursues his/her own route of development, integrating the learning of life and from life, as he/she proceeds. The image of the unheroic leader at the end of life's journey may bear no resemblance to the hesitant, unimpressive youth who embarked upon that road. The false leader provides for the negative aspect of the developed discretionary leader: possibly unimpressive at the start, learning and developing rapidly as they proceed, but driven by a darkness, wherein they see that they are the only light that shines, and all others are expendable or irrelevant to their progress.

Within each of these four categorizations, examples are provided of leaders from past to modern times, in order to assist in understanding, respecting or disregarding the leaders one has encountered in one's own life passage.

Heroic leaders

Alexander the Great

According to his historical biographers, Alexander the Great (fourth century BC), who was both king and priest, ruled and commanded, but most of all interacted with others of his period by displaying greater skill in battle and a greater capacity for discourse in debate than his fellow Macedonians or his enemies. He made himself master of the Greek world first, then dominated another, the Persian Empire, and finally ventured into India. However, whilst in India, Alexander learned that his army yearned for Greece more strongly than for new worlds to conquer. He subjugated his plans to good grace and turned his steps homeward.

Each of Alexander's leadership capabilities was an ingredient in the elaborate edifice of personality, that was the foundation to his generalship. Alexander possessed consummate theatrical skills but was also a man of daily routine even on the days he awaited battle. He rose early. He sacrificed offerings of animal blood. He, with impeccable discipline, attended to the business of the day (there was justice to dispense, taxes to be levied and distributed, pay, subsistence, and court expenses to be accounted for, appointments to be made and revoked). Aware of his own needs, he took a short siesta at noon, then rode in the hunt, practised skills at arms, and late in the day took his second bath (he also bathed in the early morning). The day's climax was dinner with his companions, an occasion, 'central to the life of the hero'.[15] The time of dinner signified not only enjoyment and relaxation, when music, poetry and songs were performed but also the time for an exchange of news, views and considerations of the future. It was the evening when the strengthening of relationships took place with advisers and soldiers alike.

Alexander's exceptional fascination arose through his schooling at his father Phillip's, court (he was princely by birth), with his tutor Aristotle's philosophy, which was regarded not as a meeting of minds, but a juxtaposition of opposites. While citizens of the ancient Greek city states, 'held their political culture of equality and of democratic self-government,[16] the kingdom of Macedonia, was hereditary in practice – the monarchy dominated. The Macedonian king was considered to be the chief intermediary between the people and the gods, as Macedonia was the result of an intermingling of disparate and uncooperative highland clans. The leaders of Macedonia in the fourth century BC, evolved close blood ties with their companions. Their relationship was one of shared hardship, arising between those who battled together and outdid each other in their exhibition of courage. In order to unite such warriors the leader had constantly to excel in battle, in hunting, in the control of their steed, in winning the attention of their paramour, in discourse, in exaggeration, in self-projection and especially in drinking. Alexander's philosophy of leadership thrived on feelings. His kingship was as much an exercise of emotion as of deed. Thus his belief that leaders should be at the front in battle was constantly exercised. Upon completing his advanced planning, Alexander would leap into battle at the head of his troops.

Although admired by Caesar, Augustus and Napoleon amongst others, very little is known about Alexander's inner emotional life. Like Socrates, Alexander was an intellectual who also never recorded in writing any of his spoken words. He left no code of laws, no theory of war, no philosophy of kingship. Although characterized by certain outbursts of violent, impetuous and unreflective actions, he was not impulsive, but incisive and strategic in his military technique. He used meticulous logistical arrangements, and a consultative approach in his staff conferences and in the management of his army. He attended to his soldiers and few complained that they were not well fed or promptly paid. Alexander used every trick in the book, flattering, bribing and granting favour. Reward for bravery was generously given, as was care and comfort genuinely offered to the sick and wounded.

The Olympian manner he adopted in battle and in the hunt, he rarely used in the management of his immediate circle. Reconnaissance and staff discussions preceded the advance to combat, highlighting precision, timing and caution. He addressed his men, sometimes the whole army, sometimes only their officers.

Overall, he excelled in the art of communication. The ability to lead and stage-manage is well shown, for after being wounded during an encounter with a local Indian tribe on the return from India, Alexander allowed the suspicion to grow that he had died of his wounds. Although he shortly sent word that he was alive, he allowed the rumours of his passing to continue. Finally, he allowed himself to be carried by ship to his troops, as though a corpse, but then suddenly raised his body and arms to the adulation of his soldiers.

Charlemagne

In medieval history, Charlemagne (Carlos Magnus, Charles the Great), the Frankish crown emperor in AD 800, stands out (Bullough 1980). Although in the tradition of the Frankish warrior-king he conquered by war, he also added a novel dimension, namely the seriousness he took to the Christian sanctification of his role, as well as the same degree of endeavour to patronizing learning and the arts. He wanted to 'magnify the grandeur and prestige of his court by filling it with evidence of Christian learning'.[17] Territorially, Charlemagne was a great builder, putting together a realm bigger than anything in the West, since Rome. Even the church was firmly subordinated to his authority. 'He presided over the Frankish synods, pronouncing upon dogmatic questions as authoritatively as had Justinian'.[18] Charlemagne's coronation, performed by the Pope, added an additional novelty, that of being one of the few monarchs to have commanded the services of his Holiness. He manipulated the church with ease, turning it into an organ of his government, thereby controlling the bishops. He was an intellectual, educated at Auchen, the centre for the copying and diffusion of the Bible. He also spoke Latin as well as Frankish, and understood Greek.

Born to be king, Charlemagne held an unbroken conviction of being at one with the divine will. He increasingly strove to create a disciplined army of mailed cavalry, out of the Frankish host of unarmoured foot soldiers. Cavalry tactics were also given another impetus, for only mailed horsemen could cope with the might of the Vikings.

In Charlemagne, politically conditioned spiritualism emerged as the basis of his empire, as church and state blended into an institutional and spiritual unity. His reforms have survived until today. He gave his state a Treasury, and gave Europe the division of a pound of silver into 240 pennies (*denarii*), which division was to survive in the British Isles for eleven hundred years.

Charlemagne's power was centred on him. Charlemagne's courtiers, advisers and ministers were bound to him by the swearing of a solemn oath, the oath of loyalty. Although by no means a new practice, he made the solemn oath of loyalty a tool of government and by his will was not resisted, but strongly acclaimed.

The anti-hero

The adulation of Alexander, for those who would be heroes, is understandable, for that is their aspiration. However, a drawback for certain would-be heroes is that they will not be great if the virtue they lack is charisma. That lack of charismatic influence then designates them as anti-heroes.

Julius Caesar

In 59 BC, Julius Caesar commanded the army of Gaul and proceeded to a succession of brilliant campaigns over the next 7 years, ending in Gaul's complete conquest. Caesar was worshipped, but was also a tyrant, was rich and stretched his influence over a loyal and experienced army. Officers and men alike looked to him for leadership, so as to continue their clamour for pay, promotion and victory. Caesar, never one to rebuff attention, was also a patient and ruthless man. His brilliant military tactics and success brought him great honour. He was voted as head of state for life, displaying his little regard for the susceptibilities of politicians. His reforms included imposing order in the streets of Rome, and undertaking steps to end the power of the moneylenders in politics. His greatest contribution, crucial to the future of Europe, was the introduction of the Julian calendar, which he adopted across the Roman empire and which began on 1 January 54 BC.

A strategist by nature, Caesar proclaimed that leaders should be at the front only sometimes, and even then seldom in combat situations. His strategies, and his remarkable on-the-ground intelligence, kept him abreast of the movements of his enemies' armies. His leadership style, copied and envied by Frederick the Great when he came to the throne in 1740, by Napoleon when he came to power in 1793, and by all other great anti-heroic leaders, had one flaw – it was not the traditional interpretation of heroic. The discipline, coldness of character, and the lack of sharing of the common soldier's plight, induced an unenviable propensity towards abstraction, which unfortunately was combined with an equal propensity for cruelty.

Oliver Cromwell

One of the most remarkable of all English military and political leaders, Oliver Cromwell rose to power particularly during the English Civil War. It was he who established the only republic in English history. Cromwell acquired a reputation both as a military organizer and a fighting man. Similar to Alexander, he required loyalty, discipline, good treatment of, and regular payment for, his troopers.

However, comparison with Alexander, from there, ceases. Born as a country gentleman farmer, educated at the local grammar school, at Cambridge and at Lincoln's Inn Bar, a devoted family man, Cromwell was brought up as Protestant but converted to Calvinism near the age of 30. Cromwell was a victim of a spiritual and psychological struggle, polarized between strong beliefs concerning virtue and morality, and the democratic rights of individuals to determine their own future. Even certain of his own actions he detested, because they either offended his sense of virtue or his belief in the right of self-determination. For example, the number of Pilgrim Fathers, who, sailing in the Mayflower, were exiled to The Americas for their beliefs, was small in comparison with the number of religious extremists sent there by Cromwell. Cromwell did not, in great numbers, ship off the High Church Protestants or Catholics, but the extremist sections of his own supporters, the Levellers, the Shakers and Quakers who had become too vociferous in their demands, and were making the reuniting of the state problematic. Although his popularity with and support shown by his own side were dented, the need for state unification was pressing, as contrary to the popular belief that there was one English Civil War, there were, in fact, a second and a third speedily to follow.

The First Civil War having disrupted the social order, it was Cromwell's intent thereafter to provide stability. However, the remnants of the King's forces were active, mustering support in Scotland and Ireland. The two ensuing Civil Wars were concerned with the flushing out of these armies and undermining their local strength. In Scotland, Cromwell reached Elgin where he destroyed the remnants of the Royal forces. His campaign in Ireland involved the scorching of the towns of Drogheda and Wexford, to pursue and neutralize the Royalists, but historically has been interpreted as the slaughter of Irish Catholics. As a result, his reputation for cruelty was established.

In fact, Cromwell was the architect of the British state, which in ensuing centuries became a dominant world influence. First, with the army he created structure, discipline, uniform, and provided the latest in technology. At the beginning of the Civil War, the only distinction that was made between the opposing sides was the colour of the plume in the combatants' hats. Initially, it looked certain that the King's forces, under the command of the daring Prince Rupert (a heroic, Alexander-type figure), would quickly emerge as the victors. However, more for off-the-battlefield reasons, to do with logistics, recruitment and quality of equipment, that was not to be. Despite setbacks on the King's side, Cromwell should still have been vanquished at the decisive battle of Marston Moor in Yorkshire. The speed and agility of Rupert and his command had the Royalist forces in place ready to do battle, whilst Cromwell's forces were still trying to bring up their supplies, and their rearguard into position. Rupert thought it 'ungentlemanly to attack before the other side was ready', and waited for approximately 11 hours whilst Cromwell formed his line; a decision Rupert was to regret. Despite other shortcomings in his army, Cromwell's strength lay in the cavalry, wherein his drilling and discipline had created a force that was able to charge, check and re-form in order to attack once more. Acclaimed as the victor of Marston Moor, Cromwell then attended to the remainder of his army and produced one of the finest fighting forces in Europe.

A further achievement of Cromwell's was the navy which, under Sir Robert Blake, set the structure for the sea power that Britain became. Cromwell's naval strength provided the confidence to engage with the great naval power of that day, the Dutch, and to emerge from what were trade wars, on balance, the victor. That would have been unimaginable in the reign of Charles I.

Cromwell, appointed commander in chief by Parliament, also accepted an 'Instrument of Government' drawn up by his fellow officers and thereby became Lord Protector of the State. Cromwell's aims were to reform the law, to set up a Puritan Church, to permit toleration of worship, to promote education, and to decentralize administration. Cromwell's new republican parliament promoted four fundamental tenets: government by a single person and Parliament; the regular summoning of parliaments, each with a limited lifespan; the maintenance of fundamentals such as liberty and conscience and the division of control of the armed forces between the Protector and Parliament. 'The result was an English republic astonishingly fertile in new constitutional schemes, as Oliver cast about to find a way of governing through Parliament without delivering to England an intolerant Protestantism.'[19] It was he who provided the term Commonwealth, a wealth common to all in the nation.

As Lord Protector, Cromwell displayed greater tolerance than many of his Puritan supporters. Once bishops were abolished and congregations allowed to chose their own ministers, he was satisfied. Outside the church, he promised that all Christians could practise their own religion, so long as they did not create disorder and unrest. In politics he did not hold fixed views, except that he was opposed to what he called arbitrary government. The irony was that in order to achieve a balance and tolerance of different interests in the state, Cromwell had to use military force to attain the local democracies he desired. His reputation as the anti-hero was now set. A cold and incisive individual, Cromwell became hated by friend and foe alike.

Frederick the Great

Frederick II, 'The Great', who ruled Prussia from 1740 to 1786, inherited from his father, the 'left overs' of an army, composed for the most part of criminals, mercenaries, unwilling conscripts and simply the poor and starving. Furthermore, the cost of this inept military machine was heavy on Prussia's budget. However, Frederick's careful housekeeping, allowed him once more to rebuild Prussia, grow a disciplined and efficient army and leave behind one of the best-filled treasuries in Europe.

As a person, Frederick was, 'malicious, vindictive and completely without scruple'. Yet, at the same time he was 'highly intelligent and cultivated, playing and composing for the flute, and enjoying the conversation of clever men'. He was, moreover, 'utterly devoted to the interests of his dynasty'.[20] His ambition for expansion and that his state should be dominant in Europe reflected his desire for glory. He not only borrowed much from the practice of Roman legions, and in particular from Cromwell's reforms, but also introduced numerous innovations of his own. Frederick introduced standardization of regulations and equipment, promoted specialization of tasks, created a common language in the Germanies, and established systematic training involving the discipline of army drill. Frederick also fostered the principle that fighting men must be taught to fear their officers more than the enemy. Basically, Frederick was determined to make 'Theory X' work. To ensure that the military machine was wisely used, he distinguished between advisory and command functions, freeing specialist advisers (staff) from the line of command, in order for staff to forward plan activities. In time, further adjustments were introduced, decentralizing control to create greater autonomy for particular units, so as to have the freedom to respond appropriately in different combat situations. Frederick's impact was long term, for his innovations in weapons technology and drill sequences remained the essentials of warfare from the third quarter of the 17th century until almost the middle of the 19th. Many of Frederick's ideas and processes found their way, in a piecemeal fashion, into the system of factory production in the nineteenth century. The so-called Protestant Work Ethic, and Max Weber's analysis of bureaucracy, are examples of the way in which Frederick's innovations were woven into management theory, just a century ago.

Napoleon Bonaparte

In the same century, Napoleon came to prominence, initially through his ability to control mobs during the French Revolution. Napoleon had highly developed, intellectual powers, an unusual gift for mathematics and an attraction to ancient history. He was obsessed with Rousseau and the cult of feelings. Despite a sophisticated mind, Napoleon was a loner, despising the rest of humanity, and impressively unpopular due to the sharpness but also penetrating nastiness of his tongue. Napoleon, for a long period, was a committed Jacobean, and although his ideological commitment was perfectly genuine, he was extreme and that earned him the reputation of being a terrorist.

Napoleon seemed to hold a profound contempt for the intense wealth of human nature. His attitude towards others was transactional, as he believed that any person could be bought. He loathed intellectuals, and entered into suppressing freedom of thought and movement by means of censorship and secret police. He briefly restored his country's prosperity through ruthless diplomacy and war, but destroyed himself by invading Russia. He advanced his career by making shrewd use of the opportunities offered by the state. In power in 1793, Napoleon secured considerable support from the church, persuading the French temporal hierarchy to tell the peasants in their pastoral region not to evade conscription.

Napoleon was still a young man when he came to power, and had already shown his exceptional brilliance and ruthlessness as a soldier. Although feigning Alexander's informality and bonhomie, he readily used grapeshot on women and children, and deserted his armies, one left to rot in Egypt, and likewise in Russia, when the campaigns turned sour.

He boasted that his armies offered a career to those with talents, and turned a blind eye to the fact that many of his officers were Louis XVI's aristocrats. Napoleon brilliantly promoted his own hybrid mix of tactics and strategy known as 'grand tactics', and in so doing not only overcame the problems of transport and supply thereby allowing for rapid deployment, but also pioneered lightning warfare. He applied the same basic principle of strategy and tactic to prevent his forces from being divided, which allowed him the freedom to concentrate all his might against the enemy at critical points. He emphasized balance, clearly targeting his forces before action, overwhelming the enemy through the weight of strike power, shock attacks, great daring and ruthless decisions in battle which often led to bloody consequences. The method was simple, direct, overpowering, even brutal.

His empire was governed by legal codes, drawn up by the revolutionary legislators. The codes determined the concepts of family, property, the individual, and public power, and were, in generality, spread throughout Europe. The codes replaced and sometimes supplemented a chaos of local, customary, Roman and ecclesiastical laws. Similarly, he imposed common administrative practices. Service in the French armies required attention to a common discipline and military regulation, and French weights and measures, based on the decimal system, replaced many local scales. Such innovations exercised an influence beyond the actual limits of French rule, providing models and inspiration to modernization in other countries. Thus, Napoleon altered the map of Europe and stamped his own political testament on the region. He may have shaped the map of Europe, but he lost it by the fear France had inspired under his leadership. History surfaced a brilliant mind, but a person deeply loathed.

The unheroic leader

Ulysses Simpson Grant

During the American Civil war in 1862, Grant rose to the rank of General in Chief of the Armies of the United States. His style was to ride to and inspect the battle front and survey its state, rather than participate in combat. When he saw disorder and a deterioration of discipline, he intervened to balance the situation.

As a person he was, 'physically slight, personally self-effacing, and academically undistinguished'[21] in his passage through West Point, or in the army. A democrat and populist, he was a keen realist, about himself and others. Grant's support team was small in number, rarely exceeding 20, largely because of his voracious appetite for work. In today's terms, he would be known as a workaholic. His sense of duty and habit of self-sufficiency left him with the view that most tasks were perfectly manageable by one individual, and he could therefore dedicate his staff not to bureaucratic routine, but to acting as his eyes and ears. Grant relied on their information. His style was open, where people would freely express their views. Grant was both a transactional and transformational leader, with an enviable capacity for attending to transactional detail. Grant also displayed another gift, namely as a writer of extraordinary capacity. He was as able to set dramatic mood, as he was sensitive in his analysis of people and their character. He could quickly summarize events or write detailed and long narrative. The result was a literary phenomenon.

Grant was quiet by nature, not given to dramatic gesture, impeccably courteous to all irrespective of their stature in life; in effect a polite listener. Grant loathed gossiping and the damaging tension that can arise when dissecting others, 'behind their back'. He rarely swore, and was careful not to reprimand subordinates and colleagues alike in public. His approach was encouragement rather than reproof. He was equally courteous in his dealings with superiors, civilians and the military. Grant, a victor crowned with laurels, shrank from the political limelight. His personal needs were so small that he had the barest of possessions and relied little on his daily help.

His unconcern for outward appearance was famous. Though scrupulous about personal cleanliness, such discipline he did not apply to the presentation of his uniform. His lack of panache in dress was replicated in his manner and personal style. Grant was direct in speech and actively disliked ceremony, drama and oratory. He rarely addressed his troops, had no appetite for the conventional rewards of war, shrank from crowds, and shunned the nineteenth-century form of twentieth-century 'spin doctors'. For him, war was won by fighting, not by evasion and strategy. The one field where he overtly displayed what others would call Alexandrian type leadership, was as an outstanding equestrian.

Ironically, Grant was sickened by the sight of blood and was deeply disturbed by his encounters with the wounded and the dead. He could not bear to see people dismembered and broken. Grant, the modest man, the unassuming hero, eventually a new nation's President, firmly falls in the category of unheroic leader.

Martin Luther King, Jr.

American clergyman and world-famous civil rights leader, King was born in 1929 into a family steeped in the tradition of the Southern black ministry of Baptist preachers (Fischer, 1977). Particularly gifted, he entered college under a special programme, eventually gaining a BA. His early interest in medicine and law was overtaken by a desire to enter the ministry. He spent three years at a theological seminary, earning a Bachelor of Divinity, graduating with the highest academic average in his class. It was at the theology seminary that King first became exposed to Mahatma Ghandi's philosophy of non-violent protest, as well as becoming acquainted with contemporary Protestant theologians. King was awarded a PhD from Boston University, where he began to elucidate and clarify his concept of man's relationship with God. His unending faith in God's guidance proved to be the foundation of his strength and resilience. In 1955, when black activists formed the Montgomery Improvement Association to boycott the transport system, King was elected their leader. In his first speech he declared that blacks had no alternative but to protest, and thereby introduced a fresh voice, a skilful rhetoric, in inspiring a new doctrine to civil struggle. A year later, the blacks of Montgomery achieved their goal of desegregation of the city's buses.

Recognizing the opportunity for capitalizing on the successful Montgomery action through mass movement, King organized the Southern Christian Leadership Conference (SCLC), which supported his activities throughout the South, as well as promoting his cause nationally. King addressed people from all walks of life in all parts of the country, discussing the problems faced by black communities, with civil, business and religious leaders, both within and outside the USA. After visiting India in 1959, King became convinced that non-violent resistance was a powerful lever available to oppressed peoples in their struggle for civil liberties.

Co-pastor with his father in his native city of Atlanta, King declared that the right moment to accentuate the drive against injustice. In an attempt to achieve the desegregation of public parks and other facilities, the tactic of non-violent sit-ins and protest marches was used. As a result, King was arrested on a number of occasions and jailed, only to be released upon the intervention of the dashing east coast Democratic presidential candidate, John F. Kennedy. From 1960 to 1965, King's influence reached its peak. King aroused the devotion and allegiance of many blacks and liberal whites, in all parts of the USA, as well as support from the administration of President Kennedy.

King's leadership in the civil rights movement was challenged in the mid-1960s as other, more militant, black activists appeared. However, in the face of mounting criticism from young blacks, he broadened his approach to include socially charged issues other than racism. He opposed the war in Vietnam and extended the platform to include the poor of all races. His focus was clear. To fight poverty and unemployment. King was awarded the Nobel Prize for Peace in 1964. On 4 April 1968 the eloquent speaker, proficient writer, and social activist, Martin Luther King, was shot and killed, at the age of 39, by an assassin's bullet, on the balcony of the motel where he was staying.

The contribution of King to the black freedom movement was that of a leader who was able to turn protest into crusade, and to translate local conflicts into moral issues of nation-wide concern. Successful in the waking of the black masses and galvanizing them into action, King won his greatest victories by appealing to the consciences of white Americans and thus bringing political leverage to bear in Washington. Just as his insistence that non-violence must remain the essential tactic of the movement never wavered, neither did his resolve to promote civil and economic justice for all Americans. The humble and the unassuming King did not take for granted his rights to leadership or that he should remain in the forefront of the cause for which he fought. His unselfish nature as a leader, his concern for the everyday life of people, his sharing of their hardships, and his preoccupation with the future and morality, place this great hero in the unheroic school of leadership; a school that some say is probably the most heroic of all.

False heroic leader

Joseph Stalin (born Iosif Vissarionovic Dzhugashvili)

Stalin ventured beyond tsarist boundaries, for by the winter of 1940, he made further gains into the west, taking over the Baltic republics and retrieving old provinces in the south-east of Europe. During his dictatorship, he rebuilt most of the tsarist empire, restructured Soviet industry and secured the help of powerful allies. In 1949, Stalinist Russia signalled its arrival as the world's second nuclear superpower by exploding the hydrogen bomb.

Notwithstanding the formidable achievements that resulted from the Second World War, namely industrialization and collective farming, few of these advances ever became available to the ordinary Soviet citizen in the form of consumer goods or amenities for improving life. A considerable proportion of Russia's national wealth was appropriated by Stalin to cover military expenditure, the police infrastructure and further industrialization. Ironically, the collectivization of agriculture did not produce an economy rich in produce upon which to feed its population but was successful in subsuming control of the section of its people, the difficult and recalcitrant Kulaks, the peasantry. Probably, Stalin's greatest achievements proved to be his intricate, surprisingly efficient bureaucratic machinery, based on the interweaving of the Communist Party with legislative bodies, with trade unions, with the police and the armed forces. All of these devices of control he manipulated.

Stalin feared and disliked anyone who, in his assessment, could be a potential threat. His approach to leadership was simple: rule by brutal force and fear. Such was his extent of persecution in the Soviet Union, that Stalin had under his control all elements of Soviet society. He eliminated his veteran Bolsheviks, colleagues, party bosses, military leaders, industrial managers, and high government officials, all of whom were already totally subservient to him. Other sections of the Soviet elite, the arts, the academic world, the legal and diplomatic professions, also suffered a high proportion of victims, as did the population at large, to a psychotically paranoid, indiscriminate persecution that fed on extraordinary denunciations and confessions. Stalin's political victims were numbered in their tens of millions.

After the war, Stalin imposed, in Eastern Europe, a new kind of colonial control, nominally independent states, that in reality were directed to follow his bidding. Diplomacy was used not only as a convenient tool but also as a weapon for the advance of ideology. Stalin drew a high cost. Commercial relations between Soviet Russia and other countries became more strained, causing a huge disruption to world trade after 1931. Domestic life in the Soviet Union after the Second World War was harsher then ever. Both the propaganda to which Soviet citizens were subjected, and the brutalities of the police system were intensified, after some sporadic relaxation during the war. The distinction between the economic systems of East and West remained a fundamental divide of world economic history from 1945 to the 1980s. Stalin consolidated the division of Europe, for when, West Germany entered NATO, the Soviet response was the Warsaw Pact, an alliance of Russia's satellites.

Stalin seems to have neither desired nor experienced satisfactory private or family life. He seemed to thrive on impromptu buffet suppers, inviting high party officials, generals, and visiting foreign diplomats. He encouraged indulgence at these events, thus revealing weak points in others that he could exploit.

On his own behalf, he engaged in the fabrication of his heroism. History books were rewritten, and any of his early Caucasian colleagues (Stalin came from Georgia) who objected were removed. Through Soviet propaganda, he made himself a legend, exaggerating his heroic deeds as a boy, as a Bolshevik conspirator and faithful follower of Lenin. In reality, he ascended to power through ruthless, self-promoting means. Unfortunately, his model of leadership was copied by many societies. Stalin was a false hero, rewriting the past glory of the Bolsheviks in his favour, accentuating his personal heroism, whilst behind the scenes millions suffered to fulfil his dreams of a world dominant Soviet.

Saddam Hussein al-Tikriti

A revolutionary assassin and terrorist from an early age, Saddam joined the Ba'ath Socialist Party in 1957. The Ba'ath Party had been founded in 1940 by a Syrian Christian, Michael Aflaq, who first established the party in Syria, which he later fled and moved to Iraq. The party promoted the ideals of pan-Arab unity, freedom and socialism. It also staged a successful *coup d'état* in Iraq in 1968, and has remained in control ever since. Saddam worked his way up the party hierarchy to become chief aide and later vice president to the then president Ahmed Hassan al-Bakr. Saddam took office in 1979, after al-Bakr stepped down, allegedly because of ill health. However, Saddam had long been the effective head of state for Iraq, displayed by the fact that in 1972, he nationalized the Petroleum Company, that being a major step to gaining effective control of the government.

The Revolutionary Command Council (RCC) underpins the presidency in Ba'athist theory, linking it to the Ba'ath Regional Command, placing Iraq as a state within the broader context of the Ba'ath National Command, the broader representative body overseeing the Arab world. However, with the absence of its wider acceptance in the Arab world, and with little sympathy emanating from Syrian Ba'athism, the RCC has little political life other than being the expression of Saddam's will. Saddam holds the position of president and prime minister, runs the country from his own presidential office, with the help of trusted advisers, keeping a tight reign over the bastion of the regime, the Ba'ath

Party, the security organizations and the armed forces. His careful manipulation of the major centres of power continues to give his regime its greatest strength, despite the narrowness of his power base.

Born in 1937 in Tikrit, Iraq, Saddam later attended the Cairo Law School, in exile in 1961–1963, and continued at the Baghdad Law College after the Ba'athists took power. He was reared by his widowed mother, who later married his father's brother.

As ascending president, Saddam's goals were to supplant Egypt as the leading country of the Arab world, and to establish a pan-Arab alliance strong enough to resist Western influence in Arab politics. He also wanted to use oil revenues to raise the country's standard of living, and to build a strong and modern defence system. Towards this end, he undertook huge and expensive industrialization projects. Further, in order to build an image of an international leader, in June 1980, Saddam held the first parliamentary elections since the overthrow of the monarchy in 1968, which resulted in a victory for the Ba'athists.

As part of his continuing expansionist campaign, and determined to gain control of the Strait of Hormuz, historically Iraqi land, Saddam declared war on Iran in September 1980. He banked on a rapid and easy victory against a demoralized and ill-equipped Iranian army caught in the throes of an Islamic revolution. In the event, the Iraqis themselves became bogged down in urban warfare in the southern Iranian cities, and ultimately found themselves ignominiously defeated on Iranian soil. The eight years of continuous fighting in a series of land offensives came to a halt in August 1988, when the Iranians agreed to accept previously refused cease-fire proposals. As the war tortuously progressed into years of battle, and the campaign for pan-Arab unity became bogged down in a war of attrition, Saddam's prestige in the Arab world declined.

Having rebuilt his armed forces and having suppressed internal criticism, in August 1990, after accusing Kuwait of border violations and of manipulating the price of oil, Saddam invaded and occupied Kuwait, claiming reunification of the original borders. Shortly thereafter, he formally annexed Kuwait, making the statement that he was prepared to negotiate. However, by mid-January, the intense military attack from the US and allied forces severely disrupted Iraq's ability to become a major player in any organized modern warfare. By April 1991, Saddam agreed to comply with UN cease-fire terms. The results for Saddam have been catastrophic. Championed by the USA, an international trade embargo currently exists, isolating Iraq from the rest of the world. After Iraq's defeat in Kuwait, Kurdish leaders launched an all-out revolt which, in the space of a few days resulted in their capture and control of Kurdistan, only to be met by a massive counterattack by government forces, using gas and napalm, resulting in the displacement of approximately 22 million Kurdish refugees, and the intervention of the United Nations and the creation of 'safe havens' for Kurds. The Arab Corporate Council has been fragmented into those who support and those who oppose the dictator. In addition, there has existed, and does exist, unrest within Saddam's own family. His two daughters and their families defected to Jordan. Their disloyalty was punished on their return, a year later, by the execution of their husbands and children. What is startling, is that an Arab killed or allowed to be killed, children, especially those of his own family, a fundamentally counter-cultural and taboo action for Arabs. Latest press reports highlight that the turmoil in the Hussein family has reached new heights whereby Saddam has imprisoned his wife, stating that he has had to tighten his own internal security.

Similar to Stalin, Saddam is also placed in the false heroic category. The contradiction between his original stated aims of Arab unity and an end to Western manipulation of Arab resources, and his subsequent actions, is too great to ignore. His focus on building the armed forces at the continued cost to the Iraqi citizens, his complete disregard for human life, the terror that his intelligence organizations create inside Iraq and with dissidents outside Iraq, and the slaughter of his grandchildren so that they, in adulthood, could not threaten his regime by wishing to avenge the death of their fathers, place him in the position of a harsh and ruthless dictator. Being a dictator does not in itself qualify him for the label of false hero, but the underlying self-oriented nature of his actions, does.

Leaders as arbiters of dialogue

Undoubtedly, various leaders in different organizations could be relatively easily categorized in any of the above leadership subdivisions. From the overtly dashing and daring to the dark and satanic; from exuding a quiet, comforting confidence, devoid of ego, to an alarmingly cold, but analytically correct figure; all of us will have judged the great and not-so-great leaders we have encountered by criteria of a wide-ranging nature and, if and when becoming better acquainted with them, will have hardened our view or changed it dramatically. Creating categories which may, on the one hand, unfortunately stereotype, but on the other, hasten understanding of those who influence our lives and by so doing improve the potential for dialogue is no bad thing, despite the drawbacks of such an approach.

But where is leadership today? Does the fourfold categorization enable a better appreciation of the leaders we may know and those who will always be a distant fascination of our attention? Do we need more sophisticated criteria to assess our leaders of today and tomorrow? Another dip into history may help, and this time a history of a more contemporary nature.

Kennedy, Cuba and decision processes

The Cuban missile crisis of 1962, through which was narrowly averted a world war, was brought about by the positions taken by the two super-powers. The military historian, John Keegan, describes President John F. Kennedy as entering into the fray in Alexander-like heroic style. However, detailed analysis of Kennedy's management of the affair did not display Alexanderian flair, but rather a cool and wise handling of process and dialogue. Despite the speed of affairs, Kennedy seemed determined not to be spun into any blind alley, the emergence from which might lead to collapse or catastrophe. Intelligence assessments indicated early deployment of Russian missiles, and that 14 days were left before a military, nuclear facility could be established in Cuba. Whether to respond through air blockade, bombardment or an invasion of Cuba, only 48 hours were required to harness to battle conditions. That left 12 days for deliberation.

Robert Kennedy's (US Attorney General and the President's brother) recollection of those 12 days was that the debate was unstructured, with no rank dividing the members of the Executive. There was no Chairman appointed to referee the debate process. The dialogue was that between equals. However, the intensity of the pressure inflicted its casualties. Dean Rusk, Secretary of State, seemingly experienced a nervous breakdown. McGeorge Bundy, National Security Advisor, by all accounts, was inconsistent in his argument; he advocated to strike, then to blockade, then to do nothing, but wait for the Russians to move, then once more he urged to strike. The military member, General Maxwell Taylor, advocated a military intervention. Despite Maxwell Taylor's insistence, it took three days to reach a decision to blockade. Three further days were devoted to discussions of a more technical nature and to further private discussions with Kennedy. By the sixth day, a clear way forward to counteract the Russian threat was in place. Within a matter of a week, the Russians responded by turning round their nuclear missile laden vessels and headed for their Soviet homelands.

Three important elements of learning emerged from this world stage encounter. First, sharpness of dialogue; even though it may be rude and personally uncomfortable, if focused to address the issues at hand, it is crucial that it be undertaken. Kennedy has often been accused of creating a climate of group think; the Bay of Pigs may have been, the Cuban missile crisis was not! Quality of dialogue is measured by its robustness to leave no stone unturned, so that all interested parties can raise their views and concerns, even if that means shifting position and shifting it again, in order to reach a cohesive view with which all, or most parties in the debate, can identify. The fear of losing face due to changes of heart or mind should be secondary; primary, is fully to unearth all relevant concerns. The leadership task in this process is to arbitrate dialogue, not to be the superhero. The task of the leader, like that of the elders of old, sitting on neutral territory managing a process of discussion designed to resolve differences that would otherwise lead to mutual, but unacceptable destruction, has re-emerged and now requires the wisdom to referee. As the leader may build up the complexities of strategy, he or she, in turn, may also be required to reduce argument to the simplicity of tactics, leaving workable strategy to subordinates. Military leadership requires filtering through voluminous and complex information. Social, business and community leadership requires tenacity and sensitivity, but by being more in the midst of combative stakeholders, managing a process of discussion, whilst each pursues their own agenda.

The theme of this book is that today's constraints and complexities duly require leaders to display strength and sensitivity, to guide discussions to resolution or just settlement, and also to have the good sense and grace not unduly to burden the process with the dominance of their ego. Maybe the elders of olden times are back, but the self-natured and tenacious side to heroism is the front we wish to see, whilst calmness and wisdom are the sensations we wish to experience. It seems that we desire of our leaders, and place our leaders in, a paradox, but leave it up to them to find their way through.

Notes

1. Quotes from John Keegan (1988), p. 9.
2. This quote can be found in Plato (1956a), p. 36.
3. This quote can be found in Plato (1956a), p. 45.
4. The quote is taken from Plato (1957), p. 26.
5. The quote is taken from Plato (1956b) p. 431.
6. Quote taken from Aristotle (1986), pp. 12–15.
7. Quote taken from Aristotle (1986), pp. 8–22.
8. The quote is taken from Machiavelli (1950), p. 56.

9. Quote taken from Tao Te Ching, in Hesse (1989), p. 132.
10. Quote taken from Watts (1992), p. 16.
11. Adapted from Ross (1980).
12. Part quote taken from Maslow (1968), p. 179.
13. The quote is taken from Senge (1992) p. 13.
14. The quote is taken from Arnold and Plas (1993) p. 18.
15. Quote from John Keegan (1988), p. 60.
16. Quote from John Keegan (1988), p. 32.
17. Quote from Roberts (1995), p. 383.
18. Quote from Roberts (1995), p. 384.
19. Quote taken from Roberts (1992), p. 565.
20. Quotes taken from Roberts (1995), p. 603.
21. Quoted from John Keegan (1988), p. 182.

References

Aquinas (1963), *Summa Theologiae*, Edited by Gillby, T., Routledge, London.

Aristotle (1986), *Nichomachean Ethics*, Translated by Irwin, J., Hacket Publishing Company, Indianapolis. Also in the same reference, see paragraphs 1140; 1142.

Arnold, W. and Plas, J. (1993), *The Human Touch*, Wiley, New York.

Bennis, W. (1993), *An Invented Life: Reflections on Leadership and Change*, Addison Wesley, Reading.

Bryant, A. (1955), *King Charles II*, Collins, London.

Bullough, D.A. (1980), *The Age of Charlemagne*, 2nd Edition, Darton, Longman and Todd, London.

Coogan, T.P. (1993), *De Valera, Long Fellow, Long Shadow*, Hutchinson, London.

Covey, S. (1990), *The Seven Habits of Highly Effective People*, The Business Library, New York.

Covey, S. (1992), *Principle Centred Leadership*, The Business Library, New York.

Deutscher, I. (1959), *The Prophet Unarmed*, Trotsky 1921–1929, Oxford University Press Paperbacks, Oxford.

Fisher, H. (1977), *Free at Last: A Bibliography of Martin Luther King Jr*, Free Press, New York.

Goldsmith, W. and Ritchie, B. (1987), *The New Elite: Britain's Top Chief Executives Reveal the Secrets of their Success*, Weidenfeld and Nicolson, London.

Hegel, G.W.F. (1971), *Philosophy of Mind*, Translated by Wallace, W. and Miller, A.V., Clarendon, Oxford.

Hesse, H. (1989), *My Belief*, Triad Parthen, London.

Hesse, H. (1995), *The Journey to the East*, Picador, London.

Horne, A. (1988), *MacMillan 1894–1956*. Volume 1 of the Official Biography, MacMillan, London.

Isaacson, W. (1992), *Kissinger, A Biography*, Simon and Schuster, New York.

Jeannot, T.M. (1989), Moral Leadership and Practical Wisdom, *International Journal of Social Economics*, Vol. 16, No. 6, pp. 14–38.

Keegan, J. (1988), *The Mask of Command*, Penguin Books, Harmondsworth.

Kelley, K. (1991), *Nancy Reagan. The Unauthorised Biography*, Bantam Press, New York.

Kouzes, J.M. and Posner, B.Z. (1987), *The Leadership Challenge: How to Get Extraordinary Things Done in Organizations*, Jossey Bass, San Francisco.

Locke J. (1971), *Social Contract*, Oxford University Press, London.

Machiavelli, N. (1950), *The Discourse*, Translated by Detmold, C. in *The Prince and The Discourse*, Random House, New York.

Machiavelli, N. (1958), *The Prince*, Translated by Marriott, W.K., J.M. Dent, London.

Machiavelli, N. (1970), *The Prince*, Translated by Adams, R.M., Norton, New York (first published in 1513).

Mair, V.N. (1990), *Tao Te Ching, Leo Tzu. The Classic Book of Integrity and the Way*, Bantam, New York.

Maslow, A.H. (1968), *Toward a Psychology of Being*, Van Nostrand, New York.

Nietzsche, F. (1969), *The Will To Power*, Vintage, New York.

Pascal, R.T. (1990), *Managing on the Edge*, Simon and Schuster, New York.

Peters, T. and Waterman, R. (1982), *In Search of Excellence: Lessons from America's Best Run Companies*, Harper and Row, New York.

Plato (1952), *The Statesman*, Routledge and Kegan Paul, London.

Plato (1956a), *Republic*, Translated by Jowett, B., in Edman, E. (ed.), *The Works of Plato*, Random House, New York.

Plato (1956b), *Apology*, Translated by Church, F.J., Bobbs-Merrill, Indianapolis.

Plato (1957), 'Theaetetus', in *Plato's Theory of Knowledge: The Theaetetus and the Sophist of Plato*, Translated by Conford, F.M., Bobbs-Merrill, New York.

Roberts, J.M. (1995), *History of the World*, 3rd Edition, Penguin Books, Harmondsworth.

Ross, N.W. (1980), *Buddhism: A Way of Life and Thought*, Knopf, New York.

Salisbury, M.E. (1992), *The New Emperors, Mao and Deng, A Dual Biography*, Harper and Collins, London.

Semler, R. (1993), *Maverick*, Arrow, London.

Senge, P. (1992), *The Fifth Discipline: The Art and Practice of the Learning Organization*, Random House, Sydney.

Summers, A. (1993), *The Secret Life of J. Edgar Hoover*, Victor Gollancz, London.

Thatcher, M. (1993), *The Downing Street Years*, Harper Collins, London.

Volkogonov, D. (1991), *Stalin: Triumph and Tragedy*, Weidenfeld and Nicolson, London.

Watts, A. (1992), *Tao: The Watercourse Way*, Avkana, New York.

CHAPTER THREE

Visioning: promoting a shared perspective towards organizational success

Andrew P. Kakabadse, Frédérick Nortier and Nello Bernard Abramovici

---

CASE I THE DIRECTORS' CONFERENCE

The directors and managing directors of a French multinational gathered for their annual conference in Geneva. The purpose of the conference was for key heads of business to report on the last year's expected performance. Equally, presentations were billed from the group CEO and directors concerning the overall position of the organization, worldwide, and the targets and strategies for the next year. As usual with such conferences, spouses were invited and had their own social programme, culminating in the annual dinner on the last night of the three-day event.

At the outset, the mood of the conference was described by one of the delegates as 'expectant, filled with opportunity'. However, such a positive attitude turned out to be short lived. Each of the key business area heads, i.e. heads of regions, made their presentations outlining their region's performance for the last year and provided a projected performance for the subsequent year. A gasp came from the audience when the figures for the current year were presented by the president of the American subsidiary. Apart from the loss, which was expected, its magnitude came as a complete surprise. Even more astounding was the projected performance – no improvement. The director of human resources (HR) of the US subsidiary highlighted a downsizing programme that did not match the reductions being introduced by some of the

European country heads. Furthermore, the HR director identified the US organization as ill prepared to introduce the group's executive development programme of off- and on-the-job training, performance-related appraisal and career pathing, and thereby felt obliged to pursue a separate US-driven HR policy. Questions from the group directors were abrupt, hostile and, at times, impolite. One of the European MDs was the most confrontational: 'In reality, who is going to pay for this? With your level of performance, you are not. We are!!'. 'The US is a very particular market. We just would not keep any good people unless we could provide the opportunities available in other comparable companies', replied the US HR director. The European MD continued his attack, 'It all depends on who is the comparison. You have been comparing the US part of our business with Brown Boveri, AT&T, Heinz. How about doing the same with American organizations who have your record. I bet their employment practices are a lot different.'

As the three days progressed, the mood of the meeting worsened, especially after the presentation of the French MD. The situation in France was not good. Despite an attractive market share, the performance of the French organization was poor. The losses were comparable to the US organization. To the amazement of the audience, the cost containment exercise did not involve any enforced staff reductions. Staff would only be encouraged to leave on an early retirement or an attractive leaving package basis. The feeling of disapproval at the conference was no longer disguised. 'What we are here to do is keep the French in jobs, whilst our people lose theirs and we make the profit', declared the Scandinavian MD. The audience showed their support by vigorously clapping the comments made and shouting 'encore'. No questions were asked by the group directors.

Finally, the presentation of the group chief executive: 'So this is the finale of our conference', mocked one of the English business general managers. Uncharacteristically, his MD turned and said, 'Yes and with a packed hall, do you know who is going to be listening – no one. No one believes anything any more – the mission, the vision the lot. This conference has been more than a waste of money. It's been depressing.'

Lack of vision: some organizational consequences

The case outlined above is true. The circumstances captured in the case are accurately represented.

The problem in the company? No one believed or behaved the vision! Yet all knew what it was. Most agreed that on previous occasions and now, the vision was made absolutely clear to the managers at the conference – to be the first choice quality manufacturer and provider of service.[1] However, clearness in the expression of words does not mean commitment nor agreement! In the end, most conference attendees had come to believe the real vision was to keep the 'French and Americans in jobs'. Further, the more assertive concluded that the only way to progress was to do 'one's own thing', until prevented. The vision for so many of the senior managers at this annual meeting was simply a mixture of words on paper repeated by the top management running the corporation.

An unusual experience? No, for research and consulting experience indicates that generating visions which people believe and are considered to work, is not an easy task. The results of the Cranfield Global Executive Competencies Survey show that promoting a meaningful vision and direction for the organization are crucial requirements of any senior manager (Kakabadse, 1991). However, the same survey identified that the generation and promotion of a cohesive and shared view of the future amongst the senior management of the organization is difficult to achieve. Yet the downside to not pursuing a coherent and shared vision is equally clear to managers. In both that survey and a number of separate consultancy assignments, the following characteristics are identified as likely to emerge in an organization that lacks any clear or specific vision.

- *Organizational turbulence* In the view of numerous senior managers, staff and lower-level management expect their bosses to provide a definitive view of the organization's future. In the absence of such clarity, direction is provided by each individual manager, guessing the top management's vision, or promoting their own view of the future and leading their own department or division to achieve specific goals, which fits with their particular vision. Such circumstances lead to splits, dissension and turbulence due to a lack of clarity. From an organizational point of view, splits of vision lead to the pursuit of poorly or, at least, contradictory thought through goals and a poor application of resources for the attainment of results.

■ *Short-term orientation* Within such a context, the only common denominator shared amongst the leaders of an organization is achieving results, making the sustenance of competitive advantage problematic as most of the top management have become short-term oriented.

■ *Paradoxical empowerment* For those in middle management roles, the communication of contradictory messages from upper management leads to confusion and a lack of willingness to apply oneself freely to motivation and challenge. After all, why bother doing what senior management wants, if the anticipation is that a different view will be communicated with a different line to pursue in the very near future. The feeling of middle management could be: 'All that I did before is meaningless.' Not surprisingly, the attitude middle management can adopt is 'Keep your head down and don't get involved, as tomorrow it will all go away and something new will take its place.' They are 'caught in the middle'! At the same time, some middle managers will use such contradictions as an opportunity to manipulate the circumstances, or their own bosses, to their own advantage. The more proactive are likely to pursue their own line of argument and try to establish an identity for their unit which suits them.

■ *In-fighting* Eventually, the managers will have to choose between the competing logics being pursued. As a result, strongly promoting one's view may lead to substantial in-fighting, resulting in the departure of one or more key managers. The morale of the rest of staff and management in the organization could deteriorate even further, leading to the departure of key staff and damaging the capacity of the organization to do business (Figure 3.1).

The necessity for generating a shared vision is recognized as vital, as is the damage of not doing so. Despite such insight, poor-quality dialogue, poor visioning and the lack of shared vision are commonplace symptoms of organizational life. In the 1990s context, where managers are focused on TQM, results and high-quality performance, where managers are more and more aware that it is almost impossible to

FIGURE 3.1   Position of middle management

Contradictory expectations from top management	'Lets wait and see' (middle management)	→ Paradoxical ← position	'I have to act and decide' (middle management)	Clear needs from line employees

consider the environment as predictable, where uncertainty and instability have become key factors of everyday management, managers tend to consider plans or organizational goals as the vision. Understandably, managers, because of the unpredictability factor may say that visioning as a concept of the long term, is unrealistic and a luxury. Such perspectives, however, place organizations in a dangerous loop for the reasons presented above. In order to prevent short termism, in-fighting and an inability to sustain advantage for any length of time, it is postulated that the need for visioning, leading to a meaningful shared vision has become even more crucial.

In this chapter, particular emphasis is placed on identifying the key elements of the visioning process. In addition, emphasis is given to an examination of the means by which promoting a shared vision can be attained. Throughout, real and heavily disguised case examples are provided to highlight the key points made in the text. Certain of the case examples are drawn from the experiences of one French multinational facing the challenge of identifying and promoting a shared vision and direction for its future throughout the organization, as well as specific examples being drawn from other organizations.

Consideration for effective visioning

1. Discretionary leadership

Most studies on top managers have tended to fall into one of two categories: those that focus on examining the attributes of individuals in terms of behavioural, attitudinal or deeper personality dimensions, or those that are driven by job, role or organization-type criteria. The original and insightful work of Professor Elliot Jaques, (Jaques, 1951) examining, in the 1950s, different cultures within the workplace, provides the conceptual bridge between individual behaviours and role requirements. Crucial to the work of Jaques is the concept of discretion. The discretionary element of role refers to the choices the role incumbent needs to make in order to provide shape and identity to their role and that part of the organization for which that person is accountable. The contrast to the discretionary element of role is the prescriptive side, namely the structured part, which is predetermined and which drives the individual's behaviour. In effect, the prescriptive part of a manager's job is that part over which the manager has little choice, other than to undertake the duties that are required of him/her. Such distinction is particularly pertinent, as providing for leadership is likely to make a considerable demand on the discretionary elements of a senior manager's role. The individual manager will need to make choices between unclear alternatives and is equally likely to need to devote considerable attention to nurturing key interfaces with influential internal and external stakeholders, in order to ascertain their commitment to a meaningful way forward.

What choices are made and how commitment is negotiated, highlights the impact the stakeholders have on the organization, as well as the capabilities of senior managers to respond effectively to such challenges. There is no reason to assume that even if the capacity of top management in the organization is considerable, each of the members of the senior executive would form similar conclusions as to the shape, size, direction, desired qualities of the total organization and thereby the shape and cost of each of the key functions/divisions/business units in the organization. Hence, senior managers, having the same challenges to address, may form different views as to the configuration of their organization and how it should be led.

2. Positional visioning

Actioning discretionary leadership by senior managers may lead to divergence of visions concerning their organization. Obviously, the varying configurations of size, shape, costs, profitability, synergies, stakeholder demands, markets, long-term positioning, does lead each senior manager to emerge with his/her own conclusion concerning the future of their organization. However, such analysis presumes all parties have reasonably equal access to data concerning the business. Reality dictates that comparable data being available to all is unlikely to be the case. Hence, in addition to differences of interpretation, the position one holds in the organization provides for differences of access to information. Apart from the differences between line and support roles and the varying interpretations that can emerge, a fundamental difference concerning access to information is highlighted by the gulf between those managers at the centre and those running parts of the corporate organization in the field. Differences of perspective that managers in the regions hold to other colleagues due to localized lines of business or just different lines of business, require that particular attention be given to the differences of interpretation of the terms 'sales' and 'marketing'. Crucial to adjusting to different external conditions is the appreciation of local differences in terms of sales and marketing. The

Cranfield surveys highlight that companies within the same industry sector, pursuing similar customers with comparable products may display quite different approaches to sales and marketing. Regional variation is one important factor. What sales and marketing means for the same product range in Greece may be different in the French market. Misunderstandings can easily arise as to the conditions and requirements of different markets in any region, or between regions, or for that matter different lines of business with no regional variation. Targets set by the head office may be considered unattainable in the operating business due to particular market conditions or a local cultural code. A newly appointed ex-patriate senior manager, who too readily buys into targets set from above and against the advice of local management, faces the prospect of losing credibility with the local team.

A common experience in multinationals is that whatever targets are set, they are prone to renegotiation, on a functional, product, line of business or regional basis. One sure sign of poor visioning is when top management removes one or more local managers but with the new appointees nothing changes. Effective visioning can help set more compatible boundaries within which managers in different parts of the organization can identify.

3. Beliefs and expectations

The obvious statement to make is that visioning involves projecting into the future, namely a future of uncertainty. In that sense, strong conviction is necessary from each leader in terms of their expectations, bearing in mind the variety of imponderables facing the organization. Hence, one element of visioning is to have an underlying conviction that one's views concerning the future and best requirements for the organization are the most appropriate views to hold under the current circumstances; therefore vision can become a kind of organizational ambition.

4. Ways of working

Senior managers, different by role, by levels of responsibility, by geographical location, can hold comparable and even virtually identical vision(s) for the future. However, they may hold substantially varying expectations concerning ways of working. Ways of working refer to styles of leadership, quality of life and quality of service. Business arguments may be used to justify concerns over ways of working. One argument would be that in order to service customers effectively, discipline needs to be displayed by staff and management within the organization. Hence, a more directive, focused, clear style of management is required, whereby little ambiguity exists in people's roles concerning their tasks, level of accountability, reporting relationships and expected and measurable quality of work.

However, the exact same issue of quality of service to customers could be interpreted by another director as requiring a style of delegation from senior management, working with loose interlinking groups, promoting a culture of freedom to manage with a far greater emphasis on networking across the organization. The argument would be that by being supportive and providing greater freedom to staff and lower-level management to respond to customer requirements, the customer would recognize that their concerns are dealt with speedily and professionally without the delay of having to refer to other parts of the organization. The assumption is that by engendering quality relationships internally, comparable high-level quality of relationships are promoted externally.

Thus senior managers both wishing to achieve the same ends, customer service, could argue from such contrasting perspectives. Within particular parameters, the business logic of both arguments may be faultless. However, to take countenance of simply the logic of each perspective would be deceptive. Both perspectives are driven by a belief and expectation concerning quality and ways of working, bearing in mind the expectations each one has concerning future market and other external developments. Ironically, the bitterness that can emerge between managers can be deeper and more aggravated on issues of ways of working than on issues of a more concrete substance such as the shape, size and direction of the organization, which in effect, hold a common platform for dialogue.

5. Confusion

Confusion is a normal element of the process of generating a meaningful vision because of:

- the realization of the diversity of beliefs on any one organizational context;
- the non-equal access to and knowledge of, organizational data;
- the very nature of visioning, which is a non-deterministic and emerging process.

Can visioning occur with no confusion? Confusion is a natural response when one's mental map is triggered by new, external or unexpected inputs. Confusion is the sign that our brain is trying to process new data. Leaders too often consider confusion as a result of something not mastered, as not professional, as something to avoid or to hide! Being clear, consistently, is seen as a virtue. It must be no surprise to report that leaders of organizations display some strong structuring and rationalizing behaviours during the visioning process or implementation, in order to reduce the level of felt confusion. In fact, such interaction tends to freeze the process! Confusion is, in fact, not only a normal but a necessary part of any learning or creating process. Leaders enhance the visioning process if they learn to use their own confusion and accept the confusion of others, in order to allow the emergence of new possibilities (Nortier, 1995; Stacey, 1995).

6. Time frame perspective

From our consulting experience, it has been observed that the way people enact their vision is linked to their personal time frame pattern, namely their relation to time. Charles Faulkner (1994) in his latest research on people's 'structure of attention' points out that people may start visioning by using the past, the present or the future as a starting point depending on the person's time frame pattern. Therefore, it is normal to observe different time frame perspectives within a board of executives. Not surprisingly, they will meet difficulties in reaching a spontaneous common view.

We once worked on a visioning process with the four associates of a consulting company. When the time came to share the four individual vision(s) of the associates, we realized that one of them described the future organizational state as if it already existed (description of a current future state). Another described the future state by starting from the present (description of a future possible scenario). The third associate expressed his vision by explaining the process to be experienced (description of the move from present to future), while the fourth took the future as a starting point to his vision to explain what had been done (description of a future history of the past). At first, they were all a little bit puzzled, thinking that they had splits of vision in their team. This temporary disturbing sense of confusion forced this team to address confusion, to share it, and to learn to use it as a part of their visioning process. In fact, these different time frame perspectives became a precious resource to create a final vision and jointly to work towards its implementation.

Divergence: the impact on strategic management

CASE 2   SHARING A TAXI

The conference was over. Now it was the morning after the ball and the speeches. Three of the senior managers at the conference, who had not been accompanied by their wives, decided to share a taxi to Charles de Gaulle airport.

'What a waste of money – God what a waste', sighed one of the three, barely seated in the taxi.

'I came from Thailand for this', remarked a sullen second.

'If you put the time we have, as senior managers spent here, and add the total cost of our time, the air fares and hotel bill pale in significance.'

'It's just that they (the centre directors) are out of touch. What's shared about this damned vision. My market in Southern Europe does not fit with their picture of the world. I don't need more sales people. I just have to make my networks work better.' He paused for a few moments.

'And you know what that means? These networks require 'lubrication' as the English put it, or more appropriately, bribery. I know that one cannot talk about that openly, but at least some recognition of the different revenue challenges we all face should have been made instead of just imposing targets from the Centre.'

'Imposing is the word. This whole conference has been an imposition. Targets, both for sales and costs have been imposed with little thought applied to what is happening in each of our areas. Then talk about asking questions and giving feedback. Anyone who dared to open their mouth was just knocked down. Only Gilles (managing director, Eastern Europe) stuck to his point. He seems to get away with it every time. It's probably because he's French!'

'No. It's because he gets results and also he could not give a damn. He is a tough nut. He'd probably resign before they could sack him.'

The murmurings and dissatisfactions continued until the airport. After a brief goodbye, the three each went their own way.

The discussion in Case 2 highlights two key issues, the differences of view of sales and marketing and the irritation over the perceived style adopted by the top management of the corporation. Being seen to set cost and revenue targets without reference to market conditions within particular localities, especially if the feeling is that certain targets simply cannot be achieved, induces a sense of loss of trust in top management. Add to that the view that top management are insensitive to or unwilling to receive feedback, the sense of isolation and loss of morale are natural outcomes of such a predicament.

CASE 3   REFLECTIONS

The chief executive asked that his immediate colleagues remain whilst the other managers attending the conference returned home. 'Well what do you think?' he asked. Some of the directors glared at each other, but nothing was said. The group HR director finally spoke, 'I am not sure what sort of answer you are looking for but at least I feel I should give you my view. Despite our preparation, I do not think the conference has been well received. Nobody really believed us. That's what I was hearing in the bar and over dinner. In fact, they quite disbelieved us. Basically, whatever we say, most of the key country managers feel that as far as their businesses are concerned, we have got it wrong.'

'I understand that we are going to have opposition. We are trying to introduce change. We are trying to improve quality. We are trying to get our people to think across the barriers that exist in the structure of the organization and in their minds', commented the chief executive.

'I understand that we have to convince people. I appreciate that we need to spend time communicating. I know we are going to get opposition and criticism. However, I also know that basically we have to talk the same language – us and the country managers', added the HR director.

'Do you think we got the message wrong?' asked the marketing director.

'Not wrong as such. It's just that I heard complaints that we did not have a good handle on the reality of running their businesses. I feel that it is not so much resistance but more that we are seen as being unrealistic. To put it bluntly, we are seen as not talking the same language as them', said the HR director.

'So what do you suggest we do?', asked the chief executive.

The top team in Case 3 see problems. They cannot see opportunity in their current circumstances. Certainly, confusion is one issue and differences in their time frame perspective is a second, the latter being seen as particularly problematic.

How common are the experiences of dissension, incongruence and a lack of shared perspective amongst the senior management of any organization? The results of the Cranfield Survey highlight some interesting results. The top management, of 20 per cent Swedish, 23 per cent Japanese, 30 per cent British, 31 per cent Austrian, 32 per cent German, 39 per cent French, 46 per cent Spanish, 42 per cent Finnish and 48 per cent of Irish companies, report that the members of the top management team hold deeply held differences of view as to the shape and direction of the organization, in effect differences of vision. Are such differences aired? Are contrasting viewpoints discussed? The Cranfield Survey results indicate that the management of 38 per cent French, 47 per cent British, 49 per cent Finnish, 50 per cent Swedish, 61 per cent of German, 63 per cent of Spanish, 67 per cent of Austrian, 68 per cent of Irish and 77 per cent of Japanese companies believe that there are issues of substantial importance to their company which should be discussed but which are felt to be too sensitive to be openly discussed in the top team.

In effect, it is felt to be easier to live with problems of splits of vision, or with no vision at all, rather than to face the uncomfortable experience of bringing such issues to the surface and to talk them through.

Normality for a third or more of the top management of the companies surveyed (over 5,000 mid- to large-sized corporations) is not to face concerns over splits of vision and for over two-thirds of these teams not to engender a quality of dialogue which could help them face up to the strategic problems they have. In effect, top managers are attending meetings, hearing agreement on key issues, walking out of meetings, recognizing that commitment is not forthcoming and knowing that the agreements reached are worthless. What do most do within such a scenario? The research results indicate little to nothing, but then equally pretend with each other that no problems exist.

Steps towards quality visioning

Such results do highlight one point which is that senior managers are aware of the circumstances around them. Both the issues that require debate and the desired manner of debate, are clear. Managers do know the nature of their problems, often holding reasonably clear views as to the appropriate ways forward, but do not address their concerns because of the personal discomfort that is experienced in addressing such issues with their colleagues. On this basis, insight (or the lack of it) is not the problem. Actioning the insights that already exist but in a cohesive manner, is the challenge.

In order to utilize effectively the insights that already exist in order to enhance dialogue amongst key managers, to promote greater cohesion of vision and a more disciplined consistency in the implementation of the vision, the following strategies towards generating a meaningful vision are identified.

1. Involve all of the top team

Unlike a middle management team, which is fundamentally a unit for the achievement of particular tasks or objectives, a senior management team can be seen as a group of individuals brought together in a forum for the purposes of debate whereby exploration, planning, recommendation and decision making are essential processes requiring their participation. Fundamentally, the number of individuals occupying roles with a high discretionary content could vary from 15, 20, 60 or even 120 persons, making the top team a variety of people who occupy membership of multiple groups or committees. Hence, who is and is not in the top team, is a crucial question to answer. The HR director, Case 3, recognized that the dissension from the senior manager audience at the annual conference was something more than just murmurings and the expression of frustration emanating from the year's pressures. He focused on the issue of sales and marketing as a crucial symptom of deeper underlying discontent. By not creating an environment for debating such concerns, the audience was in no mood to respond positively to corporate centre's wishes and requirements. In effect, the corporate centre team had not sold their policies to the general managers of the subsidiary businesses/divisions. One reason for that could be that the top management at the centre viewed the senior management of the businesses more as middle managers, who after having sat through a clear presentation about future strategy, would then go and implement that strategy.

Life, however, is not always simple. Those occupying discretionary roles need to identify personally with the strategy being proposed. Their ownership of policy is as important as its content. On this basis, a crucial aspect for creating a vision of the organization is to be clear as to who is and who is not a member of the top team, an issue that does not seem to have been fully considered in the case example of the French corporation.

In addition to membership, the quality of relationship that drives dialogue amongst the members of the top team requires examination. If the members of the top team feel that the quality of relationships, the openness of discussion, the commitment to the decisions reached and the discipline to implement the decisions reached are positive, they would probably call that group a team – a stimulating, positive, enabling forum within which to maintain a dialogue. If the members of the top management group identify the relationships, decision-making and implementation processes as tenable, but need to create a degree of formality and structure in order to ensure that the agenda is addressed, that group may be termed by its members as a committee. However, if the members of the top management group consider the quality of their relationships to be negative and the decision making to be poor, with little commitment to implementation, the group members may turn up to meetings with little expectation as to any positive outcomes emerging. For this third group, the top team is a forum which inhibits the attainment of the vision and mission of the organization.

The creation of an effective team spirit at the top requires realistically recognizing who is involved in top team work and as a consequence, formulating appropriate structures of communication and involvement in order to accommodate the expression of those issues driving the varied agendas of each of the senior managers within the structure.

2. Promote a feedback culture

Communicating downwards is an exercise of disciplined management. Allowing for a continuous flow of opinions upwards, downwards and across is tantamount to valuing openness of comment as a way of life. Hence, management's ability to invite feedback is crucial to the effective running of the organization. The skill is to invite and receive both positive and negative feedback. Positive feedback is easy to handle. Inviting and positively responding to more critical/negative feedback is far more sensitive, as what may be offered may be personally hurtful to any one or more senior managers. If permission to offer feedback is not tacitly understood by the proposer of the feedback, such feedback is not given and hence, concerns remain unspoken.

The blocks to giving and receiving feedback could be:

- Senior management have, to date, in their role and within the structure, not been required to receive feedback and hence their competence to initiate and manage the process is poor.

- Senior management have never invited feedback, and therefore confidence in others to give feedback is low.

- It may be politically inappropriate to request feedback, as the quality of executive relationships is poor, making it difficult to enter into a deeper dialogue.

- Bosses, subordinates and colleagues have not appreciated the true nature of their problems; they focus on extraneous issues, offer inconsequential feedback, and then become disappointed or even angry when senior management cannot or will not act.

- An appreciation of, and sensitivity to, managerial problems in general is low among bosses, colleagues and/or subordinates; hence there would be little value in requesting and receiving feedback. The Cranfield surveys reveal that such an orientation is particularly prevalent in product-oriented structures where senior managers report that they gain greater satisfaction from the technical/specialist side of their work than from general management, preferring their subordinates to be tidy and well disciplined. To enter into a feedback dialogue in such a working environment could generate considerable resentment or even fear.

- Senior managers may be unaccustomed to, or untrained in, receiving feedback and hence they bar the offer of information, especially that concerning individual performance.

- Senior management, irrespective of their skills, may be threatened by the nature of the feedback, feel unable to cope, and hence fail to initiate a meaningful dialogue.

In order to promote a more effective feedback process, particular consideration needs to be given to the degree of robustness of relationships amongst the managers in the organization which determines the effectiveness of the processes of giving and receiving feedback. In the communication of a vision, certain managers may exhibit the best of people-skills and seem trusted and respected by colleagues and subordinates. They allow themselves to be open to comment. Others may exhibit highly effective interpersonal skills, but are less trusted and respected and certainly receive only favourable comment as feedback. Why? In order both to offer opinions openly and still maintain a relationship without giving offence, it is necessary to have generated a quality of relationship that can cope with openness of conversation. Such openness is achieved through a consistency of behaviour which promotes effective communication, such as walking the floor, making oneself available to be with others or receive comment from others or even attending social events, lunches, dinners or out-of-work activities. It is the consistency and discipline applied to behaviour for the promotion of more open relationships that is crucial to the generation of a robustness of relationship.

To promote such a consistency it is first necessary to recognize the need for a feedback relationship. Once opportunities have been created to grow the relationship, it is important to check for views and opinions before pursuing action. Through the application of such consistency, a greater commonality of vision may occur. By enhancing the capability of people to comment as they desire and by promoting a pattern of behaviour that supports such processes, differences between people are teased out and are positively used. Diversity can contribute to the team's development. Obviously, functional and operational differences are easier to surface as the solutions to problems are more readily identified.

Promoting a commonality for vision and highlighting differences between each of the key managers, naturally takes longer and is a more sensitive process to manage. However, in terms of behaviour, nothing different is required. Making the time to check out, to discuss and to converse, can already provide the first elements of a vision amongst senior management.

3. Establish a platform for visioning

Having worked on the processes for enhancing positive dialogue, senior management are more prepared for participation in the process of generating a workable vision. However, top teams do not have to wait to establish first a positive dialogue. The process can be the 'kick off' for more positive dialogue, but would still require the active involvement of the members of the top team and the promotion of a feedback culture. Working on the processes as well as the vision places senior management in a multi-level learning process: learning to give positive feedback within a team, learning to make something out of that feedback, learning to experience confusion with others, learning to pursue collective visioning, learning to make collective strategic decisions, and learning to change and adapt their influencing behaviour to become consistent with the vision. Usually, the visioning process in itself can potentially be a way to enhance the quality of interaction between team members. But even then, senior management should be aware of the goal the team is heading for: improved dialogue or a common vision of the future?

Hence, part of the platform is having generated or generating through dialogue on visioning, a supportive context.

Effective leaders need to check their current context to make sure it is supportive enough to start a process of visioning. If working relationships are too inconsistent, if opposite or contradictory values are held by managers placing them in a double bind situation, if teams have no real positive shared experience of change, and people lack trust towards others, then no sustainable or effective vision is likely to emerge. Attempting to generate a meaningful shared vision under such circumstances is likely to lead to gamesmanship which in turn is likely to generate instability and a more chaotic environment.

If a leader, in such a context, starts a visioning process, he/she may be able to create a vision, but potentially may have problems gaining real commitment to even embark on the process. If the individual feels able to start such a process, it means that he/she has already been, for some time, in a personal process of questioning, thinking and defining new meaning. However, this might not be the case for the other senior managers who may be facing practical and more technical problems, who may be working on other priorities, and who may have other expectations regarding the focus of the team. If this is the case, the leader may be out of step with the group, but believe that the others are experiencing similar probing and questioning.

Hence, in addition to building a common platform, the leader must try to create a common experience of change and thereby build or rebuild new satisfactory milestones concerning progress during phases of change. Once a more common experience has been achieved, people are more likely and willing to look together to the future from the view of a shared perspective.

In addition to creating a supportive context, it is crucial to establish a common language. The logic of this step is to make sure one can first build an experience of changing elements of the present before starting to influence the future! The assumption behind this logic is important. Focusing on potential in the here and now will generate new energy, new beliefs and new motivation to address the future and thereby enhance the desire to change. It is obvious however that this experience is already contributing to influence the future, but senior managers do not have to be focused on the future at this stage. All they have to do is to find ways to change some elements of the present. An additional assumption underlining this logic is that time is not linear. The past is in the present and future, *and* the future is in the present! Instinctively every executive knows that. However, most decision makers seem to act along the lines of a linear concept of time, *we have to carry the past with us in the future!*

In some cases, the past can open new doors to the future by emphasizing the reasons for past success. It is unfortunate that in so many cases the past is experienced as an unpleasant burden, limiting the exploration of new possibilities. The visioning process gives a team the chance to find a new balance by creating a process whereby a second non-linear view of time can be adopted: *We have found new ways to behave through deciding now what we want to be tomorrow!*

Certain companies have experienced starting a visioning process, only to discover they have no reliable starting point in their current context. Their context may be too unstable and not ready to support the process. The end result might be no vision emerging, or splits in the top team on issues of vision, or an intention rather than a shared and committed vision, or the emergence of new ways of working which go towards creating a workable platform rather than the vision itself. (For example, the identification of the key shared values, or the creation of a management charter.) This kind of 'platforming' has a positive impact on the top team, but it cannot be considered as a vision. However, certain top managers may believe they have a vision, but what they have is a potential platform from which to pursue the generation of a vision.

Such was the case in an IT department (ITD), of a large French public health care organization. All the senior managers in the top executive were looking to generate a shared vision of their future, which could set meaningful parameters around their decisions and their daily actions. We started, as external consultants, a creative visioning process – believing that this executive team was ready for such an experience. We were quite disappointed to discover early on in the process that the team had little shared experience of acting together as a team. Each time the team came close to drafting a meaningful vision statement, through debate strong opposing points of view emerged. It became obvious that no meaningful shared vision could emerge at this stage. The team's confusion was at its peak and its members were desperately looking to the consultants for a way forward. What was happening? It became clear that an important prerequisite was missing: the team had not yet discussed nor appreciated the values held by each of its members. Most believed that their colleagues held similar values to themselves. What was emerging was that the opposite was true. We decided to stop the dialogue on visioning and switched it into an open session allowing each person to express their values concerning work, people and the nature of organization they desired. This became the starting point to team development focused on generating core and shared values. The end result was extraordinary. Morale in the team improved as did the level of commitment, enthusiasm and synergy between the team members. The process had allowed them to emerge with a common statement of their values, which they used as the keystone for focusing their decision making, and for assessing the impact of their actions. However, since they had initially started along a process of visioning, they believed for a while that their values statement was their vision. It took them a couple of months to realize that they had just reached a preliminary staging post in the process of generating their vision.

Bain (1995) argues that of all the strategic management tools being utilised by companies, visioning is number one! However, the same study reveals that despite its high utilization amongst the portfolio of strategic management tools, it is only ranked fourth when it comes to measures of satisfaction linked to its use. One reason is that once having embarked on a process of generating a vision, senior management have to adapt or modify their aspirations because a sound platform to grow a vision was missing! These exercises end up more as important team-building events, or a specification and validation of the team's values. Some top managers may be satisfied with such an experience. Others may feel frustrated, show disillusion or even become sceptical about the relevance of visioning as a strategic management tool. Such disillusion is normal if vision is considered as a tool rather than a dynamic process. Hence, visioning exercises, although talked about as processes, can become just building 'vision statements', which are bounded and restrictive in their use.

A 'real' vision, which might just be symbolised in a single word – a single sentence, or a single image – is a much more alive image of the future desired state. It will give meaning and direction, and will be nourished by every day's activity while leading and guiding this same activity. A vision is not created to be achieved precisely, but it is there to allow a company to move ahead with consistency and commitment.

Creating or enhancing a platform can be done by generating a new quality in the dialogue, by redesigning management's role, by finding opportunities to stretch everyone's role, by building a different team logic (with new team players for example), by becoming more assertive about the team's values. Many team-building and team-development techniques are contributing to the creation of a platform. In fact, the platform is just a way to help executives and their teams experience that it is indeed possible to change elements of the current context and to change ways of learning, making development to be seen as a worthwhile experience.

Building a platform will also allow executives to make a break with the past – namely past beliefs, past successes and failures, past management style, past organization – in order to become more focused on the present, in a 'here and now' logic. This is an important step in the visioning process because when no platform exists people tend to mix past events, past experiences, past feelings and emotions, past behaviours and habits, with current ones. Too often, this mix leads to the continuation of a 'messy' organization, a 'messy' understanding and awareness of the present, leading to paradoxical management behaviours and decisions!

Through disrupting an individual's or group's links with the past, the experience will help people open their minds and focus their energy into action. In order to get out of a logic where the context decides for the person, the platform will force everyone to find out new ways to influence their context. By doing so, the executive team will learn how to lead change.

Step by step, the break with the past supported by the formation of the platform will generate a new way of operating. The platform will change current logic: 'acting' will become 'contributing'. New beliefs, new roles, new time frame perspectives and new landmarks will emerge. The platform is a way of changing individual experience in order to give a common and positive experience of change!

There are many ways for a platform to emerge. It is possible to create a global platform for the whole organization, or to build first an experimental or local platform in a department, which can then be implemented in the organization. However, whatever the alternative, it is the CEO's or the senior manager's responsibility to display and to act in the way of the platform. The individual should enact the platform first, and then find a way for its conceptualization and communication. A platform is a part of the 'shadow' of the organization. As such, it is crucial that people enact it, rather than structure, formalize or rationalize it – there is no real need to state it for the external world.

However, the platform must be consistently applied for a period of time, in order to avoid a 'one shot exercise'. The platform must be stabilized to a certain extent, so that everyone can learn from these new experiences, without 'overstabilizing', in order to keep future change potential possible. Once this is achieved, the executive team or the leader might study the opportunity and the relevance of moving to the next step or not.

A visioning process puts an organization into transition. Once the initial break with the past is no longer considered as disruptive, a new way of operating has begun.

CASE 4   BUILDING A STRATEGIC TEAM

The criticisms outlined at the conference continued for the following months. The comments reached the corporate centre directors second-hand as they were inevitably 'doctored' by the time they filtered their way through to corporate centre. However, in the businesses, criticism of headquarters management was rife and verbose.

The HR director had maintained a relatively positive relationship with most the key business stream directors and was painfully aware of the lack of confidence in corporate management. He persuaded his colleagues that a weekend away for the corporate centre directors and the chief executive of the larger business units would be a valuable investment to make, so that they could sit together and discuss how to improve the confidence in the leadership of the organization.

'No' was the reply from the group CEO. 'Do you think I am going to subject myself to continuous, never ending criticism, from a bunch of pissed off managing directors? No is the answer. Absolutely not. They will do as they are told and that's that.' The HR director just got up and left the CEO, who barely glanced up from his papers throughout the conversation.

Undeterred, the HR director approached the group director, manufacturing, Henri Martin, a Frenchman, who said, 'I know the criticisms are bad. Soon we will have a disaster. Already some of my good people are leaving. I am told it is not me. It is more that they can see no future in this company. Yes something needs to be done'.

'Henri, we need one success story. Someone in the company who has really turned things round, company-wide. Two of our subsidiaries are in profit, but that is even causing a greater problem in terms of morale – those two are doing their best to distance themselves from the rest of the organization. So that someone, I am hoping, will be you. Can you show that manufacturing world-wide can create quality, unity amongst its management and the products that sales and marketing need?'

Henri nodded. 'Let's try, what do you suggest?'

The two agreed that they needed the services of an external consultant. After an intensive search, they chose one consultant with considerable experience of dealing with strategic issues. Following discussions with the consultant, the way forward became clear. The consultant would interview all the key managers, and present a brief report of his findings especially highlighting appropriate ways forward, with the probability that a workshop or series of them would be organized, as the vehicle to work towards generating a meaningful vision.

That is exactly what happened. The interviews highlighted the dissatisfaction of staff and management with the company. Henri was respected. He was seen as supportive of his people, as attempting to ensure that quality standards were maintained and people's working lives were improved. However, considerable cynicism was expressed towards any attempts from the centre towards improvement. 'Why start with manufacturing? What difference will it make if no one else in the company does anything?', were some of the comments made. However, the general consensus was that if Henri was willing to try, why not support him.

A workshop event was organized and run over a weekend, attended by Henri and his immediate subordinates. Most at the meeting felt relatively at ease to express their views, which they did even at the dinner on the Friday evening. The criticisms of the company became vociferous. Henri said little, allowing the negatively charged emotions to continue, which they did at the bar, late into the night.

Henri showed his disappointment the next morning as the criticisms of the corporation become more voluminous. He had hoped that his team may have run out of steam the evening before. The more critical they were, the more critical they wished to become. 'So why do we not all go home now?', asked Henri. 'If this company is so bad and all our lives are so miserable, and, according to some of you, so is mine – I heard the comments last night – "poor Henri, his life must be awful having to deal with some of the bastards at his level" – why don't we all go home? We spend so little time as it is with our families. Is this what you want to do, criticize, as opposed to spending your time at home?'

Pause. Henri continued, 'Yes, you may feel that you can do nothing. Defining a vision, a purpose – in effect a mission – for our part of the organization, may be a waste of time if nothing else happens in the company. All of what you say may be true! But it is not true this weekend. The whole point of being here is to see whether we can create a way forward, a set of standards for what we do and for our people. This weekend we have an opportunity to materialize with something positive. Yes, you may be right, it may all fall apart when we go back to work on Monday but not here. Here, at this hotel, we can do something because there is no-one stopping us. I am not stopping you. M. Roblait (group CEO) is not here to stop you. Nothing will be reported back to anyone, because if it was, it would have been reported to me and I am here listening. So here, we have the choice to do something or nothing. If we criticize, we criticize ourselves but we will end up doing nothing. So if this is what we all want, why not go home?'

No one responded. 'So what do we do?', asked Henri.

The manufacturing director for Germany spoke, 'So what do we do Henri? Although many of us have many ideas what to do, we actually do not know what to do as a group. That is why we can do nothing but criticize', he finished. 'Well, why not start with being clear about what we have done well and wish to continue doing well', responded Henri.

The senior managers nodded. 'Look we have success to be proud of – what about the impact of the C700 and the success that followed, on the market. On that line, we even drove marketing. We were pushing the company towards quality', remarked Henri.

The directors from the businesses and the regions discussed the positive impact of the C700 series on their part of the organization. The mood became more buoyant. With the help of the consultant, subgroups were created to explore the criteria that led to past and current successes and further where the shortfalls lay. The subgroups presented their deliberations to each other at plenaries and after further discussion went back into subgroups to continue their analyses. By Sunday afternoon, the fundamental elements of the vision for worldwide manufacturing had been agreed.

'Jim Fischer (from the USA) and Sascha Mischa (Poland) can further refine these ideas, with their teams, coordinate between them and present to us at the next manufacturing quarterly meeting, a statement which they think captures the vision for manufacturing, which, of course, we can then discuss', said Henri. 'As far as we are concerned, from now on we do what we have said here. We try to practise the standards we have agreed upon. We also work closer with marketing, which will not be easy. Our actions need to be dictated by the criteria we have set. When we next meet, we can see how we get on and whether the exercise has been in any way useful.'

Henri reflected for a moment. 'For me, I need to let my marketing colleagues at the centre know what is happening. Although we want everything to improve, I know we will be seen as, initially at least, uncooperative. We have not found it easy this weekend, so why should they?' questioned Henri.

All agreed.

The HR director's initial rebuff drove him to explore how a platform for creating a vision for the corporation could be established, if not on a global basis, then on a more localized basis within one of the core functions. Henri Martin's strategy at the workshop was to establish what had been done well, as the basis for moving forward. Once it was understood how effective that function had been, then a basis for moving forward could be established. More instinctively than consciously thought through, Henri highlighted the need for consistent behaviour from his managers, their actions driven by the criteria they had set themselves. Henri recognized how the exercise had strengthened the team. The respect of each of the managers for each other improved considerably. The confidence to express their views openly, once key issues had been aired, was a major turning point in the team's fortunes. The questions facing Henri were: Could he successfully sustain the initiative and could he help spread the vision creation process into other parts of the organization? Interestingly, Henri did not wait for a vision statement to be published, he continued with the initiative in his part of the organization and in the rest of the corporation.

4. Creating the vision

Creating a vision is a delicate but insightful exercise for any executive team, for it will allow each of its team members to share and better understand the way others imagine or wish to see the future desired shape and state of the company. An effective visioning process is an intellectual, emotional, rational, behavioural and existential process.

The first step is usually to invite each team player to take the time to express the way he/she sees the state of the organization. Best practice highlights that each of the team formalize their view into one sentence, by using 'state' descriptive verbs rather than 'process' descriptive verbs. Each word should be well considered, in order to project a meaningful sentence. This is a crucial preliminary step as all involved will experience involvement in the process of defining the future.

The second step, equally a group process, requires each member to discuss all of the individual visions expressed. Hence, each person's ambition for him or herself and for their company, their expectations, their desire to achieve specific goals, their values, their perspective regarding the team and the company, their time frame and the priorities they would wish to see the company focus on for the following years, is discussed. This step allows for a strong team development experience, as it allows for a mapping of strategic issues and perspectives. The sharing will also concretely illustrate the team's variety and richness. Team members will be able to discuss common future perspectives, and to point out new potential areas of development. By doing so, the team is moving from an individual sense of commitment to a group shared perspective.

Often, executives are surprised by the richness of this step, as a strong emotional catharsis accompanies the expression of views. Individuals express their deeply held views concerning their past experiences of the organization and the future shape, profile and culture they would wish to see. Most recognize that once views start being shared, the process is ongoing and cannot be stopped.

This is the time when people start to address, to share and discuss issues which they had never or hardly ever addressed together before, as occurred in Case 4. A feeling of confusion is normal as each team member will have to reconsider certain aspects of their views according to how they are influenced by the discussion. Personal beliefs start to be reframed, new potential actions identified, and new meanings concerning the organization and its constitution developed.

The third step could then be progressively opened by the consultant, who will lead the group to build a common vision statement. This step can be intense, emotionally and intellectually. People sometimes describe it as peak team performance whereby the feeling of being part of a cohesive team can be extraordinarily strong. Interestingly, in Case 4, Henri Martin asked two of his line managers to go towards building the final elements of the vision statement, his reasoning being that greater ownership of the whole exercise would occur through that means rather than have the consultant do this job.

The involvement of the CEO, or a key top manager, in the process, but in a non-directive manner, is crucial for generating this feeling of performance. The CEO has a key role to play, since it is usually him/her who decides to introduce this process within the team. Some CEOs struggle. They may think 'how can I ask the senior managers of the organization to do this if they do not want it? If I cannot manage this I am not a good leader!' For example, the manager of the information technology department, described earlier in this chapter, first experienced a frightening sense of failure when he realized that his team was more a group of people than a team, and that they could not build a vision together. But in his case, this feeling of failure became the trigger and driver that allowed him to create a specific situation where the group could discover their effectiveness as a team.

However, a visioning process does not have to be undertaken by the whole team. It can be developed by the CEO (in conjunction with the chairman). The information, individual views and feelings individuals observed during the platform stage, will become useful in allowing a new vision to emerge. In that case, he will have to share the emerging vision later with the team, gain their commitment, fine tune it, and coach each member of his team to help them envision their role in the new order. In a group process, the moment of peak performance will become the common reference for future action and be useful during the implementation stages. Each executive will be able to act consistently, as they are likely to identify fully with the vision which they have been involved in growing.

However, as occurred in Case 4, the CEO does not have to be involved, as a local platform had to be created. As with the CEO, the top manager of that function/department has to be equally fully involved in the process. Assuming the exercise to be successful, the challenge would be to extend the exercise, namely turn a local platform into a global one.

Too often, CEOs, managers and even consultants are too focused on the written result of the visioning process, the so-called Vision Statement. In fact, the written document has no real importance! What happens during the process of debate is important, namely the quality of dialogue that is developed, the quality of relationship that is grown, and the memory of the feeling of peak performance linked to that future desired state which will remain and drive future actions and decisions.

The written document is just the formal and immediately visible side of the visioning process. But the other side, the informal and shadowy one, cannot be put in words even if it is the heart of the vision. Like Palo Alto saying 'The map is not the territory', we can say 'The vision statement is not the vision'!

Many management gurus or OD practitioners use methodologies highlighting rational processes to help their clients build a vision. The problem with such consulting approaches is that the informal side of the vision, namely the building process, is neglected. Interestingly when these executives are asked to comment and explain their vision statement, they will usually put it to one side and start telling the story of how the vision was built. They will share anecdotes of what happened during the process, and illustrate in very concrete terms, how this vision has helped them so far. One can then notice, that by doing so, it is not the 'formal' side of the vision which is used and explained, but the 'informal and shadowy one'. If the senior manager sticks to the formal document, he/she is unlikely to be impactful. If the person uses the informal/shadow dimension of the vision, he/she will be able to demonstrate their own commitment. By doing so, the executive will give life to the vision and will have more chances to develop followership.

Since the formal aspect is just a 'key', it is normal to observe many different ways to express the newly emerged vision. Vision statements differ from one company to another varying from a sentence, a vision statement of three pages, a word, a set of words, an image, a specific place, a set of miscellaneous objects, or other mechanisms.

It is our experience that leaders usually feel excited once they have formalized their vision. They are willing to show and share it with their staff and managers. But if they underestimate the power of the non-visible part of the vision, they may experience a strong feeling of disappointment, simply because no other person will be able to grasp the whole meaning of the vision simply by reading it. Subordinates may react by saying, or thinking, 'It took them two days to write two sentences! What a waste of time!'

To illustrate the power of the non-formal aspect of the vision, we frequently observe that when we talk with leaders one year after the visioning process, they make reference to the vision in order to guide their decisions. However, when asked to spell out the vision as it was formalized, they are often unable to do so. They can talk and show the spirit of the vision, but not the details. They simply do not need the full text to behave and decide consistently with the vision. Usually, they spontaneously say that the written text has far less importance than what happened during the visioning process. The 'shadow' of the vision has become the explicit reference and guideline to team and individual action.

5. Enacting the vision

Top teams should define certain specific actions which will contribute towards implementing the first milestones of the vision. These should include individual as well as group actions. A key criterion to measure the quality of application of the vision, is to check if the vision spontaneously helps individuals to take decisions for concrete actions, helps to free people to take initiatives, and to give input to dare to do something! We believe that it is far more important first to show the vision, and the power of the vision initially through action, rather than through verbal or presentational communication about the vision. This means that the top team, once having identified the vision, has to pursue a certain number of actions, such as to define decision-making criteria consistent with the vision, to specify supportive management behaviours, and to specify how the team needs to operate in order to start acting the vision. Our experience has shown that starting to implement a vision that way allows the team the opportunity progressively to materialize some aspect of the vision at the very top of the organization, the first step in the route to successful implementation. Thus the vision becomes part of the reality of the organization and an ever stronger driver of the top team in its pursuit of organizational success.

The information technology department (ITD team) of the public health care deparment referred to earlier in this chapter realized after some months that their value system, presented as a vision, was considerably insightful. If, at the beginning, the team members were quite happy about what they had done, they became more and more enthusiastic about their vision, and could progressively provide more insight and meaning to their joint endeavour. The vision became a strong team reference to guide decisions, to initiate new projects, to redesign the organization in a more consistent way, but also to regulate conflicts, and to share emotions linked to the vision. They decided not to talk about the vision with the other members of the department, but to act it.

As in the ITD case, a 'real' vision will always inspire people. Very soon, other levels of the organization will become aware of a greater consistency in the top team, of important changes being instituted in the organization, and of new kinds of results being expected and achieved.

Conclusion

Visioning is certainly not another managerial fad, nor a guru tool. It is a fundamental component of best practice for senior executive teams. Starting a visioning process requires analysis of the current dynamic in an executive team, to make sure the team is ready to embark on a visioning exercise. Once a positive dynamic has been established in the team, a platform, or springboard from which the vision can grow, needs to be established. A platform for a vision is important to reinforce the quality and the effectiveness of the process and the organizational impact it is supposed to generate.

The way the vision is created is another key part of the effectiveness of the final result. A vision is richer than the text representing it. Executives need to be aware that visioning contains an important hidden, implicit and non-rational element, which is in fact the core aspect of any effective vision. For this specific reason it is more important that leaders act, or enact the vision, than talk about it.

Visioning provides for an important organizational force, providing a binding cohesion, initially at senior management levels, but subsequently throughout the organization, and by acting as a shared ambition, which guides and motivates people's actions and efforts. Visioning is not a predictor, but a creator of the future.

Note

1. For the sake of confidentiality, no information that could identify the organization concerned will be presented.

References

Bain & Company (1995), Survey published in *Le Mensuel Consulting* (July/August), Paris.

Bridges, W. (1980), *Transition – Making Sense of Life Changes*, Addison-Wesley, Reading.

Faulkner, C. (1994), Research Conference at Repère International Training centre for NLP, on 'Perceptual Cybernetics™', 6 May, Paris.

Jaques, E. (1951), *Changing Culture of the Factory*, Tavistock Publications, London.

Kakabadse, A. P. (1991), *The Wealth Creators: Top People, Top Teams and Executive Best Practice*, Kogan Page, London.

Nortier F. (1995), 'A New Angle on Coping with Change: Managing Transition!', *Journal Of Management Development*, MCB, Vol. 14, Iss. 4, pp. 32–46.

Stacey, R. (1995), 'Creativity in Organisations – The Importance of Mess', *Complexity & Management Working Papers*, Complexity & Management Centre, University of Hertfordshire, UK.

CHAPTER FOUR

The Cassandra complex: how to avoid generating a corporate vision that no one buys into

Philip Davies

Cassandra was the daughter of King Priam of Troy. Apollo fell in love with her but she spurned him. He gave her the gift of being able to foretell the future but of never being believed. Her most famous prophecy concerned the Wooden Horse which the Greeks had left outside the walls of Troy ostensibly as a gift to the Gods prior to their departure. She prophesied that the Horse would cause destruction to the city. She was right – the Horse was full of men and the Greek ships had only sailed over the horizon – but she was not believed.

Visioning, the process by which a corporate vision is generated, is a powerful business idea. The corporate vision articulates a view of a realistic, credible future for the organization that is in some way better than the present state. It is a target that beckons (Parikh, Neubauer and Lank, 1996). Examples include Kennedy's setting a target of putting a man on the moon by 1970 or the sense of a common vision that inspires Asea Brown Boveri (Bartlett and Ghoshal, 1993).

Visioning is important to organizations today. Employees, institutional shareholders, customers and other stakeholders need to feel that the organization has a clear view of where it is going and why it is going there. Yet achieving a clear, shared vision is difficult. One cause is the difficulty of seeing what to do. Another cause is a lack of commitment to the new vision by some in the organization because it does not match reality as they see it. Those who support the new vision are termed Cassandras – given the ability to see what is going to happen but not believed. The Cassandra Complex describes organizations whose executives can generate visions that meet external business reality but who have no internal credibility. This chapter will outline a model for developing a corporate vision based on a perception of the firm as embedded in a set of relationships within a wider institutional setting (Granovetter, 1985). But first, it may be useful to locate the social network perspective within the wider field of management theories about strategic choice and change.

Current explanations of visioning

Visioning is part of a wider literature on strategic choice and change. It explores issues around leadership, top management team effectiveness, strategic decision making and organizational change. This body of literature is concerned with the extent to which managers and organizations can make and implement choices, and who in the organization is involved in that process. Most of the visioning literature seems to be prescriptive. In addition there is a paucity of empirical research, in part because the concept is relatively new. Broadly, visioning seems to involve inspiring people, careful planning, achieving buy in and setting up a situation in which people in the oganization come to see, and identify with, the vision. From my readings there seem to be two dimensions that are relevant to visioning:

- The capacity for choice and purposeful action: defined as the extent to which managers can make choices and then carry them out, and

- The scope of the theory: defined as its unit of analysis, i.e. individual, firm or industry.

I have constructed a typology of theories that have a bearing on visioning using these two dimensions. The references are not comprehensive but rather cite the key publication, or where appropriate simply the field, i.e. classical economics. Some approaches such as structural theories span several cells, but I have placed them where they seem to be most relevant. Each set of theories are then loosely grouped along the dimension of purposeful action in terms of preferred leadership style; rational leadership; strategic leadership; and the illusion of leadership.

- *Rational leadership* This assumes that a vision is logically derived from an analysis of the various factors by top management who can then make clear plans for the vision to be implemented by middle managers. The underlying philosophy is one of a top-down model of strategy implementation. At the political level, rational leadership tries to implement big ideas. An example would be the monetarist policy of the Conservative Government in Britain in the 1980s.

■ *Strategic leadership*   This assumes that the visioning process will be highly contextual and that political and cognitive factors will influence the process. Implementation is via a microstrategic approach whereby managers at various levels within the firm construct the strategy. At the institutional level the strategic leadership approach shares Giddens' view (1984) of purposeful actors influencing and being influenced by the environment.

■ *The illusion of leadership*   Finally there are those who take the view that it doesn't really matter what individuals do. Organizational outcomes cannot be influenced dramatically by individuals. The best that can be achieved is successful adaptation to conditions. At the institutional level the main approach is that of population ecologists who view firms as if they were so many varieties of chaffinch.

Table 4.1 shows the key elements of literature grouped around these three leadership styles.

There seems to be an emerging consensus around strategic leadership, in particular, mid-range theories concerning how context influences, and in turn is influenced by, the visioning process. Yet many questions remain unanswered, or indeed may be unanswerable. These include:

■ What are the links between demographics and action?

■ What impact does context play and how can this be understood?

■ How does the decision process relate to the visioning process? Are they the same?

■ What is the impact of demographic factors on visioning. Does homogeneity suit implementing the vision, while heterogeneity fits generating the vision? If that is the case should different groups carry out these functions?

■ What role does the position of the organization in its institutional field play in visioning. Are there trends to isomorphism, in particular, copying success?

■ How can you measure the success of visioning if the result is in the future?

TABLE 4.1   Selective literature review

Scope of theory	The capacity for choice and purposeful action		
	Rational leadership	Strategic leadership	The illusion of leadership
Individual/ team/group	Visionary leadership Charisma Social exchange Blau (1964)	Strategic choice Child, (1972) Demographics Hambrick and Mason (1986) TMT competencies Kakabadse (1991) Political theory	Garbage can Cohen, March and Olsen (1972) Hypocrisy Brunnson (1986)
Organization/ firm	Core competencies Hamel and Prahalad (1994) Organizational Economics Barney and Hesterley (1996) Transaction costs Williamson (1991)	Culture Schein (1990) Institutional Scott (1995) Resource dependence Pfeffer and Salanacik (1978)	Organizational ecology Baum (1996)
Institutional/ industry	Classical economics	Structuration theory Giddens (1984) Embeddedness Granovetter (1985)	Marxism Population ecology

Clearly we cannot address all these issues here, but perhaps another perspective may help illuminate the field. One that is being increasingly utilized to explain links between individuals, ideas and organizational action, is that of social networks. The importance of understanding and managing business relationships is now increasingly seen as the main function of the executive. Firms are not autonomous entities able to choose what to do without taking anything else into account: they live within business networks (Forsgren and Johanson, 1992). The firm needs to manage a set of relationships with customers, suppliers, governments, competitors and other stakeholders. The totality of these relationships defines the individual firm and creates its distinctive identity (Kay, 1993).

Relationships may therefore be a source of sustainable competitive advantage. Visioning, as a means of crafting strategy, is influenced by these relationships, which may be better explained in terms of the social networks of those involved in the visioning process. In the next section, I will explain what is meant by the social networks perspective, outline some of the key findings, and relate them to the issue of visioning.

Social network analysis

Social network analysis[1] is a methodology that directs the analysis of relationships between individual actors in an organizational field. It measures the ties between, rather than the attributes of, actors. Typical questions that are asked by social network analysts include: What is the relationship between banks and industries? How does information pass through social networks? Do managers have different social networks to non-managers? What is the relationship between the take up of an innovation and social networks? Why did the Medicis rise to power in Florence in the 15th century? How do people find jobs? Does power relate to where the individual is located within the organization? What situations in a business network improve organizational learning? More articles are being published in mainstream journals and the perspective is proving both interesting and useful for scholars from many areas.

The power of the perspective lies in its capacity to illuminate the precise nature of structure and roles and how people perceive their place in that structure. It is also used by consultants to facilitate organizational change. The methodology is based on mathematical graph theory and uses a series of matrices to collect and analyse data. An important difference is that in social network analysis everyone in a network is asked a few questions, typically no more than four, while in probability sampling, a few people are asked lots of questions. Software to carry out the analysis is widely available.

Main terms

Before I discuss the value of the perspective, it is important to be clear about some of the key terms which we will be using which are: ties – strength and direction; density – weak and strong networks; cliques and coalitions; formal and informal structures; structural equivalence; trust; power; centrality.

Ties – strength and direction

A tie is any relationship between individuals or organizations. A tie can be a communication link, a financial relationship or a social relationship, i.e. friendship or kinship. The strength of a tie is important. It is a function of the number of ties that are present from a single tie to a multiple tie. The direction of the tie is to do with who is giving what to whom, as in the case of goods and services, while in social networks it is to do with who can influence whom, or who trusts and is seen as trustworthy.

Cliques and coalitions

A clique is a permanent set of individuals who are tightly connected. A coalition is a temporary group formed around a particular issue. Individuals can belong to several coalitions but usually only one clique. Cliques can be hidden.

Formal and informal structures

The formal structure is the organization chart. The informal structure is what lies behind the chart in terms of individual relationships. Both managing and influencing are important. As organizations delayer and decentralize, the informal structure may become more important and managing in that type of situation demands different skills. Political skills are sometimes defined as the capacity to utilize the informal structure. Of course, as is often the case in management studies, the importance of the informal organization has been recognized before. Chester Barnard wrote about these issues six years ago in the classic *Functions of the Executive* (1938).

Structural equivalence

This is a measure of the extent to which individuals in different organizations occupy a similar position in the structure. The implication, which is hotly disputed in the field, is that structurally equivalent actors will behave in similar ways. Thus accountants in London, it is argued, will behave in similar ways to accountants in Glasgow even though they do not know each other.

Trust

Trust[2] is both the specific expectation that another's actions will be beneficial rather than detrimental and the generalized ability to take for granted the features of the social order. Trust is embedded in social and economic relationships and often takes the form of professional norms, i.e. doctors behave like this, airline pilots like that. The obverse of trust is opportunism. High trust organizations probably have lower transaction costs than low trust organizations. This applies especially to interorganizational relationships such as partnering or joint ventures (Davies, 1997).

Centrality

The *centrality* or otherwise of an actor is a measure of where they are located in the network, as measured by the number of ties they have with others. Someone who has many ties is more central than someone who has few ties. A person with no ties is an *isolate*. Someone who connects several disparate groups is the *broker*. The direction and intensity of the tie are also important.

Power and influence

Power[3] is an important concept. It can be split into three areas: direct, indirect and mind-set power. Direct power is where A gets B to do something. Indirect power is where A controls the process so as to prevent B from getting their issue on the agenda. Mind-set or institutional power is where neither A nor B can think in any other way.

Density – weak and strong networks

In weak networks, the density of ties is low. Individuals know many people but not that well. As a result, new data is more likely to flow into the organization. In contrast, strong network organizations are characterized by frequent contact between individuals both at work and socially. There exist many friendship ties and relationships go back over many years.

But therein lies the paradox. Strong networks require considerable investment in terms of time to service them. Also, because people know each other well, little new information is available. In contrast, weak ties are an excellent way of finding out what is important. Granovetter's classic study (1972) of unemployed men in Boston found that individuals picked up important data, in this case a job opportunity, more from casual acquaintances than close friends.

How networks change from weak to strong is interesting. There is probably a link to time and history. As individuals interact more, and as the present becomes history, so some ties are seen as preferable to others in terms of the benefits gained from the relationship and in terms of the nature of the social interaction, i.e. was it enjoyable, or not. It is likely therefore that some ties will be developed at the expense of others which will then be discarded. A study of research and development (R&D) groups found that there was a curvilinear relationship between performance measured in terms of performance and time. For up to 18 months and after five years, R&D groups were recognized as ineffective. The findings are that new and strong networks are less able to innovate (Katz and Allen, 1982).

Social network analysts (Granovetter, 1972) have also found that there is a curvilinear relationship between the strength of ties and access to new data, defined as information that others in the network do not yet know. In a new network there are few ties but they do not carry much data. The strong network has multiple ties but will not be the source of much new data. The best network for new data is a weak network.

In practice, of course, individual actors will belong to a variety of network types. These networks are often turbulent and can fragment as people leave, or as organizational structures and roles are changed, for example following downsizing. The loss of social network connections, under such conditions, may well contribute to the loss of organizational wisdom, especially tacit knowledge.

The spectrum of network types is therefore:

- *Low*   This is an isolate who has no ties to anyone else.

- *New*   This is a network where few actors know each other and so there are few ties. An example would be someone who has just joined an organization.

- *Weak*   Here individual actors are loosely connected to each other but have a wide circle of acquaintances. An organizational example would be a consultancy, or a partnership or medical practice.

- *Strong*   In a strong network, individual actors know each other well and have multiple ties. A classic example of a strong networked organization would be a military unit.

- *Total*   This is a like a black hole where no new information can enter. Religious cults are one example of total networks, although possibly, groups can become total networks when they refuse to accept outside advice. Groupthink may be a form of temporary total network.

The curvilinear relationship between access to data, high or low, and the network type is illustrated in Figure 4.1.

FIGURE 4.1   Curvilinear relationship between access to new data and density of network

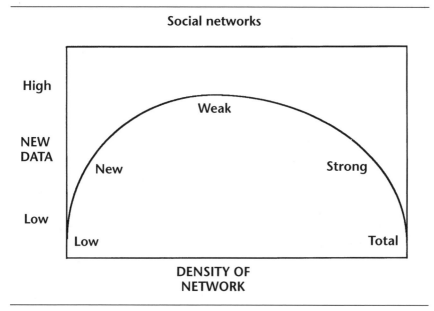

What links are there between networks and the visioning process? Weak networks will probably have better connections to external environments and so should be better at understanding what is happening in the wider business world. By contrast, strong networks should be better at maintaining cohesion during implementation. Total networks may reject an alternative that does not fit their world-view, while new networks have insufficient data to understand what is going on.

Value of the perspective for visioning

In terms of the key issues for managers who are involved in visioning, what are the main questions and how can social network analysis help? First, social networks define organizational reality. As one of the early theorists pointed out: 'A person's network forms a social environment... it is a reservoir of social relations from which and through which he recruits support to counter his rivals and mobilizes support to attain his goals.' (Jeremy Boissevain, *Friends of Friends* (1974)). Access to suitable networks helps managers take account of that environment so that new ideas can be developed and implemented. Different parts of the organization, depending on their demographic profile as well as organizational history, are likely to have different perceptions of both external business reality as well as what is acceptable within the organization.

At certain stages of the visioning process, a social network analysis approach may help draw attention to what managers should take notice of, and what could get in the way. I have applied a social network perspective to Parikh, Neubauer and Lanks' (1994) excellent model of visioning. They argue, based on work with top teams, that visioning involves a combination of reflection on experience and intuition. Reflective visioning generates ideas based on experience while intuitive visioning uses imagination unconstrained by reality. There seems to be a clear link with social networks. For example organizations with weak networks may find sensing their external environment easy but may be less effective at reaching consensus as to what to do next.

I have combined their visioning model with a force field model (Table 4.2). The force field approach sees change as a matter of increasing the enabling forces while at the same time weakening blocking forces. Like all such models, it is simplistic but it may help in better understanding where social networks may help or hinder. The networks

TABLE 4.2   Force field model

Steps	Enabling	Blocking
Step One: Group reflective visioning	Weak networks Good external data Reliable internal performance data	New/strong networks Blinkered external data Poor performance data
Step Two: Individual reflective visioning	Weak networks	New/strong networks
Step Three: Group shared reflective visioning	Strong networks Trust	Lack of trust
Step Four: Individual intuitive visioning	Weak networks Trust	New/total networks
Step Five: Group shared intuitive visioning	Strong networks	New/total networks
Step Six: Group integrative visioning	Strong networks	New/total networks
Step Seven: Group current reality	Strong networks	New/total networks
Step Eight: Group process action plans	Strong networks Cohesion	Lack of cohesion

are for those involved in the visioning process – normally but not necessarily the senior executive group.

An additional paradox arises here. The very conditions – weak networks – that lead to a good understanding of external business conditions may in practice make it harder to deliver on the vision. Parikh, Neubauer and Lank's model (1994) provides valuable insights concerning the visioning process itself but, I believe, it does not go far enough down the road of implementation. Here, I will use insights from the strategy process field to take the argument a stage further. We also need to keep in mind that this is not an intellectual exercise as at some point, the vision has to be turned into reality.

Conceptual versus realized vision

All big business ideas from business process reengineering (BPR) to shareholder value are only beneficial once implemented. What happens on the ground in terms of sales and results is what influences business performance. A criticism of management education is of fields rich in ideas, that are poorly implemented in business. This has led some executives to question the value of academic concepts for effectively addressing their problems in the real world. So, for visioning to deliver the potential that it has, and not be seen as another big idea that never works out in practice, we need to consider how the vision will be implemented as well as how the vision itself is generated. Henry Minztberg (1976) was concerned with a similar problem when, with his colleagues, he analysed how often, in practice, strategic decisions were implemented as originally planned. He found that generally they were not and that decisions either emerged out of the planning process, were imposed, or arose from unexpected opportunities. Some of course failed. I have adapted his insight to visioning and suggest a four-phase process for visioning:

- Phase One: generating the vision.

- Phase Two: debating the vision within the executive.

- Phase Three: testing the vision out.

- Phase Four: realizing the vision in terms of business performance.

In practice the process is likely to be iterative and messy. This is illustrated in Figure 4.2. Let us look at each stage in more detail.

- *Generating the conceptual vision* This is both a group and an individual process in which those responsible, normally the executive group, produce the vision. The vision is compared to current reality and then action plans are prepared. Executive team dynamics and demographics influence strategic decision making. It is clear that demographic factors such as the background of the group, their industry experience, functional role as well as communication processes will influence group processes (Ireland et al., 1987) The philosophy or ideology of the executive (Child, 1972) will also have an impact in terms of selective attention to strategic issues. This is likely to be significant when going through the reflective visioning

FIGURE 4.2   Conceptual versus realized vision

Phase one	Phase two	Phase three	Phase four
	2. Debated vision ⇔	3. Tested vision ⇔	⇒ Failed vision

⇈⇈⇈⇈   ⇊⇊⇊⇊

| 1. Conceptual vision | ⇒⇒⇒⇒⇒⇒ | ⇒⇒⇒⇒⇒⇒ | 4. Realized vision |

⇈⇈⇈⇈⇈   ⇈⇈⇈⇈⇈   ⇈⇈⇈⇈⇈   ⇊⇊⇊⇊⇊

Executive group dynamics · **Social networks and business reality** · **Business performance**

⇐   ⇑   ⇑   ⇐

⇐⇐⇐⇐   ⇐⇐⇐⇐

MAIN INFLUENCES ON PROCESS

stage. The extent to which the group trust each other is another key factor. Low trust groups may be loath to share 'off the wall' intuitive visions.

■ *Debating the vision*   This is the point when the vision starts to be debated. The debate may be restricted to direct reports of the executive group or it may be much wider. From the strategic leadership perspective, there is an expectation that the strategy process will involve a significant portion of the organization and may even extend into stakeholder groups. Even if no formal debate occurs, informal debate is inevitable as different interest groups try to make sense of what has happened and work out the implications, in practice, for them. In extreme cases, leaks to the media can be used. Institutional shareholders are especially significant at this stage.

The more complex the activities of the firm and the more widely dispersed its activities the more the debate may lead to some questioning of the vision. This can make CEOs naturally nervous because of the adverse effect such questioning can have on their own position. However, restricting conflict at this point, especially if there are genuine concerns, is dangerous. Conflict should be welcomed first because it may surface unforeseen issues and secondly because unresolved conflict is more dangerous. The reputation of the CEO, especially if he or she has enjoyed success elsewhere will be an important factor in securing consent. Once the debate is concluded the vision will start to be tested by events.

- *Testing the vision*   This phase can either be explicit or implicit. An explicit testing process involves checking results against predictions made in the action planning phase. Explicit testing has the advantage of clarity but can become bogged down in detail and blame-seeking behaviour. Implicit assumptions as to what constitutes success may initially feel more comfortable, however, there is a danger that individual executives will make judgements based on their own perceptions of success rather than shared views. Thus the marketing director will notice improved performance only in terms of more sales leads but will not notice problems in quality. The power of the vision may then weaken. What is needed is a sufficiently robust set of assumptions that are shared and can be discussed. The emotional strength of the executive group is vital here. But there is always the possibility that conditions may alter so drastically that the vision cannot be fulfilled. At this stage the vision fails.

- *Realizing the vision*   The point when the vision is realized is when it becomes embedded into the routines and processes of the organization. It is simply the way *we do things around here.* A successful vision needs to retain the capacity to direct present action towards a future goal. I would argue that the vision has been realized when it informs the actions of everyone in the organization. Visions cease to be a target that beckons once you have got to the Moon. The failure of NASA in the 1970s and 80s to capture the imagination of the American people may in part have been due to a sense in which it was felt that they'd done what they had said they would do. The war was won. The great challenge for leaders is how to sustain that sense of common purpose and vision over long periods.

I have argued that visioning involves sensing what possibilities exist in the wider business environment and then embedding this vision within the routines and processes of the whole organization. I have also argued that different social networks exist in organizations and that they have distinctive characteristics which can help or hinder effective change. How then can an understanding of social networks help? And how can you avoid becoming an organizational Cassandra – crying *I told you so* – after disaster has struck!

How to avoid the Cassandra complex: balancing internal and external social networks

Peter Senge, when discussing what skills leaders would need in the future included, along with systems thinking and surfacing and testing mental models, the capacity to build a shared vision (1990). He broke that skill down into: encouraging personal vision; communicating and asking for support; visioning as an ongoing process; distinguishing between positive and negative visions; and blending extrinsic and intrinsic visions. The contribution of the social networks perspective is in the need to balance the benefits of weak, external networks while retaining sufficient cohesion to make and implement a vision that will be accepted by the organization. I propose, following Senge, that leaders need to establish and maintain a balanced network – what I have called 'Where Extremes Meet'. The phrase is not mine. I first heard it used last year by the chief executive of a large NHS hospital to describe how he managed to deal with the difficulties of leading such a complex organization. The extremes he had to deal with were expressed as a series of choices between:

■ patient care and limited resources;

■ professional autonomy and the need for control;

■ research excellence and avoiding legal consequences of risky procedures.

The chief executive had no answers! For him, what mattered, was the ability to deal with specific situations by means of good processes so that no single incident could overwhelm the capacity of his team to manage.

In order to understand what is involved in developing a balanced network two aspects need to be considered, the extrinsic or external vision, and the intrinsic or internal vision. The extrinsic vision concerns the way in which the organization understands what is happening in the wider business environment while the intrinsic vision concerns the extent to which the vision can be delivered. The two questions that need to be asked are:

■ *Can top management deliver the vision?* This concerns the extent to which the executive have the confidence and respect of those within the organization. This perception will be based on past experience but may also be affected by whether or not the organization is in crisis. This dimension is concerned with understanding context and leadership.

FIGURE 4.3   The Cassandra complex

Does vision meet future needs?

	Low	High
Low	Cell 1 **Dead in the water** New or isolate internally Fragmented externally	Cell 2 **Cassandra complex** Isolate or new internal Weak networks external
High	Cell 3 **False dawn** Strong/total internal network Isolate/new external network	Cell 4 **Where extremes meet** Balanced network Weak external network Strong internal network

Can top managers deliver the vision?

- *Does the vision meet future needs?*   This concerns the extent to which the vision is related to what is happening in the wider business environment, in particular, issues such as changing bases of competition, customer perceptions or unexpected opportunities. This dimension is concerned with opportunity costs and strategic thinking.

From a consideration of these two issues we can derive a model of visoning Figure 4.3). Let us look in more detail at these types. In practice of course no single organization will fit precisely into any box, however, as ideal types they may be useful in noticing where organizations are going, or where they have come from!

Dead in the water

There exists at senior and middle levels of management a poor understanding of what is happening in the industry as a whole and a reluctance to learn from others. Internally, managers are either seen as fools or dangerous dictators. Strategy is disconnected from everyday activity. Everyone leaves the organization if they can. Leaving parties are the most common form of ritual. Leadership is someone else's problem.

Problems are attributed to a lack of resources. Individuals either accept the situation or set out to create secure niches. Such organizations can be surprisingly resilient if their market is in growth or if they are protected by a monopoly. When this changes, however, they will either taken over, transform or die. Very large organizations, or ones from the public sector often display certain of these characteristics.

Cassandra complex

In this organization some of the executives are usually new, brought in to 'sort out' an organization in trouble. They have a good idea what to do but don't know how to make it happen. In this situation, external consultants are often used to show what needs to happen but their intervention is unlikely to be effective unless senior managers, with strong internal networks, visibly support change. There may be a strong professional or technical bias, with management historically seen as 'bean counting'. In this situation the vision may be sabotaged by existing managers. There may be an initial acceptance of the new vision but, during the debate and testing stage, problems will emerge. Often managers will request more data, more analysis and more consultation, but this is only a delaying tactic. The motives for doing this vary from a genuine belief that the new ideas are unworkable to a cynical interest in retaining power but the net effect is the same: the vision will fail. In Cassandra organizations, the visionary is right but no one listens. If the visionary lacks power he will be ignored and leave.

False dawn

False dawn organizations have secure and well-liked executives. They have been successful in the past and there is no reason why they should not be so in the future. Current problems are temporary. When a vision is needed it will be seen as sensible and likely to work. The vision is popular and is listened to. The vision seems viable, but in practice it doesn't work because it has not taken into account what is happening outside. In fact false dawn organizations are in strategic drift and at some point will have to face up to reality. However, the strength of internal relationships, especially if change involves downsizing, will make the process uncomfortable. Such organizations invest tremendous energy in maintaining strong internal relationships with office parties and social events. Leadership is traditional and paternalistic and employees are expected to stay for life. Information is controlled and outsiders are distrusted because *this organization is different*. Institutional shareholders in particular are blamed for problems. People are promoted more on considerations of soundness than any other reason, while those who study for business qualifications are seen as academics and so are suspect. There is likely to be a myth of the golden age when things were better. Banks in the UK have exhibited some of these characteristics in the past.

Where extremes meet

The vision is compelling and the executives are viewed as likely and able to make it happen. Everyone wants to be part of the success. Conflict is welcomed and part of the normal process of management. Groups may well be deliberately broken up to prevent relationships becoming too close. This type of organization is never satisfied with the way things are and can be seen as difficult and unreasonable. But there are a set of core values which bind the executive together.

Summary

We began this chapter at the siege of Troy. Cassandra's warning to 'fear the Greeks, especially when they bear gifts'[4] had not been heeded. The wooden horse that the Trojans believed was a sign that the Greeks had given up the siege of their city was hauled inside the gates by the rejoicing citizens. Later that night, when everyone was asleep, the Greeks hidden inside the Horse emerged to open the gates to the waiting Greek warriors. The city was sacked and Cassandra made a captive. The Trojans had endured many years of fighting and wanted to believe that it was all over. The tragedy was that the one who could see the danger was not believed.

Organizations are facing tremendous pressures. Under such conditions there is always the temptation to believe what we want to believe and to ignore different voices – the organizational Cassandras. We need to ensure that those different voices are heard and that their warnings, or indeed unrealized opportunities, are built into the strategy process and not ignored.

Visioning will always be an uncomfortable process because it involves working on complex issues with colleagues who are different. It may mean giving up a pet project or admitting that a past decision was wrong. Building a balanced network does not mean that conflict will disappear either. More conflict is likely. But there should be less hidden conflict and a greater emotional robustness about debates.

Executives need to accept dilemmas and not seek to resolve them in one neat solution. In practice the realized vision will be adapted on the basis of debate and experience. The nature of social networks influences how, as well as what is considered. Executives need to build balanced networks which can sense the external environment while at the same time retaining the capacity to implement their vision.

Notes

1. This section is based on a wide variety of articles and texts. The best single account of the perspective is currently Wasserman and Faust (1994) *Social Network Analysis*. The trade journal is *Social Networks*. See also Burt (1992) and Gulati (1995).
2. The field of trust studies is growing rapidly. A good summary of recent research is Kramer and Tyler (1996), *Trust in Organizations*.
3. Power is a separate study. This section draws on a recent survey by Hardy and Clegg (1996) in the latest Handbook of Organizational Studies.
4. Timeo Danaos et dona ferentes. Virgil, *Aeneid*.

References

Barnard, C. (1938), *The Functions of the Executive*, Harvard University Press, Cambridge, MA.

Barney, J. and Hesterly, W. (1996), 'Organizational Economics: Understanding the Relationship between Organizations and Economic Analysis' *Handbook of Organization Studies*, Edited by Clegg, S.R., Hardy C. and Nord, W.R. Sage, London, pp. 115–147.

Bartlett, C.A. and Ghoshal, S. (1993), 'Beyond the M-Form: Towards a Managerial Theory of the Firm *Strategic Management Journal* Volume 14: pp. 23–46.

Baum, J.A.C. (1996), 'Organizational Ecology', *Handbook of Organization Studies*, Edited by Clegg, S.R., Hardy, C. and Nord, W.R. London, pp. 77–114.

Blau, P. (1964), *Exchange and Power in Social Life* Wiley, New York.

Boissevain, J. (1974), *Friends of Friends: Networks, Manipulators and Coalitions*, Basil Blackwell, Oxford.

Brunnson, N. (1986), 'Organizing for Inconsistencies: on Organizational Conflict, Depression and Hypocrisy as Substitutes for Action', *Scandinavian Journal of Management Studies* May pp. 165–185.

Burt, R.S. (1992), *The Social Structure of Competition*, Harvard University Press, Cambridge, MA.

Child, J. (1972), 'Organizational Structure, Environment and Performance: the Role of Strategic Choice', *Sociology*, Vol. 6, pp. 1–22.

Davies, P. (1997), *How Social Network Analysis can Help in Understanding Cooperative Relationships between Organizations: the Case of Partnering in Service Industries*, Paper presented at the International Conference on Multi-Organizational Partnerships and Cooperation. Held at Balliol College, Oxford, July.

Forsgren, M. and Johanson, J. (1992), 'Managing in International Multi-Centre Firms', in Forsgren, M. and Johanson, J. (eds.), *Managing Networks in International Business*, Gordon & Breach, Philadelphia, pp. 19–31.

Giddens, A. (1984), *The Constitution of Society*, Polity Press, Cambridge.

Granovetter, M. (1972), 'The Strength of Weak Ties', *American Journal of Sociology*, Vol. 78, No. 6, pp. 1360–1380.

Granovetter, M. (1985), 'Economic Action and the Problem of Embeddedness', *American Sociological Journal*, Vol. 91, No. 3, pp. 481–510.

Gulati, R. (1995), 'Social Structure and Alliance Formation Patterns: A Longitudinal Analysis', *Administrative Science Quarterly*, Vol. 40, pp. 619–652.

Hamel, G. and Prahalad, C.K. (1994), *Competing for the Future*, Harvard Business School Press, Boston.

Hardy, C. and Clegg, S. (1996), 'Some Dare Call It Power', *Handbook of Organization Studies*, Edited by Clegg, S.R., Hardy, C. and Nord, W.R., Sage, London, pp. 622–641.

Ireland, R.D., Hitt, M.A., Bettis, R.A. and De Porras, D.A. (1987), 'Strategy Formulation Processes: Differences in Perceptions of Strength and Weaknesses Indicators and Environmental Uncertainty by Managerial Level', *Strategic Management Journal*, Vol. 8, pp. 469–485.

Kakabadse, A.P. (1991), *The Wealth Creators*, Kogan Page, London.

Katz, R. and Allen, T.J. (1982), 'Investigating the Not-Invented-Here Syndrome', *R & D Management*, Vol. 12, No. 1, pp. 7–19.

Kay, J. (1993), *Foundations of Corporate Success*, Oxford University Press, Oxford.

Kramer, R.M. and Tyler, T.R. (1996), *Trust in Organizations*, Sage, London.

Mintzberg, H., Raisinghani, O. and Theoret, A. (1976), 'The Structure of Unstructured Decision Processes', *Administrative Science Quarterly* June, pp. 246–275.

Parikh, J., Neubauer, F. and Lank, A.G. (1996), 'Developing a Vision', in Bennis, W., Parikh, J. and Lessem, R. *Beyond Leadership: Balancing Economics, Ethics and Ecology*, Oxford, Blackwell, pp. 62–86.

Pfeffer, J. and Salancik, G. (1978), *The External Control of Organizations: A Resource Dependence Perspective*, Harper and Row, New York.

Schein, E.H. (1990), *Organizational Culture and Leadership*, Jossey-Bass, San Francisco and Oxford.

Scott W.R. (1995), *Institutions and Organizations*, Sage, London.

Senge, P. (1990), 'The Leader's New Work: Building Learning Organizations'. *Sloan Management Review*, No. 7.

Wasserman, S. and Faust K. (1994), *Social Network Analysis*, Cambridge University Press, Cambridge.

Williamson, O.E. (1991), 'Comparative Economic Organization: The Analysis of Discrete Structural Alternatives'. *Administrative Science Quarterly*, Vol. 36, pp. 269–296

CHAPTER FIVE

Bridging the S-curve gap

Mike Jeans

Organizations are likely to be, if they not already are, operating in an environment where:

- the marketplace is international or even global;

- their vision becomes more about long-term sustainability;

- their strategy must be to ensure flexibility and creativity – and do so rapidly;

- knowledge, and easy access to that knowledge, is key in terms of systems;

- technology continues to be a key resource, but information (knowledge) and people become more important;

- formal structures, even if matrix-based, break down and networks take their place.

Endemic in such developments is change, not just evolutionary change, but transformational change that requires management to make major leaps. The question is how?

Making the leap

Much has been written about S (sigmoid)-curves over the past few years, particularly by Dick Nolan (co-founder of Nolan, Norton & Co – now part of KPMG). This was primarily devoted to a hypothesis of how organizations need to adapt to stages of the technology revolution (Figure 5.1).

FIGURE 5.1   Sigmoid curves

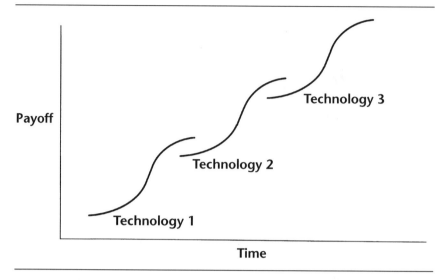

FIGURE 5.2   Nature of adjustment

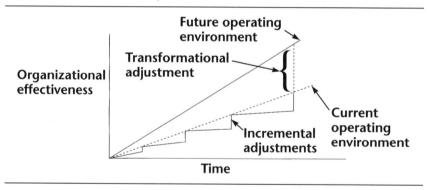

More recently, this model has been used to explain the need for organizations to undergo radical transformation. The argument runs along the lines of saying that incremental adjustments are insufficient (Figure 5.2); even if these adjustments tend to become bigger and bigger.

When one then maps on the future operating environment, the adjustments, it is argued, can no longer be seen as incremental but as transformational. This is equivalent to an organization moving from operating in one age of man to the next age.

This idea can also be shown in terms of S-curves (Figure 5.3).

The argument here suggests that it is necessary in transformational terms to leap from the old S-curve to a new one. It is also argued that this

FIGURE 5.3   The leap

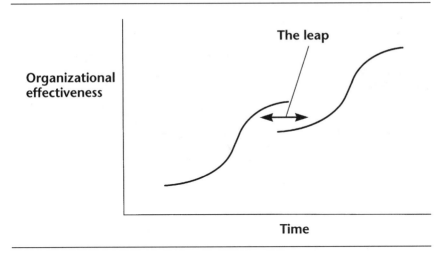

FIGURE 5.4   Going backwards

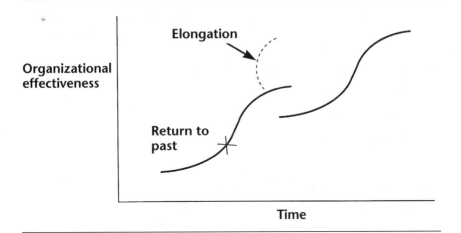

leap should take place before the old S-curve begins to flatten – the logic being that the longer you leave it, the bigger the leap; indeed you may eventually face a precipice which could result in a very hard landing!

Whilst there may be some legitimacy to this approach, there is the risk that it will cause a return to an earlier point on the S-curve when the organization was successful (Figure 5.4). This could mean a return to a model that worked, but which ignores the possibility that the environment has changed. It could be argued that this was the error made by the UK Conservative Party and Prime Minister John Major's

FIGURE 5.5   Migration

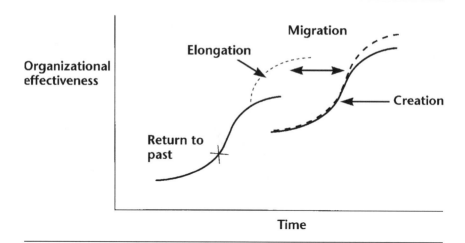

famous line 'Back to basics' – possibly the only vision statement ever to begin with the word 'Back'!

What has perhaps been forgotten in these arguments is that during the transformational process, three tasks need to be considered (Figure 5.5):

- Elongation of the current S-curve whilst not returning to an earlier point.

- Creation of the new S-curve.

- Managing the migration from one S-curve to the next.

In marketing-oriented organizations, this phenomenon of managing S-curve migrations should be well understood in terms of managing a portfolio of products some of which are new and some old. How often one hears of the issue of 'managing the brand trial' (the old products – or S-curve).

But an analogy can also be drawn with corporate transformation. When Midland Bank (now part of Hong Kong and Shanghai Banking Corporation) decided in the late 1980s to set up a telephone banking operation, it did so by creating a separate organization, First Direct. This was arguably a second-curve operation, bearing little resemblance to Midland Bank's existing traditional branch banking operation. This did not, however, mean that the latter was ignored. Indeed Midland engaged in a great many first-curve initiatives, such as branch closure/ amalgamation or staff reduction to elongate the life of that operation.

Another example is that of UK utility companies. Many, if not most, utilities in the UK have their origins in privatized organizations. Their development could, perhaps, be divided into three key stages:

■ Privatization.

■ Commercialization.

■ Development.

The tasks of privatization were, in essence, structurally and financially driven to ensure that the companies were in a position to be floated.

The tasks of commercialization were arguably far more numerous and were driven by the need to become more competitive. This involved many exercises concerned with reducing the cost base (BPR, delayering, profit centre accounting, overhead reduction, headcount reduction, etc.). Most, if not all, of these activities can be seen as 'first curve elongation' with, possibly, a move onto the migration path.

The development stage is more likely to be concerned with migrating to, and operating on, a second curve. If this is the case, then some far more fundamental changes in operating structure, style of management and culture need to be considered. During the transformation, it may well be necessary to separate teams and projects to look into:

■ elongating the current S-curve; projects are likely to include cost cutting, BPR, (business process re-engineering), TQM (total quality management);

■ migrating to the new S-curve; projects might include cultural change, programme management, acquisition of new competencies;

■ creating the new S-curve; projects could be out-of-the box visioning, Delphi thinking, mergers, acquisitions, divestment.

The people involved in each of these teams are likely to be different in behaviour, attitude and skills. The challenge is to make them all feel valued, and contributors. Each of the three teams is making the leap.

Blanchard and Waghorn (1997) look at two teams of people operating in a transformational context. The first is called the 'P Team'. Its focus is on the present and upon improving the existing organization. The second is the Team 'F', whose task is to create the future. Both teams operate at the same time. Blanchard and Waghorn describe this as a World Class Organization. Such an organization, they say, is working effectively not just on one curve or the other, but on both at the same time, and learning from both.

Look before you leap

The processes of elongation, migration and creation probably sound difficult and potentially fraught with dangers for the organization. Indeed, many chief executives, when faced with a decision as to whether or not to set such process in motion, ask two self-searching and fundamental questions: 'In order for the transformation process to start, I shall have to let go. How can I prevent corporate anarchy breaking out and the organization self-destructing?' and 'How can I take my people with me?'

To begin to answer these questions, it is necessary to understand that there are three stages to the transformation process. These are articulated by Tichy and Sharman (1993) as:

- Awakening.

- Envisioning.

- Rearchitecturing.

Blanchard and Waghorn (1997), similarly identify a sequence of three steps – envision, prepare, deliver. This sequence appears to assume that the awakening stage has already occurred.

During the awakening process, as described by Tichy and Sharman (1996), agreement is sought amongst the senior managers that a continuance of the corporate status quo is not an acceptable option. It is, however, more complex than that, since not only should the need for change be agreed, but also the causes of that need.

Take, for example, a hypothetical manufacturing company that by common assent is 'bleeding to death'. Margins are down, staff turnover is high, market share is being lost, management is pressured – all resulting in a disastrous bottom line. The board is unanimous – 'We have to change!' A project team of middle managers is formed and charged with drawing up recommendations and reporting back to the board. The report is duly presented and at its heart is the recommendation that a massive cost-cutting exercise is embarked upon, primarily based upon headcount reduction. One can imagine the consequent dialogue amongst board members:

Finance director:	'Marvellous, just what we need! That should increase margins and profitability.'
Marketing and sales director:	'Fantastic, but only if it enables us to retain current margins, reduce selling prices and increase market share.'
Personnel director:	'What's that going to do to staff turnover – increase it still further.'
Production director:	'Not only that, but most of the people are in my area, so I'll be the one having to cut back. Fat chance of meeting any increased product demand.'
Chief executive:	'!!!! ???? .....'

Perhaps it was the right recommendation, but now not only is the company bleeding to death but there is also blood in the boardroom. This outcome was the result of managers not taking the time to understand and agree the *causes* of the need to change before embarking on the next stage of visioning.

In his book *Who Knows Wins*, Ketan Patel (1996) looks at some of the great, ancient strategists (Sun Tzu, Miyamoto Musashi and Alexander the Great) and compares them with leading strategic thinkers and analysts of our time. He also draws on lessons to be learnt from current corporate strategies. Patel says:

> Strategy is the result of assimilating information, processing this against our accumulated knowledge bank, and planning the utilisation of resources and how to move and position them to achieve our goals.

> The master strategist is that unique person who is better able to assimilate knowledge than his opponents and thereby forms superior strategies.

Knowledge has always been vital in developing vision and strategies. What has changed, and continues to change at an ever-faster pace, is the increase in availability of that knowledge.

KPMG's approach to the awakening process comprises a number of activities designed both to gather knowledge and to achieve consensus on the causes of the need to change. These activities include:

■ Meetings with top management as individuals.

- Collection of internal and external data.

- Top team and, possibly, middle management workshops on the case for change.

- Collection of data on likely areas of resistance to change.

- Feedback to top team, and search for consensus.

This may appear a tedious process in which to engage before moving on to what might seem to be the more exciting stage of visioning. But without a thorough awakening, experience shows that visioning becomes sterile, inappropriate, superficial or an academic exercise – or all of these!

Conversely, it should be recognized that there is little point in commencing an awakening process unless there is commitment to following it through to the subsequent stages, regardless of whether first- or second-curve change results. 'Hares' will have been set running, perceptions formed, aspirations raised, and fears begun. A process has started and needs to be led.

Visioning: a mechanism for bridging the S-curve gap

Visioning is a process. It is about finding a way of arriving at a statement of how the organization would like to describe itself, and be described, at some point in the future. Exactly what that vision should be will depend upon each individual organization and its marketplace.

This is not the place to debate the crafting of vision statements. The statement is, of course, important but, as previously stated, so are the causes (drivers) of the need to change, and the timescale. Figure 5.6 draws upon a number of sources to summarize 11 different examples, that have arisen over the past decade or so of cases of drivers of visions.

The process of visioning is often based upon what has been learned in top team workshops. It can frequently prove difficult to enable such teams to focus on the future without being overly constrained by the present. If the latter occurs, at best only a first-curve change in vision will occur.

There exist a variety of methods facilitators can use to draw individuals' minds into the future. The use of case studies such as those summarized in Figure 5.6 can be helpful. Other external generic studies such as the Royal Society of Arts inquiry into tomorrow's company can

FIGURE 5.6 Drivers of vision

Organization	Driver	Timescale	Future
Xerox	Losing share to Japanese	Survival	Leadership through quality
British Telecom (UK)	Future competition	Long-term prosperity	Global player orientation
GE (UK) (privatization)	Market turbulence in future	Success-enabling future	Flexibility and customer
Conservative Government (UK)	Opinion poll ratings	Re-election	Back to basics
SmithKline Beecham (US/UK)	Globalization/restructuring of industry	Medium-term survival	World's best healthcare company
Massey-Ferguson (Canada)	Impending bankruptcy and market collapse in farm machinery	Medium-term survival	Varity Corporation (US) Automotive and industrial parts
SAS (Sweden)	Deregulation and recession	Medium-term survival	Cost-efficiency
Shisheido (Japan)	Falling market share	Long-term prosperity	Customer driven and flexibility
Barclays (UK)	Falling customer and market share: losing money	Restore short-term profitability	Focus on core business
Groupe Bull (France)	Steady decline in revenues	Recovery within two years	Cost-efficiency
Ahlstrom (Finland)	Global competition while linked to Finnish economy	Long term	Global company

FIGURE 5.7   What will future organizations look like?

Factor	Yesterday's companies	Tomorrow's companies
Performance measures	Financial returns related to future success	Achievement of purpose not based on past measures of success
Relationships	Adversarial	Reciprocal and communal
Management style	Us and them	Collaborative
Organization	Top-down bureaucracy	Learning and adaptive
Perspective	Inward	Global
Customers	Source of revenue and profit	Value creating relationships
Suppliers	Interchangeable vendors	Extension of company
Employee competencies	Effort and conformity	Diverse skills, learning and creativity
Shareholders	Disclose minimum information	Share information
Community	Neutral or interfering	Interdependence
Environment	Peripheral issue	Importance of sustainability

stimulate debate. Figure 5.7 summarizes some of the findings of that important inquiry.

Other techniques might include asking the team members to draft out articles that they would like the financial, trade, and tabloid press to carry when their annual results are announced in, say, three years' time. An addition to this could be the article they would seek to draft for the organization's own in-house paper. Whatever techniques are used, it is important that the visioning process itself is valued. Tony Page (1996) talks about a vision as something emergent, not mechanistic.

Giving substance to principles

Visions are, to an extent, dreams and it is all too easy to wake up from a dream only to find it impossible to put substance to it. Corporate visions are also about how an organization looks and operates.

We need a way of describing an organization and thus a means of analysing it. KPMG developed its model of an organization that links the marketplace and vision with five elements:

FIGURE 5.8   KPMG organization system model

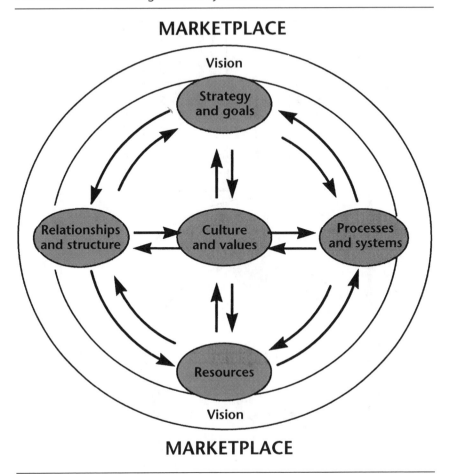

- Strategy and goals.

- Processes and systems.

- Resources.

- Relationships and structure.

- Culture and values.

The model can be represented as a globe (see Figure 5.8).

This globe model can be further analysed in order to look at the generic component parts of each element (Figure 5.9). It is important to remember that:

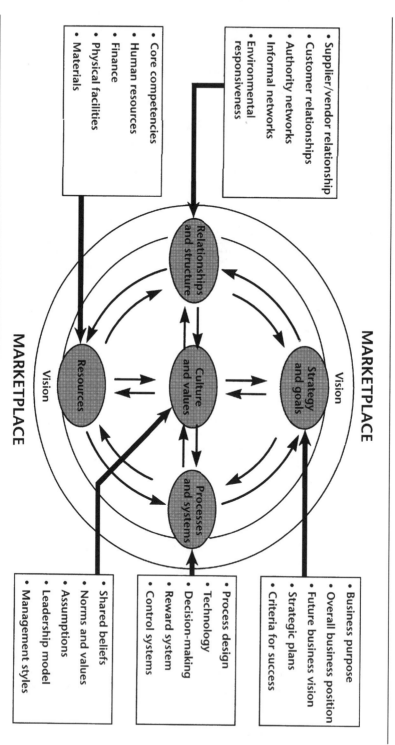

FIGURE 5.9 Globe model

■ some of the component parts may appear, to a greater or lesser extent, in more than one element. The model shows where they might expect to be predominantly placed;

■ the model represents a dynamic in which the elements and component parts interact.

Ideally, these elements combine to create an organization that is aligned to achieve its vision which, in turn, is appropriate to the marketplace (external environment). If this is the case, the organization is probably operating successfully on its first curve; if not, then it is either in regression, on the downward point of its first curve, in migration with no view of the second curve, or at the start of creation but with no ongoing operation on its first curve.

The globe model can be used in part to describe the process of moving from the first to the second curve (see Figure 5.10):

■ *Step 1*   Looks at what the future operating environment may be.

■ *Step 2*   Is the process of describing/defining a vision for the organization in that future operating environment or marketplace.

■ *Step 3*   Describes the component parts of the organization needed to achieve the vision; this is done using the globe model.

■ *Step 4*   Describes, in terms of the globe model, the components of the organization in its current state.

■ *Step 5*   Analyses the differences between the current and future components of the organization. In so doing, a series of projects will be identified as being required to be undertaken to move the organization from its current to its future state.

This series of steps is primarily focused on determining the projects needed to migrate an organization from a position on its first curve to the beginnings of a second curve position. Step 2 is essentially a creative activity. If step 4 is taken without the comparison with step 3, there is a risk that the existing organization will wither faster than the new one is created. If step 4 is taken in isolation, the best that can be achieved is elongation and the worst, regression.

Finally, in terms of the globe model, the systemic interaction between the component parts needs to be considered (Figure 5.11). Culture and values are, to a large extent, determined by strategy and

FIGURE 5.10   Moving from first to second curve

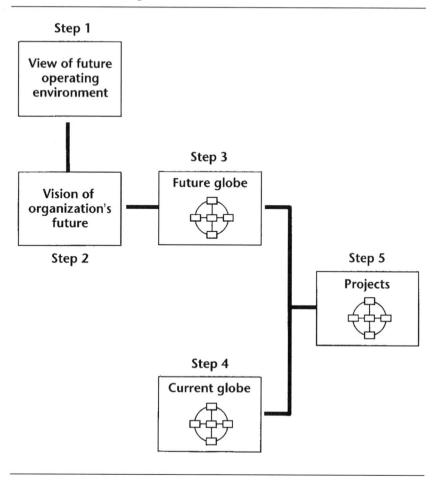

goals/relationships and structure/resources/processes and systems. The manner in which an organization is structured, the resources at its disposal, and the processes and systems that are used have a major influence on 'the way we do things around here' – its culture and values. This element, in turn, can constrain its strategy and goals, and consequently, the organization's vision.

In creating a new vision, there is that need for a new strategy and goals, and a new culture and values. The difficulty is that the current culture and values may be so strong and embedded that they destroy or severely inhibit the ability to achieve a new vision. In this case, a frontal assault may be required to change the current culture and values.

FIGURE 5.11   Interaction between the component parts

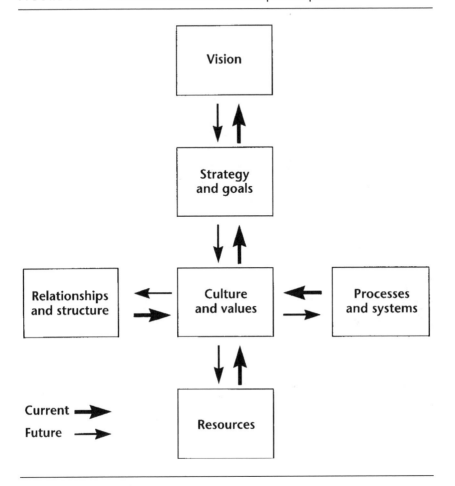

The final step

Step 5, as described earlier, moves into Tichy and Sharman's (1996) re-architecturing stage. By comparing the components of the existing organization with those of the future, it becomes possible to identify the changes that will require to be made. These changes are likely to necessitate various projects being instigated. These projects can, of course, be identified with the components of the organizational model; this is shown, in terms of typical projects, in Figure 5.12.

Whilst this approach may appear somewhat theoretical, it is one that has been used in practice. This representation gives a much clearer

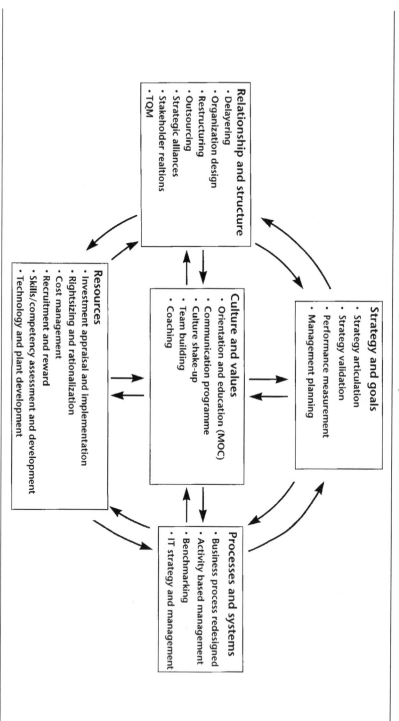

FIGURE 5.12 Examples of projects in the KPMG organizational systems model

Strategy and goals
· Strategy articulation
· Strategy validation
· Performance measurement
· Management planning

Relationship and structure
· Delayering
· Organization design
· Restructuring
· Outsourcing
· Strategic alliances
· Stakeholder realtions
· TQM

Culture and values
· Orientation and education (MOC)
· Communication programme
· Culture shake-up
· Team building
· Coaching

Resources
· Investment appraisal and implementation
· Rightsizing and rationalization
· Cost management
· Recruitment and reward
· Skills/competency assessment and development
· Technology and plant development

Processes and systems
· Business process redesigned
· Activity based management
· Benchmarking
· IT strategy and management

picture of what is trying to be achieved, coupled with a demonstration that there is cohesion between the projects. An additional benefit is that it shows if insufficient attention is being paid to any of the components of the globe model.

Once projects have been defined, implementation can be planned, project interfaces identified, resources defined, and time-scale reviewed.

In summary

This chapter has drawn upon various academic sources in order to describe a visioning process. The process has also been shown to work in practice through the cases highlighted. A few key messages emerge:

- Visioning is part of an overall process, and not a one-off event.

- For a vision to be realized, commitment must be gained; the process is a key ingredient in gaining that commitment.

- Any organization/business change creates turbulence and uncertainty. The use of a proven process reduces that uncertainty.

- The visioning process can be more important than the vision statement itself.

References

Blanchard, K. and Waghorn, T. (1997), *Mission Possible*, McGraw-Hill, New York.

The Conference Board (1994), *Change Management: An Overview of Current Initiatives*, Research Report 1068 by Kathyrn Troy, The Conference Board, New York.

Economist Intelligence Unit (in collaboration with Gemini Consulting) (1994) *Transforming the Global Corporation: How the World's Leading Companies Create and Manage Change*, EIU, London.

Page, T. (1996), *Diary of a Change Agent*, Gower, Aldershot.

Patel, K. (1996), *Who Knows Wins*, Jordans, Bristol.

Royal Society of Arts Inquiry (1995), *Tomorrow's Company*.

Tichy, T. and Sharman, S. (1993), *Control Your Destiny or Someone Else Will*, Doubleday, New York.

■ CHAPTER SIX ■

Leadership and the NHS: working together towards best practice

Andrew P. Kakabadse and Andrew Myers

A recent NAHAT update (NAHAT 1996) outlines guidelines as to best practice for NHS boards, covering NHS Trusts, health authorities and health boards, namely the gamut of the previous provider/purchaser institutions. The update highlights best practice in terms of roles and accountabilities, attributes of effective boards, clarity as to the roles of boards, the contribution of management and that of board members, ways of enhancing relationships with key stakeholders and the inhibitors to effectively performing boards (the inhibitors fundamentally being organizational, time related, lack of clarity of roles and poor use of meetings). Although attention is given in the document to the induction and development of the skills required for the effective directorship of NHS organizations, no meaningful attention in this and most other works is given to examining the nature of leadership required for the enhancement of health service organizations. Most works helpfully emphasize role and organizational clarity in areas such as clinical management (Harwood and Boufford, 1993), general management (BAMM, 1995) and the involvement of clinical staff in management (Scott 1996).

However, other than in health, the requirements for the effective leadership of service organizations and other government agencies have been given attention. Goffee (1996) emphasizes the importance of identifying and prioritizing key managerial and leadership competencies in order for firms of professionals (stockbrokers, insurance brokers, investment bankers) to continue to survive and prosper in rapidly changing, divisive markets. Dixon (1996) equally highlights that for federal/central government civil servants to continue to provide desired levels of service, the development of individuals and not their roles, requires greatest attention. In effect, the wisdom emerging from professional and government agencies is that the leadership issue is a vital consideration, followed only secondly by structural and demographic concerns. The emerging predominant views in NHS organizations run contrary to other walks of organizational life, with the word leadership spoken in the corridors and coffee bars, but far less in the official bulletins promoting best practice and pathways forward for NHS organizations.

Bearing this lacuna in mind, this chapter explores the impact of leadership on NHS Trusts through a study which examines organization culture, job satisfaction, communication practices and perceptions of patient care which are linked to the manner in which leadership is promoted and actioned, thereby making the point that leadership practice has a profound impact on the development of NHS Trusts. The survey results highlight the nature of strategic leadership in the NHS, emphasizing the contrasting philosophies of leadership that pervade NHS Trusts. Further, the performance of individuals in particular leadership roles is analysed, with the view emerging that clinical directors are perceived as needing greatest attention in terms of training and development. Following the analysis of survey findings, pathways to attaining leadership best practice are identified and discussed.

Overview of leadership

Leadership is one of those few topics of management and organization behaviour that has a history far greater than the subject matter heading within which it is housed. The writings of Confucius, Aristotle and Plato emphasize the transformational interpretation of leadership, highlighting the visionary or superhero nature of the great man or woman. From the ancient philosophers, to more modern great philosophers such as Hobbes and Nietzsche, to current scholars, transformational leadership has dominated thinking. Further through postulation and/or enquiry, the search has been on to identify those elements that lead to superhuman drive and extraordinary impact, in the hope that others can replicate or be trained in such attributes. Historically, it is assumed that transformational leaders make the big strides and break out of existing moulds to go on to new worlds.

With the onset of large, structured work organizations needing to be responsive to market and/or community/political influence, leadership has equally been viewed from jointly, the perspective of action and making major strides forward, and the point of view that it, leadership, is strongly influenced by context. The contextual interpretation assumes that different circumstances in different organizations substantially influence the manner in which the leadership contribution is applied. Effectiveness of leadership would be determined by being able to recognize appropriateness of action and influence relevant to the dynamics of different contexts. Hence, in any analysis of leadership, when taking into account context, attention needs to be paid to understanding followership and culture of organization. Unless the requirements of colleagues and subordinates are appreciated, any leadership effort could be ineffective or even counterproductive, as the followers would not have given their tacit 'permission' for their leaders to act. Add the modern-day phenomena of speed of information, the rise of multinational and multicultural organizations, the fact that revenue streams and key client accounts can be enhanced or damaged by subordinates irrespective of the behaviour of the boss, then contextual considerations can be of paramount importance.

The theoretical framework adopted in this study attempts to capture the reality of demands made on senior managers and their response and contribution to improvements and changes of their circumstances. In effect, context and person are intertwined. Further, from a developmental perspective, exploration is undertaken as to whether managers can be grown to be effective leaders, sensitively balancing their wishes with the dynamics of the demands they face in their situation. Taken into account are the individual manager's attitudes, values and behaviour, organizational circumstances and the feelings and views of others within the organization. Such analysis provides insights as to current leadership practice and its impact on present-day dynamics. In turn, such enquiry highlights pathways for improvement that would be contextually relevant and useful.

The underlying assumption of this chapter is that leadership in today's work organizations requires an examination of attributes of individuals, namely behaviour, attitudes or deeper personality dimensions, and job/role-related dynamics or pressures which would take account of context. As already highlighted in Chapter 3, the concept of discretion provides the conceptual bridge between individual behaviours and role demands (Jaques, 1951). The discretionary element of role refers to the choices the role incumbent needs to make in order to provide shape and identity to their role and that part of the organization for which the person is accountable. The contrast to the discretionary element of role is the prescriptive side, namely, the structured part, which is predetermined and which focuses and restricts the individual's behaviour. In effect, the prescriptive part of a manager's job is that part over which the manager has little choice, other than to undertake the duties that are required of him/her.

Hence, a senior manager's job is unevenly split between the leadership elements (discretionary) and the managerial elements (prescriptive), with the discretionary component predominating.[1] Such distinction is particularly pertinent, as providing leadership in circumstances of substantially conflicting priorities is likely to make considerable demands on senior managers. The individual senior manager will need to make choices between unclear alternatives and is equally likely to need to devote considerable attention to nurturing key interfaces which influence internal and external stakeholders, in order to ascertain their commitment to a meaningful way forward.

Hence, senior managers' beliefs concerning what to lead, how to lead and when to lead, highlights one key question, to what extent do senior managers share their views and concerns with each other?

On this basis, fundamental to leading an organization effectively is to ensure a high quality dialogue amongst the members of the 'senior executive'.[2] The preliminary results of interviews and case study analyses of private and public sector organizations conducted at Cranfield School of Management, examining the behaviours and capacities of senior managers, indicates that where the quality of dialogue is high and the relationships amongst senior managers is positive, the issues and concerns facing the organization are likely to be more openly addressed. Where, however, relationships are tense and the quality of dialogue restricted, certain issues and problems tend not to be raised, because to do so would generate unacceptable levels of discomfort amongst certain or all of the members of the senior executive. In effect, such discomfort would be experienced as unwelcome and too overwhelming to face up to the problems confronting the organization. Ironically, the original case studies which underpinned the learning eventually emerging formally as survey instruments, in both the private and public sector highlight that unless the top team is working reasonably effectively, issues which need to be addressed are not.[3] Namely, the senior management of the organization knowingly allows the organization to deteriorate because they feel too uncomfortable jointly to discuss and attend to key issues and challenges facing the enterprise.

The survey

The survey conducted amongst NHS Trusts is an adapted version of the results of considerable research carried out by the Cranfield International Management Development Centre team over a number of years in the private and public sectors. In fact, over 5,500 general managers (GMs), directors, managing directors (MDs), chief executive officers (CEOs) and chairmen spanning 12 countries, and 750 senior staff from the Australian Public Service (APS) spanning senior executive service (SES) bands 1, 2 and 3 and senior officers (SOs) levels A, B, C and their equivalents initially provide a benchmark database against which the behaviour, attitudes and perspectives of 550 chairmen, CEOs, directors (executive and non-executive) of NHS Trusts, are examined. Additionally, a number of interviews have been conducted in order to explore the key issues to have emerged from questionnaire analysis.

The Cranfield/NHS survey covers four key areas:

- Demographics, namely size of organization, organization structure, gender, age, background of respondent, years spent on the job, years spent in organization, years spent in the service, qualifications, and the number of senior management appointments held by each respondent.

- Culture of organization, identifying the shared views and attitudes medical and non-medical senior managers hold towards their organization, their role and work, decision-making capabilities, communication practices, ways of coping with change and bureaucracy, keeping abreast of new developments, the personal discipline to discharge effectively one's duties, and the degree of support and constraint they experience in the discharge of their duties. Equally explored are values, namely the more deeply held feelings of the respondents concerning professionalism; quality of relationships, internally in the NHS and externally with clients, communities and other agencies; the orientation towards provision of service to clients, communities and other agencies and quality of patient care.

- Leadership, namely particular attributes of leadership displayed in the NHS and whether such attributes are universal throughout the service or particular, according to whether specific factors influence leadership orientation and behaviour.

- Organizational performance indicators, such as the effectiveness of service delivery, the opportunity for development for people, the effectiveness of the top team, the clarity of strategic direction, and the quality of internal interfacing and the effectiveness of utilization of change management techniques in the organization.

Factor, cluster and regression analyses are used to identify discernible elements of culture, shared values and leadership orientation and correlation analyses are utilized to explore the relationship between elements of these characteristics.

Strategic leadership

Two crucial themes repeatedly emerged from the original semi-structured interviews conducted with senior NHS managers, senior civil servants (APS) and private sector executives, namely, do the senior management of the organization share the same view(s) as to the future shape and direction of the enterprise and, second, have the senior management nurtured an internal culture of openness of dialogue?

The reason that these two perspectives are considered important is that, in the exercise of discretion, it is likely that the members of the senior management of the organization can meaningfully form substantially different views as to the future shape and direction of their enterprise. Whether they would equally have formed any sense of collegiality which would serve as the platform for in-depth examinination of those views which would then be used as the vehicle for the consistent application of an emerging shared view, is another matter. It is considered that if sharing of views or openness of dialogue are non-existent, chaos is likely to reign. Hence, two issues are explored, the degree to which there exists shared/ unshared vision at senior levels and second the quality dialogue amongst the members of the senior executive.

Shared/unshared vision

One key question is asked, namely 'Do the members of the senior executive (president/chairmen/CEOs/MDs/EDs/directors/GMs/SESs/SOs)[4] hold different views as to the future direction of the organization?' (Table 6.1)

Fifty-six per cent of the SESs and SOs (Australian Public Service) who completed this questionnaire consider that members of the senior management group hold fundamentally different views as to the shape and nature of the APS in general, and of their department and the future

TABLE 6.1 Fundamentally different views concerning the direction of the organization (%)

	Japan	UK	France	Ireland	Germany	Sweden
Yes	23	30	39	48	32	20

	Spain	Austria	Finland	USA	China	Hong Kong	APS	NHS Top team	Board
Yes	40	31	25	39	33	42	56	20	21

Adapted from Kakabadse et al. (1996).

pathways that should be pursued, in particular. Of the NHS Trusts, distinction is drawn between the executive committee (top team) and the main board, as constitutionally, only two executive committee directors sit on the main board, accompanied by three non-executives including the Trust chairmen. Twenty per cent of the top team members and 21 per cent of the board members highlight that fundamentally different views on vision future direction and shape of organization are held by members of their respective groups.

Of the private sector respondents, the Irish (48 per cent of respondents), Hong Kong Chinese and expatriate (42 per cent of respondents), Spanish (40 per cent) and French top managers (39 per cent) compare with such diversity of view as expressed by the Australian civil servants. The Swedish (20 per cent) and Japanese (23 per cent) respondents highlight the least differences of view concerning strategic direction at senior management level, comparable to NHS Trust top teams and boards.

Quality of dialogue

Dialogue is explored as the capability to address and, or resolve issues of sensitivity at senior management levels. One question was asked, namely 'Are there issues or sensitivities that merit attention but do not receive attention at senior management level?' (Table 6.2).

The Chinese (80 per cent) and Japanese (77 per cent) private sector respondents highlight the greatest number of concerns indicating that important but unattended issues predominate at senior management

TABLE 6.2 Sensitivity of dialogue (%)

	Japan	UK	France	Ireland	Germany	Sweden
Yes	77	47	36	68	61	50

	Spain	Austria	Finland	USA	China	Hong Kong	APS	NHS Top team	NHS Board
Yes	63	67	49	62	80	58	66	70	66

Adapted from Kakabadse et al. (1996)

levels. The senior managers of the APS (66 per cent) follow the Irish (68 per cent) and Austrian (67 per cent) private sector senior managers. The British, Finnish and French senior managers identify the least number of sensitive issues impacting on the quality of dialogue at senior levels.

The NHS top team respondents also report inhibited dialogue at senior levels (70 per cent). The executive committee of NHS Trust organizations is viewed as a slightly more restrictive forum for dialogue than the main boards of Trusts (66 per cent).

Basically, other than for the French respondents, one-half to two-thirds of respondents report outstanding issues remaining unaddressed at senior levels but which need to be addressed in order to progress the organization. The NHS and APS respondents (public sector) are no different from the majority of the other private sector top managers, emphasizing the strain senior managers are likely to experience in responding positively to difficult challenges. In essence, strain, tension and inhibition at senior levels in attempting to address sensitive and difficult issues, is viewed by the respondents as normality.

Philosophies of leadership

Benchmarked against the responses of private sector senior managers and senior civil servants from the APS, NHS top teams and boards emerge favourably in terms of displaying the least degree of divergence of vision. However, the NHS sample seem to be in keeping with responses of the senior managers from the private sector and government samples, in that attaining a high quality of dialogue is no easily won process. Therefore what are the dynamics of leadership to have induced such responses?

TABLE 6.3   Demographic distribution with three leader groups

Function	Directorate (%)	Medical Manager (%)	Stakeholder (%)
Chief Executive	15	4	
Medical Director		20	
Finance Director	24		
HR Director	9		
Clinical Director			14
Non-Executives			9
Chairmen			5
Percentage Total	48	24	28

Percentage (%) refers to percentage of total sample

An analysis of leadership within NHS Trusts interestingly highlights three fundamentally different philosophies and practices of leadership. These differences of leadership are varyingly driven by six demographic variables, namely gender, age, length of time in the establishment (i.e. hospital, DHA, etc. prior to becoming a Trust/purchaser organization), length of time as a senior manager of the Trust, being a member of Trust top team, and job function. The contention is that the influence of demographics on individuals is likely to engender differences of view over issues as, how should diversity and tension with NHS Trusts be managed, how to change ways of working, how should the organization be structured and what is the shape, content and direction of the future strategies and mission to be pursued? Of the six demographic factors, the most significant differentiator is that of job function (Table 6.3), whereby CEOs, finance and HR directors fall into one group (the directorate), medical directors and a small number of CEOs medically qualified fall into a second grouping (medical managers) and clinical directors, chairmen, non-executive directors fall into the third grouping (stakeholders).

The reason these terms are used is that the directorate group is composed mainly of executive directors, the medical manager is mainly composed of clinicians (including medically qualified CEOs) and the stakeholders because they have a stakeholding in the management of the Trust, but do not hold executive responsibility. The perspectives, philosophies, attitudes and ways of working of the three different groupings are outlined below.

Directorate

Personal style

- Team oriented
- Job satisfied
- Effective communicators
- Disciplined
- Committed

Views of Trust structure/strategy

- Strategy of trust needs attention
- Mission of Trust not clear
- Leadership requires development
- Top management are dependable

Views on health care management

- Clinicians viewed as positive/supportive
- Patient care requires more attention

Those senior managers who adopt the style and philosophy of a member of the directorate, are team oriented and attempt to evolve positive relationships with their colleagues. Such a positive attitude is carried over to their job in that they declare themselves as well satisfied with their role, enjoying the challenge of contributing to the enhancement of the Trust. They feel themselves to be positively stretched and similarly attempt to challenge and develop their colleagues and subordinates. These senior managers see themselves as effective communicators, attempting to promote clearly the objectives of the Trust. Their capability to establish positive relationships is shown by the fact that they feel themselves to be regularly informed about how new developments and initiatives are progressing. Directorate senior managers see themselves as well disciplined, attempting to introduce an equally structured and disciplined way of managing the Trust. Their level of commitment to the Trust, its objectives, the enhancement of patient care and the development of its staff and management, is high.

The directorate equally display a positive attitude towards clinicians. They consider that clinicians relate well to each other, as well as to the directors on the Trust management team. Equally, it is felt that management's relationship with the Trust's clinicians is positive. However, directorate executives feel that patient care requires attention. It is recognized that the budgeting practices and other internal procedures in the Trust adversely affect the quality of service provided, hence undermining patient care.

The greatest degree of attention is considered as needing to be given to the development of the leadership and strategy of the Trust. It is considered that further work in terms of clarifying the Trust's mission and strategy needs to be undertaken. The objectives and strategy of the Trust are considered as unclear and require further clarification, resulting in the Trust top team not providing sufficiently clear direction. On this basis, the quality of decision making at senior levels within the Trust is considered as also requiring improvement. It is considered that improvements in the areas of mission and strategy will only take place if investment in the development of the leadership of the Trust occurs. Further, senior management view themselves as needing to become better listeners, thereby minimizing the accusation that they are too distant from what happens on a daily basis. Attention equally needs to be given to enhancing understanding as to what are the areas of weakness in terms of patient care, highlighting the need to be more in touch with what is happening within the Trust. The view that emerges is that through improving the performance of individual top managers and equally the Trust team, progress in the areas of mission strategy and service provision (patient care) will equally occur. By investing in senior level training, both the Board and Trust management team are likely to have a more powerful impact on the management and growth of the Trust.

Medical managers

Style

- Open management style
- Job satisfied
- Supportive of colleagues
- Feedback oriented

- Disciplined

- Committed

Views of Trust structure/strategy

- Trust strategy needs attention

- Trust mission not clear

- Out of touch leadership

- Leadership requires development

- Top management are dependable

Views on health care management

- Clinicians viewed as positive/supportive

- Patient care requires attention

Comparable aspects of leadership style are identified for those top managers of Trusts that are identified as falling into the medical manager category, as those in the directorate category. The medical managers value displaying an open management style whereby colleagues and staff feel they can speak freely. Further, medical managers consider themselves as easy to talk to and as people consider they encourage their subordinates to discuss with them their work problems.

Through facilitating more open channels of communication, medical managers indicate they expect to be kept informed of progress on agreed initiatives. Equally, medical managers indicate that they are satisfied with their job and find the challenge of their role in the Trust stimulating. Medical managers equally declare themselves as supportive of colleagues, in particular, clinical directors. Medical managers consider that, overall, the relationship between the Trust and clinicians is positive and that clinical directors relate well to each other. Further, they consider that a positive team spirit exists in the Trust and that they are instrumental in promoting positive relationships between different groups and departments in the Trust.

Medical managers consider themselves as disciplined, paying attention to details, following established work procedures and displaying considerable discipline at following through on commitments made. In essence, attention to detail and completion of projects is an essential aspect of their working philosophy. Such behaviour is so highly valued that medical managers indicate they respect staff and management who display equal competence at being disciplined, tidy and paying attention to detail. All in all, medical managers highlight their commitment to the Trust, what it stands for, its people and their development.

However, one key area of health care management they consider requires attention is patient care. Medical managers consider that excessive time is spent on management-related issues at the expense of health care. As a consequence, clinician attention is not appropriately directed to patient care but diverted by committee and administrative activities and also by spending too much time attending to internal political relationship issues.

In terms of issues of Trust strategy and structure that require attention, similar to the directorate group, the medical managers feel that the mission of the Trust and the strategies being pursued, require attention. They consider that the Trust management team are not providing sufficiently clear strategic direction. Hence, certain of the assumptions held by senior managers driving foward change are misguided. An additional reason identified for poor strategic direction is that of poor quality of decision making by the Trust top team. The top is viewed as too distant from the operational problems and frustrations with which people at lower levels in the Trust have to contend. Equally, the senior managers in the Trust are viewed as poor listeners. As a consequence, the needs of patients and staff are not well understood by the senior managers of the Trust. Hence, the leadership of the Trust, are recognized as needing to improve the impact they have on their organization. Interestingly, the views of the directorate and medical managers coincide on issues of strategy and leadership. Medical managers consider that if Trust leadership improves, so too would the clarity of the mission and objectives of the Trust, as would the resolve to pursue more ambitious strategies for the organization. Further, attention to patient care and to certain frustrating operational problems within the Trust would improve.

Stakeholders

Style

- Independent
- Job satisfied
- Pressured

- Briefings-oriented (follow through)

- Disciplined

- Details-oriented

- Committed

Views of Trust structure/strategy

- Internal environment requires attention

- Leadership requires development

- Strategy should be clearer

- Top management are dependable

Views of health care management

- Positive team work

- Patient care requires attention

- Top management should be totally supported

The third group, primarily composed of chairmen, clinical directors and non-executive directors, indicate that they value their independence. They state that they resent being told what to do and find the systems and controls in the organization a hindrance. They feel there are too many constraints placed on them in their role. Equally, this group of varied stakeholders feel themselves to be considerably pressured at work, an experience which not only undermines their performance at work, but equally impacts negatively on their home life. They report that they find it difficult to 'switch off' at the end of their day's work. In fact, the pressures of work have an adverse effect on life outside the Trust. A number commented that the pressures of the job are at times too much to handle. It should be noted that these comments are more driven by the clinical directors than chairmen or non-executive directors.

However, as far as their job is concerned, high levels of job satisfaction are reported. Chairmen, clinical directors and non-executive directors report that they enjoy the challenge of their role in the Trust and are motivated by their work. They recognize that in order to cope effectively with their demanding work circumstances they need to feel positive and display a positive attitude. They consider that a well-run disciplined organization is fundamental to success. In order to enhance efficiency, they feel that is also important to follow established work procedures. As such, they consider themselves as disciplined at follow-through, ensuring that projects and activities are effectively completed, but are concerned that the members of the Trust team do not display sufficient discipline in their management of the Trust.

In addition to being disciplined, this group of senior clinicians and non-executive directors insist on being regularly briefed concerning new developments. They state they expect to be kept informed of progress on agreed initiatives and consider that they are regularly updated as to how new developments and initiatives are progressing. With such attention to briefing and discipline, it is not surprising that the stakeholders report they pay particular attention to detail. They indicate that they respect people who stick to the rules and encourage the traditions of the Trust to be respected. Overall, these clinical directors, chairmen and non-executive directors highlight their commitment to the Trust. They indicate that they feel themselves to be part of their Trust and accept the responsibility for projecting a positive image for their organization. They consider that the staff and management of their Trust are dedicated to its success. One reason for such a positive perspective is that the quality of staff at the Trust is considered as excellent. A further reason is that staff development is taken seriously, hence promoting improved performance and a more positive attitude by the staff to their employing organization.

The views of the stakeholders concerning health care management issues is that teamwork, in particular, is a positive experience. Clinicians are seen to work well with senior management and in turn, management's relationship with clinicians in the Trust is positive. Equally, clinical directors are seen as relating well to the directors on the Trust management team.

However, and similar to the other two clusters, patient care is viewed as requiring further attention. The stakeholders consider that attention is diverted away from patient care in the way the Trust is managed. In addition, they consider that the politics within the Trust have an adverse affect on the quality of service provided. The reasons given for diminished levels of quality of service are threefold. Clinical directors, chairmen and non-executive directors indicate that more time is spent on management-related issues at the expense of patient care. Second, the current budgeting practices adversely affect patient care. Third, the majority of standards laid down by the government are not being fully met.

As far as the views of the stakeholders concerning the structure and strategy of Trusts are concerned, two dominant themes emerge, namely, that the internal environment of Trusts is seen as inhibiting and that the leadership of Trusts requires further development. Clinical directors, chairmen and non-executive directors consider that the long-term objectives of the Trust are not clear and that the management are losing sight of these objectives. Hence, the Trust management team are seen as not providing clear strategic direction and that the Trust has been misguided about many of the changes it has carried out. The reasons given for the poor strategic development of the Trust is that there still exists a considerable level of political in-fighting in the Trust. As a result, decisions are made behind closed doors and are seen to change from one day to the next. A considerable number of respondents highlight that they are motivated to enhance the workings and status of their Trust, but others in the Trust are not and need nurture and attention in order to improve their motivation. For these reasons, the culture of Trusts and their leadership are viewed as problematic.

An additional reason as to why the internal environment is not sufficiently stimulating, is that the current leadership is seen as 'out of touch'. Overall, those at the top are viewed as too distant from what happens on a daily basis. Both the Trust management team and the board are seen to have little impact on the daily running of the Trust. One particular area seen as problematic, is that the needs of the patients are not well understood by those in senior management positions. Another issue requiring attention is that senior management are considered as poor listeners. Overall, the senior management of Trusts are viewed by the stakeholders as not performing sufficiently effectively and to be in need of development. However, the senior management are equally viewed as highly motivated, trustworthy people with every intention of promoting the Trust. For this reason, the stakeholders declare their support for senior management.

Scrutinising leadership

The three different approaches to leadership share similar philosophy and views, broadly similar perspectives on style of leadership, level of job satisfaction, personal discipline applied to the task of managing and overall commitment to their Trust. Similarity of opinion also emerges on issues such as the need to improve patient care, and on the fact that the leaders of Trusts require further training and development.

Bearing in mind that cohesion exists on most aspects of Trust leadership at senior management levels, further enquiry is pursued as to which areas of leadership are recognized as needing particular attention.

Two areas are explored, effectiveness of leadership performance and cohesion of opinion on key strategic issues.

Leadership performance

A number of key roles are rated by the respondents in terms of effectiveness of leadership performance (Table 6.4). In addition, the roles of medical director and clinical director are also rated on the dimensions of perceived contribution to the management and development of the Trust (Table 6.5) and quality and appropriateness of executive behaviour (Table 6.6). It should be noted that no particular aspects of performance, contribution and executive behaviour are identified, as the intent is to gather impressions, but impressions that can strongly drive opinion concerning the effectiveness of the incumbents in their identified roles. In so doing, the examination is to ascertain whether the occupants of the roles scrutinized are respected.

Hence, in attending to issues of policy and strategy, it is possible to determine whether the leaders pronouncing on matters of importance to the Trust and its future survival, will be believed and respected by the staff and management of the Trust and influential external stake-holders.

Table 6.4 identifies that Trust chairmen are rated highly in terms of effectiveness of performance by the three leader groups, with the stakeholders indicating a lower but still positive rating (66 per cent). Similarly and even more highly rated across the three leader clusters are

TABLE 6.4   Views on effectiveness of leader performance

Positive	Directorate (%)	Medical managers (%)	Stakeholders (%)
Trust chairmen	77	74	66
Chief executive officer	81	87	85
Finance director	86	80	63
Human resources (HR) director	61	53	48
Medical director	60	73	61
Director nursing	60	65	54
Director quality	53	52	56
Director operations	70	73	72
Non-executive directors	66	66	62

TABLE 6.5 Views on quality of contribution

Positive	Directorate (%)	Medical manager (%)	Stakeholders (%)
Medical director	71	79	62
Clinical director	49	70	55

TABLE 6.6 Views on effectiveness of executive behaviour

Positive	Directorate (%)	Medical manager (%)	Stakeholders (%)
Medical director	55	73	64
Clinical director	49	52	48

Trust CEOs. Finance directors equally receive a high rating, especially by the directorate (86 per cent) and medical managers (80 per cent) and slightly lower by the stakeholders (83 per cent). A somewhat different picture emerges for HR directors, whereby the directorate rate them as 61 per cent effective, the medical managers as 53 per cent effective and the stakeholders as 48 per cent effective. In contrast, medical directors are viewed as effective leaders, with the medical managers rating themselves more highly than the other two groups. Similarly, directors of nursing are viewed positively, but less so by the stakeholder group, who provide a 54 per cent score. Rated lowest of all are quality directors, with the scores from all three groups being in the lower to mid 50 per cents. Directors of operations are scored highly, with all three groups placing them above 70 per cent. Finally, non-executive directors are viewed positively, and only rated slightly lower by the stakeholder group, in comparison to the other two groups, at 62 per cent.

Overall, the respondents rate highly the leader performance of the key directors of Trusts, with the exception of the HR and quality directors. Directors of quality are comparatively downrated. One reason for the mixed views concerning quality directors, is that the role may not be clearly understood by its role incumbents and by others. Private sector experience highlights that a director of quality may need to behave almost as an internal consultant towards his/her colleagues and staff and management in the organization, facilitating new approaches and new ways of thinking in order to address and improve quality issues within the company. As circumstances change, even in the same organization, the very same quality director may need to behave more in an executive manner, championing and pushing through reforms, at times under opposition. The juxtaposition between facilitator/friend, as opposed to director/reformer, is no easy balance to maintain. Ironically, similar contrasting role experiences have been identified for HR/personnel directors and managers, with them sometimes needing to behave as administrative line managers and at other times, as internal consultants.

The contribution of medical directors to the growth and development of the Trust is rated as highly positive by the directorate and medical managers, but less so by the stakeholders (62 per cent) – (Table 6.5). In contrast and on the same criteria, clinical directors are only rated as highly positive in terms of contribution to the development of the Trust by medical managers (70 per cent). The stakeholder and directorate groups view clinical directors ambivalently, offering ratings of 55 per cent and 49 per cent positive.

In terms of effectiveness of executive behaviour of medical directors (Table 6.6), medical managers and stakeholders rate them more positively (73 per cent and 64 per cent respectively) whereas the directorate respondents rate them less positively, at 55 per cent. Similarly, on effectiveness of executives behaviour, clinical directors are rated far lower by all three groups, with the directorate and stakeholder respondents providing scores of 39 per cent and 48 per cent respectively.

Strategic issues: cohesion of opinion

Table 6.7 highlights six issues of importance, as identified by the senior management of Trusts, concerning strategy and managerial practice.

All three groups of respondents support the formation of Trusts, with the directorate grouping providing the most positive score (96 per cent in favour). However, all three groupings do not feel that the purchaser/provider relationship has effectively promoted an internal market, rating this item lowest of the six, with scores of 35 per cent, 25 per cent and 31 per cent respectively.

In terms of managerial practice, the three groups indicate that they hold a reasonably strong shared view as to what is required to market their Trust's services. Equally, reasonably strong and supportive views are expressed as to whether senior managers are fully accountable and responsible for the management of budgets, with the directorate group expressing considerable satisfaction (95 per cent) but the medical managers being less enthusiastic (66 per cent).

Similarly, strong and supportive views are expressed concerning the level of spend within budgets. Again, the directorate indicate the highest degree of satisfaction (90 per cent), but with the stakeholder group

TABLE 6.7   Strategic/managerial Issues

Positive	Directorate (%)	Medical (%) managers	Stakeholders (%)
Support formation of Trusts	96	81	82
Purchaser/provider promoted internal market	35	25	31
Shared view of marketing trust's services	70	76	69
Manage budgets	95	66	76
Satisfied with level of spend	90	81	63
Difference between financial accounting/managerial accounting	94	40	53

expressing less enthusiasm, but nevertheless, still positive (63 per cent). The greatest degree of discrepancy occurs in the responses to the question, 'Do you know the difference between financial accounting and managerial accounting?' The directorate grouping strongly indicate they recognize the difference between the two accounting procedures (94 per cent), but the medical managers indicate they do not fully appreciate such distinction, as only 40 per cent indicate they appreciate the difference.

The degree of cohesion of view across the three leader groups is considerable. The only areas of divergence are in the freedom and capability to manage budgets and differences of understanding concerning accounting, both highlighting a training concern.

NHS leadership in action

What is the impact of leadership on NHS Trusts? What difference does leadership make on the organization, its people and the services offered externally? The following sections highlight the evidence that has emerged concerning the impact of leadership on staff and management, the running of the organization and the development and promotion of strategy.

Four key areas of impact are identified: quality of senior level relations, quality of decision making, issues that are considered as sensitive to address and the opportunity gains that could emerge if improvements in leadership practice were to be pursued.

- *Senior level relations* This area includes assessing the quality of relationships between the members of top management team, as well as the quality of relationship directors and other senior officers have with the CEO and chairman. Equally included in this category is the level of shared understanding and cabinet responsibility held by senior management and the degree to which their influence in the organization has promoted a 'macho' management culture.

- *Quality of decision making* This area involves subdividing decision making into quality of debate, the clarity of thinking prior to making a decision and the quality of follow-through having made a decision. Included under this category are improved understanding of the Trust's structure, and understanding the nature and purpose of key senior roles in the Trust (i.e. chairman, CEO, medical and clinical directors). Further, senior management adopting a more responsive style and being able confidently to address conflicting demands, are considered as additional elements of quality of decision making.

- *Sensitive issues* This category covers people, structural, strategic and operational issues, such as morale of clinicians and nursing staff, internal relationships, issues of costs and control, private and elective work, allocation of beds, junior director hours, how to enhance relationships with GP fundholders, quality of service to patients and the community, differences over reorganization and the willingness of clinicians to market services in the community.

- *Opportunity gains* This category addresses such issues as improved external interfacing with different stakeholders; improved response to new initiatives; improved quality of service; fewer inaccurate commitments to patients, to GP fundholders, clinicians, or other interested parties; greater trust between colleagues and employees; improvements of communication within the Trust; a better under-standing of how the Trust operates; improved quality of decisions taken and implemented and fewer people leaving.

Directorate

Key elements of the leadership philosophy and practice of the directorate group are correlated against the four key areas of impact identified in Table 6.8.

Having job-satisfied directors of a Trust, who are committed, team-oriented and wish to communicate effectively and extend positive

TABLE 6.8 Impact of directorate

Leadership	Areas of impact			
	Senior level relations	Decision making	Sensitivities	Opportunity gains
Job satisfaction	**	**	_**	**
Team orientation	**	**	_**	**
Commitment	**	**	**	**
Quality interfacing (clinician)	*	**	_**	**
Patient care			_**	_**
Communication	**	**	_**	**
Discipline				
Strategic orientation	_**	_**	**	_**
Identify with trust	_**	_**	**	_**
Objectives				
Leadership style	_**	_**	**	_**

* = 05 level
** = 01 level
− negative correlation

relationships laterally, is seen to enhance relationships at senior level, improve the quality of decision making reducing the number of difficult-to-address sensitivities in the organization and enhancing the opportunities for patient care and service to the community.

Comparable results emerge concerning the quality of interfacing with clinicians. The quality of interfacing with clinicians is viewed as high and as such is seen to enhance the existing positive relationships senior managers already have with each other, thereby improving the quality of decision making, generating more opportunities that can be capitalized upon and more comfortably bringing to the surface those issues that undermine the development of the organization and that people find too sensitive to discuss and address. In contrast, the perceived poor quality level of patient care is viewed as a damaging influence and identified as a sensitive issue which people find difficult to address, which in turn undermines the willingness to pursue opportunities.

Further, issues such as clearly communicating objectives, effectively applying change management skills, improving quality of decision making, promoting greater clarity and consistency of decision implementation and

TABLE 6.9   Impact of medical managers

	Areas of impact			
Leadership	Senior level relations	Decision making	Sensitivities	Opportunity gains
Job satisfaction	*		_*	
Supportive relationships	**	**	_**	**
Patient care	_**	_**	**	_**
Commitment				
Feedback orientation				
Open management style				
Discipline				
Strategic orientation		_*	**	_*
Leadership behaviour		_*	*	
Aware leadership	_**	_**	**	_**

* = 05 level
** = 01 level
− negative correlation

a belief that the Trust has identified a clear direction, are seen as inadequately addressed.

The directorate respondents emphasize that their leadership style requires improvement. The three elements of strategic behaviour, leadership behaviour and identity with the Trust's objectives are seen to be damaging of senior level relationships, quality of decision making and undermining the will to pursue new ideas and opportunities. As these issues, which are viewed as sensitive and difficult to address, gain prominence, the fear is that their inability to be addressed slowly undermines the fabric of the organization.

Medical managers

Similar to the directorate group, the key elements of leadership orientation and practice for the medical managers are correlated against the four areas of impact (Table 6.9).

Being satisfied with one's job is seen only somewhat to improve the quality of relationships at senior level and only partly to reduce the sensitivities that inhibit dialogue and the drive to pursue new opportunities. However, sincerely evolving supportive relationships at senior levels is seen to impact positively on top team relationships and on the quality of decision making, and to generate opportunities that can be capitalized upon and minimize those difficult-to-address issues that undermine motivation and morale.

Perceived poor quality patient care is viewed as a damaging influence, undermining of senior level relationships, undermining of quality of decision making, reducing the willingness to pursue opportunities and increasing the number of difficult-to-address issues that can damage the development of the Trust.

Similar to the directorate group, the medical managers recognize that the way the leaders behave and discern between key issues has an impact on their Trust.

The strategic orientation of the top management of the Trust is seen to partly undermine the quality of decision making at senior levels and not motivate people to capitalize on new opportunities in order to gain advantage externally in the community. The seeming inability to adopt a more strategic view is seen as particularly damaging to the organization, as staff and management become more inhibited and do not raise, discuss or address known concerns.

Further, the behaviour of the leaders of the Trust is seen as needing improvement but not to the extent highlighted by the directorate group. Thereby, the impact of the behaviour of leaders of Trusts although viewed as undermining the quality of decision making and increasing the sensitivities that inhibit dialogue, is viewed as less problematic.

However, the awareness of the leaders of Trusts of important issues, is seen as a particular concern. Little or no listening, a lack of tolerance displayed towards other senior managers and a senior management that are seen as too distant from what happens on a daily basis, are viewed as damaging to the organization, its staff and the quality of service provided. Such a leadership is seen to strain relationships at senior levels, promote poor quality decision making, not to motivate people to wish to pursue further opportunities and to magnify those sensitivities that people find inhibiting and unwilling to address.

Interestingly, medical managers indicate that being committed, disciplined, having an open management style and being feedback-oriented are, as leadership capabilities, valuable in themselves, but have little impact on the continued effectiveness of the Trust. Generating supportive relationships between senior managers and between staff and management, having leaders who are aware of issues and concerns prevailing in the Trust and improving patient care, are considered as making a more powerful impact on the positive development of the Trust.

TABLE 6.10   Impact of stakeholders

Leadership	Areas of impact			
	Senior level relations	Decision making	Sensitivities	Opportunity gains
Independence	_**		_**	_*
Job satisfaction	**		_**	
Commitment	**		_**	
Strain	_**		**	_*
Clinician relations	**	*	_**	_**
Patient care	_**		**	_**
Follow through	*			
Open communications	**		_**	*
Attention to detail				
Internal environment	_**	_**	**	_**
Leader awareness	**		_**	

* = 05 level
** = 01 level
− negative correlation

Stakeholders

Similar to the directorate group, having senior managers who are satisfied with their job and who have evolved positive relationships with clinicians, is perceived to improve relationships at senior management levels and reduce the number and nature of the sensitivities that inhibit further dialogue (Table 6.10). It is also considered that positive relationships with clinicians are likely to improve the quality of decision making in the Trust and motivate people to be more willing to pursue new opportunities. Further, adopting an open style of communication and being committed to the Trust is seen considerably to improve relationships at senior level and to reduce those uncomfortable areas of debate.

In keeping with the results of the directorate and the medical manager groupings, patient care is viewed as a perturbing issue, undermining of senior managerial relationships, the will to pursue opportunities and increasing those issues considered as sensitive which distract people from actively pursuing their objectives.

However, underpinning the organization is the stakeholders' need for independence. Chairmen, non-executive directors and clinical directors who display a high need for independence, are recognized as disrupting relationships at senior levels in the Trust and promoting an internal environment of not wishing to address issues. Further, the internal environment of Trusts is viewed as unsupportive and the leadership is considered as out of touch. The influence of these two phenomena is recognized as further loosening relationships at senior level, reducing the quality of decision making and decision implementation, reducing the drive to pursue opportunities and nurturing an internal environment of suspicion and poor quality debate.

Experience of seniority

The message is that the leaders of health care organizations in the UK indicate that they share substantial cohesion of purpose and focus. Shared vision emerges as a strength of health service Trusts. On the other hand, inhibition of dialogue is viewed as a serious and detracting problem.

Ironically, all those interviewed intuitively knew the situation they faced. More often than not, the anguish, and the seeming powerlessness to overcome what are tense but demanding human relationship challenges emerged as a common theme. What is highlighted is that the feeling of 'not getting one's act together', is in fact an experience of normality. For each individual, recognizing the nature of the circumstances they face and having the insight to appreciate the nature of the tensions and concerns which block conversation and slowly erode the essence of the organization and its people, is an equally shared experience. Not entering into areas of restricted dialogue because the emotional discomfort experienced has emerged as a shared experience of seniority and not of medical or non-medical professional specialism.

As dialogue is identified as problematic, what is the impact of restrictive dialogue?

Impact of poor quality dialogue

Respondents across the three sectors were asked to identify those areas of concern that are perceived as particularly difficult and which inhibit attending to particular challenges in the organization.

For NHS Trusts, people, structure and strategic process issues are considered issues worthy of attention (Table 6.11). The morales of clinicians and nursing staff are seen as the two primary concerns. The

TABLE 6.11   Inhibition of dialogue: NHS Trusts

Issues	Percentages
The morale of clinicians	23.3
The morale of nursing staff	22.9
Issues affecting the long term	20.2
Relationship between functions/departments	18.6
Differences of opinion concerning reorganization	14.4
Private work by consultants	14.0
Issues concerning competition	13.6
The structure of the Trust	13.4
Relationships amongst clinicians	13.2
The future of the Trust	13.0

Percentage refers to percentage of responses identifying key issues requiring attention, with the respondents having the opportunity to make multiple responses. Adapted from Kakabadse and Korac-Kakabadse (1997) and Kakabadse and Korac-Kakabadse (1998b).

TABLE 6.12   Improvements: NHS trusts

Would there be:	Percentage
Improved clinician/nursing morale	32.2
Greater trust	26.4
Better understanding between clinicians and management	24.7
Improved interfacing internally	22.1
Improved quality of decision making	21.6
Improved ability to deliver a quality service	19.8
Overall, better performance from the Trust's employees	19.8
Improved clarity of decision making	19.0
Improved ability of managers to handle conflicting demands	17.3
Better relationships with external bodies	16.5

Percentage refers to percentage of responses identifying key issues requiring attention, with the respondents having the opportunity to make multiple responses.

relationships between departments and the future are also seen as important concerns. The private work of consultants and issues concerning competition are viewed as reasonably sensitive issues. Less pressing concerns are the structure of the Trust, the future of the Trust and relationships amongst clinicians.

Respondents were also asked to identify how much better the Trust would be if such sensitive issues had been resolved earlier. The top ten responses are highlighted on Table 6.12, with nearly a third of responses indicating improved morale and a quarter indicating an improved understanding between clinicians and management.

Best practice leadership[5]

The results highlight that the top managements of NHS Trusts are transformationally cohesive but transactionally suspect. In effect, being clearly focused on the mission and goal of improved heath care is not replicated by the more operational managerial skills of achieving such aspirations. Taking into account the importance of context of organization, namely in a decentralized environment, every Trust is quite different to each other, and in order to be responsive to client and community needs, six 'best practices' of leadership are identified, which from experience, both shield the organization from damaging splits and help management effectively work towards implementing strategy. The strategies recommended assume cohesion of purpose but consider that attention to the tactics to improve provision of service to the community, is the area requiring improvement.

■ *Providing example* The reasons why issues pertinent to the organization may not be effectively addressed may be due to poor quality of relationships between individual senior managers in the organization. Equally, such inhibitive tensions could be due to the territorial instincts of individual senior managers. If territory is distorting dialogue, the recommendation is to concentrate on organization-wide issues and not territorial concerns. A number of Trust CEOs highlighted the planning process as a mechanism for breaking down functional barriers and promoting an organization-wide perspective.

... we asked them to nominate a clinician and head of department to sit on this core group ... basically, there is a mixture of clinical directors, heads of departments and other directors having away-days to talk through issues and make up the plan, so what we now have is a formal document into which we all have contributed. (CEO, NHS Trust)

If the example provided by top management is that of being able to take an overview of a situation, such a perspective is more likely to emerge from staff and management lower down the organization.

However, if the example from the top is to preserve one's territory, that pattern of behaviour is equally likely to be replicated lower down.

- *Promote the qualities of leadership*   Apart from intellectually recognizing that need for a helicopter view, the challenge emotionally to accept and address sensitivities and concerns, is considerable. Two words capture the qualities for effective leadership – maturity and wisdom. Maturity can be defined as the capability to invite, receive and handle feedback well. Wisdom can be defined as the capability to identify appropriate pathways forward when direction is obscure(d). In effect, the robustness and courage to stand back, recognize the nature of the current dynamics within the organization and then identify the best ways forward where guidance seldom exists, are the nature of the qualities of leadership.

- *Get the dialogue right*   As stated, within any larger organization setting, differences, diversity and tension are normality. Not allowing for the emergence of undermining constraints requires the establishment of a common language within the organization. That starts with a common language at the top. The question is, do senior management sufficiently respect themselves and the responsibilities of their roles to stand above daily frustrations and allow for the emergence of a process which helps them approach and meet current and future concerns? Process, how we talk to each other, is as important as content – what do we talk about? The skill is to stimulate a debate in a manner that is workable to the key managers of the organization. Promoting a 'grit' in dialogue has to be matched with maintaining a level of comfort that allows for conversations to continue.[6] High quality dialogue needs to be crafted as much as any new service or product.

- *Get the interfaces right*   Making complex structures work is dependent on the quality of interfacing within the organization. Effective interfacing is a crucial lever to making strategies and policies work. If such practice is not held dear at the top, then distortion of policy during the phases of implementation is an expected and natural outcome. Hence, it is important to portray a consistency of message, so that in a disciplined way, important initiatives are effectively cascaded down the organization. The question is, do the managers at the key interface points in the structure recognize their degree of responsibility in terms of consistency and discipline? The response is yes, if those managers feel themselves to be responsible members of the executive. Having clarified who is and is not in the broader executive, then such feelings of responsibility are inculcated by the setting of ground rules concerning dialogue and behaviour, such as be responsive to feedback and above all respect meetings and the manner in which issues are represented at meetings.

■ *Promote high quality dialogue*   Policy and organizational agendas are set at the top. Promoting a positive climate for debate requires engendering a culture of enquiry, sensitive to different environments and promoting the feeling of confidence to seek varying but cohesive ways through diversity and challenge. In effect, an appropriate attitude is, 'we are here to learn from each other'. The process takes time, requires patience and is achieved by displaying discipline, consistency and honesty at meetings and showing humanity and concern outside meetings. Effective dialoguing needs trusting relationships which are evolved over time. In addition to time, a further issue to consider is security. For any public servant, political intervention could disrupt job placement, but similar dynamics exist in private sector organizations, whereby issues of profitability, meeting cost and revenue targets could place a question mark over any senior/middle manager's future. People in both sectors can just as easily lose their jobs. Experiencing vulnerability and insecurity over job tenure is normal. Hence, maturing into the senior role and evolving a sense of resilience to represent issues without undermining colleagiateship is the fine dividing line so many top managers straddle daily. Promoting an environment where the qualities of leadership are enhanced is the platform from which high quality team dialogue emanates.

■ *Promote cabinet responsibility*   A prime test of high quality leadership is the pursuit of cabinet responsibility. Do the members of the top team display that they desire cabinet responsibility in terms of how they behave rather than what they say? If certain senior colleagues disagree with a new initiative, do they fully challenge and debate the issue at meetings, or do they undermine and block the venture, displaying their resistance to the rest of the organization, and/or even the outside world, but outside the meeting? Staff, lower level management and external stakeholders need to witness the active support of all of the top team for key policies and initiatives. It is only through the communication of good example that demanding new ways of doing are accepted and cascaded down the organization. Attaining cabinet responsibility is a two-step process. First, a conscious decision needs to be made, do we really want cabinet responsibility and intend to practise it or not? Second, its continuation is the result of having promoted a feedback culture. Could one, for example, face a colleague and say, 'You said you were going to do that and you have done the opposite!' Only when there is a quality of dialogue which allows for such comments to be made and is seen as positive, does full cabinet responsibility exist. Otherwise, one is playing with words. Attaining and maintaining cabinet responsibility is a fraught process, but once achieved it does provide invaluable results.

Developing leaders

As highlighted, the internal culture of NHS Trusts is viewed as positive. However, as identified in the NHS, the telling difference for achieving outstanding performance is effective leadership. Despite the positive results of NHS top managers, one common area needing development emerges, that of dialogue. NHS top managers, so similar to other senior executives, require training, development and confidence building in order to address fully the concerns and challenges they face in their organization. To not do so would be damaging and demotivating. As NHS top executives have shown, they know what is wrong, but do not display the maturity, robustness and trust in their team colleagues to enter into debates which may prove to be unsettling, but nevertheless, necessary.

The overwhelming conclusion is that there is a great deal right with the top management of the NHS provider organizations in the UK. Further, the pessimism expressed over market forces is not extended to the support that is expressed for the creation of Trusts. Basically, improving the performance of Trusts requires some good old fashioned investment in the development of its senior management, most of whom would enthusiastically grasp the opportunity with open arms.

Notes

1. Certain sections of this chapter are adopted from Kakabadse et al. (1996) on Japanese business leaders and Kakabadse and Korac-Kakabadse (1996) examining leadership effectiveness in the Australian Federal Government.
2. The term senior executive embraces those senior managers who occupy discretionary leader roles. These managers may be members of one team, a number of teams (e.g. boards of a company and the committee of executive directors who may not sit on the board), a number of interlinking committees. It is assumed that the manner in which discretionary leader roles are configured varies from organization to organization.

3. Top team refers to the members of the senior executive and as such is used as a shorthand term to refer to those senior managers who occupy discretionary leader roles.

4. CEO   Chief executive office   MD   Managing director
   ED   Executive director   GM   General manager
   SES   Senior executive service   SOs   Senior officers

5. Adapted from Kakabadse and Korac-Kakabadse (1996).

6. Grit in dialogue refers to openness of conversation even when addressing issues that are sensitive and unwelcome to handle.

References

BAMM (1995), *Principles in Practice: Management Arrangements in Demonstration Trusts*, British Association of Medical Managers, Barnes Hospital.

Dixon, J. (1996), 'Recruiting Civil Servants: Public Management Development and Education to Meet the Management Challenge in Australia', *Journal of Management Development*, Vol. 15, No. 7, pp. 62–82.

Goffee, R. (1996), 'Managerial Capability in the Professional Firm – Assessing Competencies in the City', *Journal of Management Development*, Vol. 15, No. 7.

Harwood, A. and Boufford, J.I. (1993), *Managing Clinical Services: A Consensus Statement of Principles for Effective Clinical Management*, Institute of Health Services Management, London.

Jaques, E. (1951), *The Changing Culture of the Factory*, Tavistock Publications, London.

Kakabadse, A.P. and Korac-Kakabadse, N. (1996), *The Kakabadse Report. Leadership in Government: Study of The Australian Public Service (APS)*, Unpublished Report submitted to the Public Service Commissioner (APS), May.

Kakabadse, A.P. and Korac-Kakabadse, N. (1997), 'Best Practice in the Australian Public Service (APS): An Examination of Discretionary Leadership, *Journal of Managerial Psychology*, Vol. 12, No. 7, pp. 431–491 MCB publication.

Kakabadse, A.P. and Korac-Kakabadse, N. (1998a), *Essence of Leadership*, International Thomson, London.

Kakabadse, A.P. and Korac-Kakabadse, N. (1998b), *Leadership in Government: Study of the Australian Public Service*, Ashgate Publishing, Aldershot.

Kakabadse, A.P., Myers, A. and Okazaki-Ward, L. (1996), *Japanese Business Leaders*, International Thomson, London.

NAHAT Update (1996), *What Makes for Effective NHS Boards?*, Issue 14, April.

Scott. T, (1996), *Principles in Practice: The Involvement of Clinical Staff in the Management of NHS Trusts*, British Association of Medical Managers, Barnes Hospital, Stockport, Manchester.

CHAPTER SEVEN

Vision and renewal

Stephen P. Colloff

Allen Sheppard and GrandMet

The situation

In 1986 Allen Sheppard[1] became group chief executive, and subsequently chairman of Grand Metropolitan (GrandMet).[2] An economics graduate, he is an accountant by training, whose career was in the motor manufacturing industry before he joined GrandMet. He says that before becoming chief executive he had received a thorough grounding in large company management styles and controls.[3] But he had also come to know the shortcomings of large proceduralized companies especially the way procedures and controls can stifle the questioning born of common sense. He had developed an aversion to short-termism and to 'rule by quarterly results'; and developed a dislike for the stifling of initiative that may develop in a culture in which 'no one dares move for fear of making a mistake'.[4]

Allen Sheppard experienced the problem, not of turning round a failure, but of renewing and revitalizing a successful company.

As he put it, 'There was nothing radically wrong in the first place. We had to take a successful company, ensure it continued to be successful, and make it more successful.' 'Often', he said, 'this situation is *more* difficult than a typical turnaround, because you run into the kind of comment, "Why do you have to make any changes?"' Sheppard was not alone in this view; John Akers of IBM experienced a similar problem when he tried 'to create a sense of urgency' in IBM long before it went into the relative decline from which it is now recovering.[5]

GrandMet was a conglomerate, with activities ranging from Scotch whisky to nursery schools; from home nursing to chewing tobacco; from keep-fit bicycles to oil wells; from yoghurts to casinos and hotels. The company had no unifying element except asset-value and property. It had experienced an opportunistic growth having been built up by the genius entrepreneur Maxwell Joseph. It had a geographically determined structure, which recognized little connection between the UK and US businesses. It had, for example, entirely separate strategies for the UK and the US.

The development of the vision

Allen Sheppard took some significant steps on becoming chief executive. He appointed Peter Cawdron as strategy director, and took him out of his previous finance and planning functions. He was put on the executive committee of GrandMet and given a small department of three, with responsibility for strategy and vision and all the major business development activities which were not delegated out to the subsidiary companies. This meant that a very high profile was given to vision and strategy; but, significantly, Peter Cawdron's role was not just to develop vision and strategy; he was also responsible for its implementation at corporate level. Developing the vision was more than just a management exercise, it was a vital component in the development, redirection and renewal of the company. This situation in GrandMet is in sharp contrast to companies and organizations which allow groups of senior managers to identify, enunciate and sometimes even communicate mission and vision statements, but without any commitment at the top to fulfilling them. The exciting element in this GrandMet story is the total integration of the visioning activity with the setting of the business direction; and the fact that this was done under the direct leadership of the CEO and at the very top of the company.

Consultants were appointed to work with the top group of senior managers, but in a *process* role. As Peter Cawdron put it, 'We used them to probe and dig and delve and to collect the data by talking to each person individually, as well as in a group.'

The top group started with a blank sheet of paper. The project was called 'Vision 2000'. Cawdron said , 'We looked at the world economic scene, the political scene, social trends and the way the world was getting smaller and more individual. At the same time we looked at GrandMet and asked, 'What is GrandMet? What is it good at? What is its competitive advantage over others?'

The top group developed a set of criteria for a statement of vision:

GrandMet's Criteria for a statement of vision

Crystal clear	Only good if clear and unambiguous.
Comprehensive	Must cover everything – type of business, geography, assets, skills, culture, outlook, personality – a complete definition.
Realistic	Not hope or wishful thinking. Not unambitious. Achievable but challenging.
Brief	Clarity, simplicity, brevity. No 'flim-flam' or embroidery. A few short sentences.
Unique	Must belong exclusively to GrandMet. Recognizably GrandMet to an informed outsider.
Relevant	To GrandMet's present and future. Only relevant if we know where we are going: Who are we? What are our assets, skills, personality? Where are we going? Where is the business world going? What are the future opportunities for sales and profit growth?

The vision

These criteria were then honed into the following vision statement:

GrandMet's vision statement

Grand Metropolitan is an international group which specializes in highly branded consumer businesses, where its marketing and operational skills ensure it is a leading contender in every market in which it operates. These businesses – in food, drinks and retailing – which are few in number but large in size, have complementary features thus ensuring that GrandMet can add value to the parts.

Its style is about winning – never satisfied and always innovative. GrandMet strives to be a good employer and a good neighbour and to contribute actively to all the communities in which it operates. (Grand Metropolitan Annual Report, 1992, p. 2)

Achieving the vision

GrandMet had a problem with publishing their vision. Many of their businesses did not fit the new concept, and so the vision had to remain a management tool at the top of the company for the first two years. Such was the reality of the vision and its implications for the businesses that it had to be kept 'under wraps' for two years until the strategy began to unfold. About 25 businesses were sold off including catering, the keep-fit company, children's play schools, the subcontracted nursing service, the cigarette business, the chewing tobacco business, and the hotel business including the Plaza in New York and over 100 other hotels. There was no more severe test of the determination of Allen Sheppard to carry through the vision and strategy than this sale and there was no more startling example of the reality of the vision.

The strategy continued with the acquisition and subsequent turnaround of Pillsbury the then ailing US foods group, the exits from bookmaking and from brewing, and the disposal of the Express Foods UK and Irish dairy interests.

The 'good neighbour' and 'active contributor to the community' components of the vision statement were realized in a £20 million contribution to community activities worldwide in 1992. An environmental committee was also set up in 1992 to ensure that each operating business had a published environmental policy and would promote a 'beyond compliance approach' to safeguarding the environment.[6]

The 'winning style' became part of the company culture, as Ian Martin, then head of the US operations, was reported by the *Financial Times* of 1 November 1991 as saying, 'Sins of commission are far more preferable to sins of omission'. Allen Sheppard and his top team set a clear direction for GrandMet. He had a thorough grounding in large company styles and controls and had learnt the importance of standing up for one's views and of exercising common sense. Allen Sheppard and his top team used vision as an integral part of setting a clear direction for the business and following that direction. Visioning was not a public relations exercise; this is emphasized by the fact we have already mentioned; that the implications of the conclusions of the top group were so far-reaching they could not be publicized for two years. GrandMet achieved a rank of 27 in the *Financial Times Top 500* companies in Europe as reported in the *FT 500* of 10 February 1993; and the company's operating profit grew steadily from £365 million in 1988 to £902 million in 1992, in spite of the world recession which halted, but did not reverse, progress in 1992.[7]

Having seen how GrandMet integrated visioning in the development and implementation of strategy by the leader and his top team we will now try to examine what vision is and the management concepts involved in the creation and use of vision.

The need for vision

Vision has become highly fashionable and even desirable. Political leaders look for a vision to convince their electorates that their brand of the future is more desirable than that of their opponents. A lack of vision is regarded with concern. In his first inaugural address President Clinton quoted Proverbs, 29: 18 'Where there is no vision the people perish'. People are beginning to expect their leaders, whether politicians or businessmen, teachers or civil servants, volunteers or trades unionists, to be able to create an image of the future, to have some idea of goals and aspirations, and to be able to communicate these and be seen to be achieving them.

Business leaders use the concept of vision to underline what Frances Westley and Henry Mintzberg of McGill University called a 'desired future organizational state'[8] for their companies. This may involve an improved and changed company, perhaps more profitable, or more global, or more diversified, or more focused on particular markets, or with a higher reputation, or having beaten the rival market leader. This vision when communicated, is something for employees to aim for, it motivates and inspires, it encourages effort and achievement.

Politicians and business leaders whose concept of what they are trying to achieve lacks imagination and inspiration but instead is procedural, bureaucratic, or unclear, are likely to find their leadership abilities being questioned. Jay Conger in his inspirational book *The Charismatic Leader* describes the roles of leaders as 'meaning makers': 'They must pick and choose from the rough materials of reality to construct pictures of great possibilities. An effective leader's persuasion is of the subtlest kind, for he or she must interpret reality to offer images of the future that are irresistibly meaningful.'[9]

David Herman, then president of Saab Automobile, described the concept of a feeling of continuity in the process of turning round a company, 'If there are two words to describe the challenges of the industry they are "continuous improvement", which implies that you never get there but you are always trying to do better... what we did that was most important was to provide a vision and that implies continuity.' Herman talked about the motivating element in having future products in the company's strategy:

A key thing is to have a long-term product plan and the resources to do it; because that channels your engineering objectives, it also provides excitement, it encourages your sales and marketing people. In the plant the idea of doing something new and improving your facilities to do it is another opportunity, because everybody likes to do something for the future.[10]

For Herman the very existence and enunciation of the vision and the product plans associated with it meant there was a future for the company and its employees, however hard the process of realization might be. Personal effectiveness and transactional skills are important, but they are no longer enough. Noel Tichy and Mary Anne Devanna in their 'blueprint for instituting change', *The Transformational Leader*, wrote

> Transformational leaders must not only diagnose their organisation's strengths and weaknesses and match them against environmental opportunities, but they must also find ways to inspire employees to meet these challenges. This vision of the future must be formulated in such a way that it makes the pain of changing worth the effort.[11]

What does 'vision' mean?

In the example of Allen Sheppard and GrandMet with which we began this chapter, we saw how vision was integrated into the strategy of the company. But how does vision relate to *mission* and where does *strategy* fit in?

In 1987 the Ashridge Strategic Management Centre undertook a two-year research project on understanding what mission statements are. Two hundred companies worldwide provided mission statements, and managers from 40 organizations in Europe and the USA were interviewed.

The researchers found that two emphases were emerging. One view was that mission was 'about defining the business you are in and the strategy you want to follow', the other also involved 'culture, values and behaviour' as part of the picture. The authors of the subsequent report resolved the problem by deciding that mission involved both strategy and culture; and they recommended the 'Ashridge mission model'[12] shown in Figure 7.1.

As we can see, the model shows that *purpose, values, standards* and *behaviours*, together with *strategy*, all interrelate. The authors even produced 'Guidelines for Managing Mission' and a questionnaire aimed at helping companies to measure the quality of their mission statements: 'Do You Have a Good Mission Statement?'[13] However, of the 34 mission statements published in the report only two contain the word 'vision'.

James Collins and James Porras of Stanford Graduate School of Business have tentatively resolved some of the problems that surround the term 'vision'. In their paper, 'Organizational Vision and Visionary

FIGURE 7.1   The Ashridge mission model. (*Source*: Campbell and Yeung, 1990)

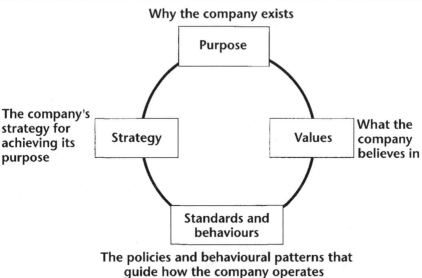

Why the company exists

Purpose

The company's strategy for achieving its purpose

Strategy

Values

What the company believes in

Standards and behaviours

The policies and behavioural patterns that guide how the company operates

Organizations',[14] they reported one CEO as saying: 'I've come to believe that we need a vision to guide us, but I can't get my hands on what that vision is. I've heard lots of terms like 'mission', 'purpose', 'values', 'strategic intent', but no one has given me a satisfactory way of looking at vision that will help me sort out the morass of words and set a coherent vision for my company. It's really frustrating!'

The authors found that organizational vision consists of two major components: guiding philosophy and tangible vision. They eschewed bland statements which don't motivate and they developed the framework shown in Figure 7.2.

Guiding philosophy often comes from the firm's founder or from a single visionary leader. Collins and Porras emphasize that it may have to be institutionalised once the company has passed beyond 'excessive dependence on a few individuals'.[15] *Core values and beliefs* are what the people in the organization feel is important. A good example is the seven basic commitments spelt out for all employees of International Computers in 'The ICL Way'; such as 'commitment to change' and 'commitment to the customer'.

Purpose is why the company exists, it comes out of core values and beliefs and 'not only reflects the importance people attach to the company's work but taps their idealistic efforts'[16], for example: 'The

FIGURE 7.2 Overview of the framework of organizational vision. (*Source*: Collins and Porras, 1991)

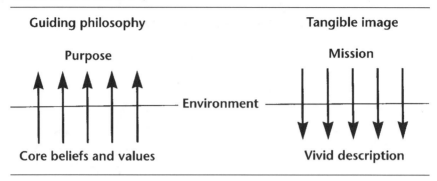

purpose of McKinsey and Company is to help corporations and governments be more successful.'[17] *Tangible image* involves the 'clear compelling goal' of mission with setting definable targets. The authors cite Bob Miller, CEO of the MIPS Computer Company. 'To make the MIPS processor architecture the most pervasive in the world by the mid-1990s. Every decision is subservient to that aim.'[18]

By developing this framework of organizational vision, Collins and Porras do overcome to some extent the problem of the 'morass of words' and help CEOs to see vision as a kind of overarching concept; GrandMet's vision fits this quite well.

Vision – a convergence model

It is important to keep both the drama and the tangible realism in vision. When vision is used mainly as a motivator or as a way of developing managers' leadership capabilities, it will almost certainly be less successful than when it is an integral part of the company's strategy; both are preferred. And when strategy and vision are effectively communicated to stakeholders, success is more probable. Most of us are familiar with the situation in which groups of managers debate vision statements with the help of a training consultant and end up with something so bland that it has no meaning – 'to be the best railway in the world', and often so excessively ambitious that their bosses become concerned about their sanity. The involvement of the top is essential though it is possible for subunits and subsidiaries with clear identities to have vision.

Vision is primarily about the future and that is what makes it exciting. The ability to envision 'the desired future state' is very important.

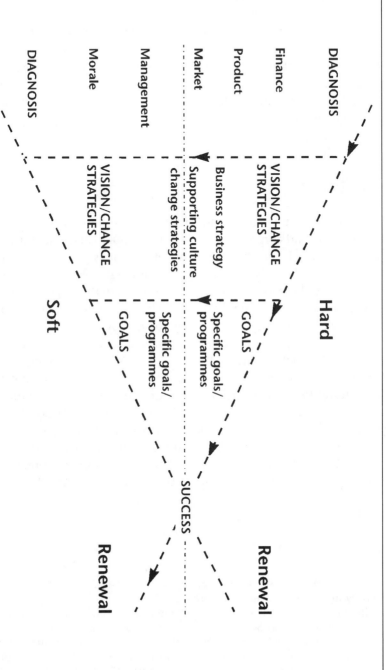

FIGURE 7.3 A convergence model of 'visioning'

The process could be developed as a kind of convergence model as shown in the diagram in Figure 7.3. In this model the 'hard' elements of *finance, product,* and *markets* have their own vision or change strategies with supporting business strategies and specific goals; these 'hard' elements converge with the 'soft' elements of *management* style and *morale* and their supporting culture change strategies and programmes. The vision and change strategies for the 'hard' and 'soft' elements are mutually supporting and relate to the needs of the business; the process is then subject to renewal (rather than abandonment in favour of the next management fad).

Conclusion

'Vision' is an exciting concept for businesses. The appearance of vision on the industrial and corporate scene is not just as a management technique for enhancing leadership and the effectiveness of a company or organization. There is as well a link between the inner motives of individuals and the expression of those motives in the drive to achieve, to be part of a successful team in a worthwhile and purposeful enterprise.

People in industry seek answers to the question 'Why am I doing this?' For doctors, teachers, priests, politicians, and other vocational jobs the answer is usually clear. For thinking businessmen the clarification and definition of the purpose, mission and vision of their company in environmental, social, financial, survival, growth, product and developmental terms, can elevate business to a higher context. It can give greater meaning to the lives of those who work in the company. The clear exposition and communication of the strategy and vision can harness energies in a clearer direction to the greater benefit of the company, and may help people to be 'caught up' in the spirit of the enterprise.

Notes

1. Later 'Sir Allen' and now 'Lord Sheppard'.
2. Now merged with Guinness as 'Diageo'.
3. Quotations and extracts in this chapter are taken from an unpublished Cranfield University School of Management research study (S.P. Coloff (1993), *Interventions of Chief Executive Officers to Achieve Turnround*, Cranfield University, Cranfield, Bedfordshire, UK) by the author based on structured interviews conducted in 1991–1992, with 13 CEOs and/or chairmen

responsible for substantial businesses based in the UK, France and Sweden. Extracts and quotations which originate from published material are separately annotated. The study aimed to discover what these business leaders actually did, and what interventions they made, to achieve the turnround or renewal of their companies.

4. *Director* magazine (1992), 'The Man Who Beat the Management', August, London, Institute of Directors, pp. 32–35

5. Tichy, N. M. and Devanna, M. A. (1990), *The Transformational Leader*, John Wiley and Sons, New York, p. 47.

6. Grand Metropolitan (1992) Annual Report, p. 5.

7. Ibid., p. 9.

8. Westley, F. and Mintzberg, H. (1989), 'Visionary Leadership and Strategic Management', *Strategic Management*, Journal, Vol. 10, p. 17.

9. Conger, J.A. (1989), *The Charismatic Leader*, Jossey-Bass, New York, p. 44.

10. When David Herman of General Motors was appointed president of Saab Automobile in December 1989, he was the first CEO of the company under the joint ownership of General Motors and Saab-Scania. An article in Scanorama by David Barton entitled 'Saab's New Big Wheel' stated, 'When Herman came on board Saab, it was like appointing a new captain for the Titanic after it struck the iceberg.' (Scanorama (1991), p. 30). Herman brought Saab out of crisis into a stage where recovery was possible. He was subsequently promoted to senior posts in GM.

11. Tichy and Devanna (1990), p. 122.

12. Campbell, A. and Yeung, S. (1990), 'Do You Need a Mission Statement?', Ashridge Strategic Management Centre, Special Report No.1208, Economist Publications, London, p. 6.

13. Ibid., p. 24.

14. Collins, J.C. and Porras, J.I. (1991), 'Organizational Vision and Visionary Organisations', Stanford Graduate School of Business, Research paper No.1159, p. 31.

15. Ibid., p. 35.

16. Campbell and Yeung (1990), p. 99–103.

17. Collins and Porras (1991), p. 40.

18. Ibid., p. 43.

CHAPTER EIGHT

The practical side to visioning: the case of Toray Industries Inc.

Lola Okazaki-Ward

'Vision is tenbô in Japanese, a wide and distant vista of the future in which the desirable image of the company is set, directing its course and generating strategies for getting there.' (Katsunosuke Maeda, President, Toray Industries Inc.)

Introduction

This study illustrates the remarkable success story of Toray Industries Incorporated, and the role that visioning played in the transformation of the company in the decade from 1987, particularly under the strong leadership of Katsunosuke Maeda, its president. His achievement was initially to restore the company to a leading position in the 'mature' fibres and textiles sector under the implicit strategic intent of 'beat Asahi Chemical' . He accomplished this by completely reversing the direction in which both his company and the industry as a whole were then going. Once the recovery was firmly established, Katsunosuke Maeda led the company through a more comprehensive and explicit vision, to become a world-class, comprehensive, chemical group as stated in the vision statement of AP-G2000 in 1991, by way of strategies of growth through globalization and group management. By the time Maeda handed the baton to his successor in June 1997, the Toray group had achieved this vision by becoming the world's largest producer of fibres and textiles, carbon fibre and polyester films, and clocking up a consolidated revenue of ¥1 trillion, an increase of 80 per cent since 1987. Under a freshly revised New AP-G2000 of 1997 which endorsed the current direction and strategies, and a new president, the Toray group has embarked upon the road to fulfilling its vision of becoming the world's leading comprehensive chemical group in the new millenium.[1]

The remarkable story of Toray's recovery and its subsequent growth as a world-class industrial group, was centred on strengthening its core competencies of synthetic fibres technology, and on building up competitive advantages against its competitors, under what Hamel and Prahalad term the industry foresight of its exceptional leader, Katsunosuke Maeda. (Hamel and Prahalad, 1994). The importance of the role of vision, in this case expressed in the Japanese term of *tenbô*, throughout in its successful process of transformation is unquestionable.

Today Toray is a diversified group of over 200 companies, producing, apart from fibres and textiles, carbon fibres and polyester films, for which it is the world's largest producer, plastics and chemicals, housing and engineering products and services, pharmaceutical and medical products, new materials and other businesses, and electronics and information-related products. Toray Industries Inc. employs just over 10,000 employees, but the group comprises 121 companies in Japan employing another 15,000, and a further 84 companies in 17 countries overseas with approximately 25,000 employees. However, the drama of transformation began well before Maeda's presidency in 1987.

A brief history (to 1987)

Established in 1926 as an artificial fibre manufacturer, Tôyô Rayon Company, with Mitsui & Co's capital attained autonomy after the war and changed its name to Toray in 1970. It is a member of Nimoku-kai, the presidents' council of the Mitsui Group.

Toray's initial post-war expansion began with the introduction of synthetic fibres technology, and the near monopoly control of the market, granted under the MITI industrial policy,[2] in the production of nylon and polyester fibres, in a period of rapid expansion in the demand for textiles worldwide throughout the 1950s (Suzuki, 1995). Together with Matsushita and Toyota, Toray was quoted as one of 'the big three in Japan', clocking up ¥100 billion in revenues, in the late 1950s, and in 1964 was ranked first in a league table of those companies most sought after by new job seekers (Chiba, 1996). These years spelt the 'golden' age of the company.

However, during the following 20 years, its performance continually declined, with the growth rate of its sales until 1985, consistently underachieving the rate of economic growth, so that at the end of this period it was well behind its major competitor, Asahi Chemical. Apart from the maturity of the domestic fibre market, the major cause of the company's decline is said to have been the overreliance on the efficacy of technical competency to the extent that the development of marketing capabilities took second place. Toray had always had a strong research and development tradition which contributed to the pioneering of new products and new businesses, but it tended to ignore the end users of the new products (Suzuki, 1995). This meant unfocused investment in R&D which, while technologically innovative, turned out to be less fruitful in terms of added value.

Another aspect of the decline was the quality of the corporate culture, in which the members of the corporate planning and support functions, under the successive presidents who were science- and engineering-oriented, had the leading hand in influencing company policy. As a result, the voices of those who worked in the front line of production and marketing gradually fell silent, as the head office staff who, whilst brilliant strategists, had little practical, on-the-shopfloor experience, were able to influence corporate decisions by presenting highly plausible and cleverly formulated arguments (Maeda, 1997). Unfortunately, they proved themselves incapable of operationalizing policy decisions. (Seimaru, 1997) As a result, apathy and discord were widespread throughout the company, and Toray suffered from a typical 'large company' malaise, a *nurumayu* (pervasive, lukewarm environment) culture.

Policy direction

The policy direction of Toray during the ten years before 1985 was to 'withdraw' from the textile business gradually and to fill the gap by developing new businesses. At the time, this was a general trend in a textile industry which had suffered a severe decline as a result of the end of the Bretton Woods Agreement, the two oil crises of 1973 and 1979–1980, and was designated by MITI as one of the structural recessionary industries in the early 1980s. All textile companies rushed to increase the ratio of non-fibre businesses by investing heavily in new areas, thereby reducing the ratio of their fibre and textile business. Toray was no exception and put a huge annual investment amounting to ¥50 billion into new businesses in order to diversify. Early in the 1980s, a decision was made to withdraw completely from fibres and textiles production in

Southeast Asia. A further blow was dealt to the ailing fibre and textile industry by the revaluation of the yen through the Plaza Accord of 1985 which 'practically wiped out the future of the industry' (Suzuki, 1995). The problem facing Toray at that time was that it believed that the only way out of corporate decline was to start an array of new businesses, particularly those which had the appearance of being immediate winners (Seimaru, 1997).

Toray, which had already acquired the unwelcome distinction of being 'weak in recession', was down on its current profit, at the end of March 1987, by 40 per cent on the previous year, because the textile division which accounted for 70 per cent of the total sales had posted a loss of ¥60 billion. Its current profit was kept in the black only from the sale of a piece of land that Toray had owned in the expensive Roppongi district of Tokyo. Even so, at ¥17 billion, its current profit was far behind Asahi Chemical's ¥34 billion, and even came after Teijin with its ¥25 billion (Chiba, 1996). These facts dealt a severe blow to the pride of Toray's employees and to their hopes of regaining industry leadership, imbuing them with a sense of crisis.

A change of president

This was the situation, when the fortunes of Toray were at their nadir, when Maeda became the company's new president. It was an exceptional event, not only because his appointment occurred in April rather than in June, when it would have usually taken place after the AGM, but also because he, then the most junior executive director and, at the age of 56, the third youngest director on the board, became president over the heads of 14 directors who were senior to him. He had served only two years on the board (K. Maeda, interview, 1997). Also, his predecessor, Masakazu Itoh, having earlier made clear his intention to hand over the reins of the company in 1987, had nominated his successor, a vice-president, but had faced the problem of having his choice accepted by the major stakeholders of the company, particularly by the members of the *Nimoku-kai* and Toray's own company union (K. Maeda interview, 1997). In the light of the dire results of March 1987, Itoh had to find a speedy and acceptable solution, that choice being Maeda. Maeda, a graduate of Kyoto University with a MSc in industrial chemistry, had long been known in the company by the nickname of 'fighting Maekatsu'[3] for speaking his mind when he felt justified in criticizing his superiors, even in his days as a junior manager, knowing that it could endanger his promotion prospects, and had been popular among his colleagues and subordinates in the textile section of the company. Maeda had also brought his name to the notice of senior directors in 1984 when he created a storm at a management meeting on the pretext of reporting on the state of the subsidiaries in Southeast Asia. He, a then non-board director, had been given the job of closing down these struggling factories in accordance with a decision made earlier in the year, and had been visiting the sites frequently in preparation for their final closure, for almost a year. During this time, however, he became convinced that it was a myopic measure which might have brought short-term relief, but in the long run would set back the chance of future growth. With the domestic market being saturated, and with the US government, which was struggling with the twin deficits, moving towards devaluation of the dollar, he could see that what the company needed was not the closure of the Southeast Asian businesses, but the rebuilding of them to take advantage of the cost competitiveness they would offer. But there was no avenue open in the company through which he could bring to the notice of the board the urgent need for major change in policy direction. Thus he resolved to gain access to the management meeting under false pretences. Instead of reporting on the progress of his appointed work, he presented his case, passionately pointing out the folly of their policy, to a group of astonished and rather bemused senior directors. A fierce debate ensued. In the end, Chairman Fujiyoshi, who was then in overall charge of the overseas businesses, adjudicated, and the implementation of the decision was deferred for one year. In the following year, Plaza Accord arrived, and Maeda, who spent the intervening period quietly turning these subsidiaries round, was vindicated (Chiba, 1996). These Southeast Asian subsidiaries were to play an important strategic role in the recovery and subsequent growth of Toray in the years of Maeda's presidency. In the critical situation in which Toray was in 1987, perhaps Maeda, young by the Japanese standards, energetic, not easily cowed by superiors, and determined, with some proven quality of leadership, was seen as the most likely person to rid the company of its current problem. Whatever the reason, Maeda's election caused a sensation both within and outside the company, as it was the first time such a choice for president was made among the blue-chip firms since the selection of Yamashita, over the heads of 24 directors, by Kônosuke Matsushita, the founder of Matsushita, in 1977 (Yoshida, 1996).

However, in a traditionally seniority-conscious Japanese, corporate board, a junior member suddenly promoted over the heads of so many of his superiors would have found it extremely difficult, if not impossible, to lead the board effectively unless backed by a tremendously authoritative figure such as the founder, as was the case at Matsushita. Maeda accepted the presidency only on condition that all the senior directors would support him, and personally saw each of them to obtain a pledge of support before he finally accepted (K. Maeda, interview, 1997). At the first board meeting after his appointment, he characteristically declared that the primary task of the board was to rebuild the company through working closely together under his leadership, and that the fact of his (relative) youth was immaterial in this endeavour (K. Maeda, interview, 1997).

'For the company' became the rallying call which immediately united the board, all the more effectively because all the directors had known the glory days of Toray in the early 1960s. Their desire to work for the recovery of company fortune was strong. The strategic intent of 'beat Asahi' became the implicit vision shared by them.

However, their loyalty was severely tested from the beginning when Maeda astonished everyone by declaring that he would turn round the fibres and textile division and produce a healthy result within one or two years (Chiba, 1996),[4] for it was generally accepted that once a company was on the slippery road to decline, it was impossible to check its downward momentum. However, Maeda had already drawn up an action for survival plan (ASP) for the fibres and textile business the year previously but had been unable to implement it because the Tokyo corporate office had not been interested.

Change programme for recovery

The major policy implication of the ASP was to completely reverse the direction of the company and go for strengthening rather than withdrawing from the fibres and textiles business, based on Maeda's firm belief that it was a growth industry with huge market potential. He argued that, whilst the domestic market had matured, there was a vast market in Asia as a whole, and China in particular, where potential demand for textiles was high and consumption growing. Those who did not believe Maeda, namely the majority of the company members, could be forgiven, for this core business on the domestic front had been on the decline for several years, even producing a loss of ¥60 billion at the end of the previous year, and the subsidiaries in Southeast Asia were none too healthy. What the company needed, however, Maeda expounded, was a strategy of differentiated marketing. The domestic and the Western markets, where the growth would be only 2 or 3 per cent, could be increased by targeting products with high added value, whereas in the developing market in Asia as a whole, a growth of 10 per cent was possible. The potential of the Chinese market was huge. Taken together, the total textile market was capable of 5 per cent or more growth, annually. It was a matter of a strategic choice of policies.

However, in order to achieve such growth, the company had first to become much more efficient, through a programme of change, in the areas of cost, organization, personnel, and corporate culture. Maeda immediately began a series of drastic top-down measures to rebuild competitiveness, and to change corporate culture to support it. Many of the policies he introduced also bucked the fashionable management trends, earning him the epithet 'maverick', but were proved to be rooted in sound orthodoxy and based on his personal philosophy of *genba*-ism, the belief that the 'shop floor' holds the secret of all sound corporate decisions.

Rationalization[5]

- The first thing Maeda ordered was a close scrutiny of the entire textile range, running to over 3,000 items, with regard to production's performance for the previous several years, to determine whether their production should be increased, curtailed or scrapped, in terms of the added value they were likely to bring, thereby rationalizing the product range. The result was fed into production and marketing strategies.

- Another activity undertaken was the drastic reorganization of the textile subsidiaries in Southeast Asia, to improve their productivity, quality and volume through rationalization and massive investment, replacing old machinery with state-of-the-art equipment, by training employees, thereby increasing productive capacity and improving product quality.

Cost reduction measures

- Apart from the drive to reduce cost by the routine means of cutting down on waste and improving productivity, Maeda changed the transfer pricing of goods from the raw materials production division to the product division to be based on cost-based price rather than on the existing market-based price, thereby stimulating efforts to reduce the production costs of these divisions and thus to improve the cost competitiveness of Toray products.

■ A more unorthodox cost-cutting measure implemented immediately was the programme to reduce the workforce by 3,300 in the following five years through a mixture of natural wastage and voluntary early retirement with an enhanced severance pay. These were the years of economic expansion, now called the 'bubble', when the average rate of growth was about 5 per cent and reduction of the workforce was the last thought on the minds of the personnel directors of most companies, as they were occupied with the problem of how to get enough new recruits to apply for the increased number of vacancies which were created by the boom.

Maeda's argument was that a period of economic expansion was the best time for rationalizing, to prepare the company for the trough in the cyclical movement which was bound to follow, for both the company and the employees would benefit. Those who decided to leave the company would have a far better opportunity to obtain a good job to go to, and the company could afford a much more generous severance package. Downsizing during the time of recession, often done under pressure, benefits nobody, as those employees made redundant have less of an opportunity for finding an alternative job, and might feel bitter towards the company, for which rationalization in recession costs more and damage to the morale of the remaining employees is greater (K. Maeda, interview, 1997).

In this Toray exercise, the lower age limit for early retirement was brought down to 45 years, as Maeda was of the opinion that by the age of 45, most white-collar workers knew whether they had a future in the company, and yet were young enough to find an alternative future outside of the company (Seimaru, 1997). Thus, Maeda established a personnel placement office to assist employees in finding new employment.[6] This also helped to ease the problem of the shortage of management posts which most companies were facing. By 1992, when the recession was beginning to bite, Maeda declared that Toray no longer needed to reduce its workforce.

At the same time as this was going on, Maeda continued the policy of recruiting a steady number of new school-leavers and graduates, annually, irrespective of the prevailing economic situation, in order to maintain a smooth, employee-age profile. This policy was also against current trends, because most companies stuck to the policy of varying the annual intake of people in accordance with the level of that year's profit. Maeda also established a practice of recruiting mid-career applicants to fill those gaps in the age profile left by any past unevenness of recruitment, as well as to obtain specialists which were needed by the expanding business. During the 1990s, Toray's internal labour market became much more fluid, though long-term employment remained as the basic policy.

Investment policies

- Toray maintained a stable level of investment in plant and equipment at around ¥50 billion on average, annually, throughout the decade (Chiba, 1997). Maeda stuck very firmly to the policy of keeping it within the limits of cash flow, and firmly resisted internal pressure to increase it beyond that level during the 'bubble' years, whilst the company's major competitors rushed to increase their productive capacity of long-polyester fibre. Production increase was managed by buying in the yarns.

- The difference thus created in the production capacity between Toray and the rest of its competitors, by the differential rates of investment on plant and equipment during the 'bubble' years, brought Toray in conflict with them in the spring of 1993 when there was a large fall in the price of synthetic fibres. The seven major synthetic textile manufacturers who now found themselves with large overcapacity, tried to form a specific agreement to reduce production. Toray refused to yield to their combined pressure and was accused of wilfully acting to disestablish the synthetic fibres and textiles industry. Maeda countered this by pointing out that Toray had not undertaken a reckless increase in capacity during the years of high demand as they had done, and that he did not see any need to reduce output (Chiba, 1996). As Toray's depreciation cost was markedly lower, this helped increase its cost competitiveness relative to its competitors. This controversy brought the spotlight upon his so-called '*Maekatsu-ryû keiei* (Maeda katsunosuke way of management)'.

- Part of the plant investment was channelled into expanding production facilities abroad, to gain the advantage of the high yen. Toray began to locate in the market abroad from 1989, beginning with the UK, then a project of going into China was mooted in the early 1990s.

- The company also maintained a steady level of focused investment in R&D irrespective of the economic situation. Traditionally, R&D had always been regarded as the key to the future of the company, and both 'underground' research and innovative development were encouraged.

- At the same time, Maeda forbade speculative investment (*zaiteku*) during the 'bubble' years, by the company, because he believed that that was not what the company was in business for, though there was strong pressure from within the company to go with the general trend. It turned out to be an astute strategy, because reckless speculations left many companies with great liabilities after the 'bubble' burst.

Measures for crisis management

- During the 'bubble' years, when the company was in a seller's market, Maeda forbade the factories to break delivery agreements with the customers, and to raise the price of the goods. A close check was kept on the factories to make sure that this order was complied with. Maeda's point was that such predatory actions would be remembered by customers, and when a recessive time followed, they would either drop such suppliers or put pressure on them, before others, to reduce the price of goods (Chiba, 1996).

- In order to be able to anticipate a forthcoming crisis in the market, Maeda ordered the company's management control department, during the 'bubble' years, to examine the level of inventory of individual products for a period of two years just before any large reduction in profit occurred, or when the company bottom line was close to zero in the past, as well as the average annual price of every product in stock year-on-year, for several years in the past. His hunch was that there had to be a hidden signal for an approaching crisis within these figures, and he was right. The inventory index jumped every time before a crisis occurred. Also, there was a trend for a recession to follow a year after the level of inventory of each product had risen to a given point. The result was the setting of a ceiling for the inventory level of each product, and a rule was laid down firmly to keep the control of inventory at a level about 10 per cent below that ceiling (Chiba, 1996).

Reorganisation of the structure

- One of the strategic changes in organizational structure was the separation of a basic research capability, which had long-term 'underground' research aims, from a product development capability aiming to produce new products in the short period. This separation enabled different sections of the R&D division to concentrate on their disparate aims and timespans and improved the investment efficiency of each of the sections (Dempsey, 1997).

- Another important organizational change was the creation of the related businesses headquarters (RBH) at Toray, in April 1988, to reorganize its relationship with the subsidiaries and affiliated companies. In the past, these related companies, then running to some 113 both within Japan and abroad, were positioned below each of the business divisions which absorbed their profits or transferred their own losses, and forced excess labour on to them. They could neither act autonomously nor expect assistance from the business departments above them. This was the main cause of the poor performance by the overseas affiliates and domestic related companies, and ultimately stunted the growth of the profitability of the group as a whole. Through the concept of federal management, Maeda brought all the related companies under the direct control of the RBH, and formalized the rights of the subsidiaries, such as the discretion of the presidents over investment on projects below the budgetary level of ¥300 million, making it a mere reporting matter afterwards, and clarifying the boundary beyond which lay matters that required Toray decisions. Under the new federal management system, the RBH practically acted as a holding company of the subsidiaries, taking on a joint responsibility with them as a profit centre. It borrowed money from the company and capitalized the related companies, paying the given rate of interest on the capital. If the related companies did well and their dividends were higher than the internal interest which the RBH had to pay the company on borrowed money, it made a profit. All related companies were required to draw up a five-year business plan to ensure both that the evaluation of their performance was not done on a short-term basis, and that the direction in which they were going was in line with that of the parent company, reviewing their plans every three years. Given that the contribution from the related companies accounted for a substantial percentage of the consolidated results, their development was extremely important for the group as a whole (Nishikawa, 1995).

This change prepared the basis for group management, which was one of the key strategies for the transformation.

The outcome

Through these top-down measures designed to strengthen corporate competitive ability, the company's performance began to show improved results.

At the end of March 1987, Toray had been lagging behind the top performers, Asahi Chemical and Teijin. However, by the end of March 1988 Toray overtook Teijin, with a current profit of ¥37 billion closing the gap with Asahi Chemicals. Also, the recovery of the fibres and textiles business was nothing short of astonishing. It earned a current profit of ¥9.5 billion, an increase of about ¥70 billion from the previous year when it was in the red to the tune of ¥60 billion, and contributed 25 per cent towards the total profit. Maeda's prediction was amply realized. Nor was it just a flash in the pan, for its current profit at the end of March 1989 was ¥15.7 billion, making a 30 per cent contribution to the total profit. The frown of disbelief on the faces of its employees began to be replaced with a gleam of optimism and determination in their eyes. The company's performance, relative to its major competitors, continued to improve, and in 1993, with a current profit of ¥49.2 billion, it finally vanquished Asahi Chemical by a 20 per cent margin, to take the leading position in the industry, after ten years (Chiba, 1996).

Changes to the corporate culture

Maeda also implemented a series of fundamental changes to the basic values and attitudes of the workforce. One of the main management philosophies which supported Maeda's push for these changes aimed at reinvigorating the organization was '*genba*-ism', which placed great stress on policy decisions and actions that were rooted in the knowledge and experience of the 'shop floor'.

Maeda took firm action to establish '*genba*-ism', first by reorganizing the corporate planning office, the nerve centre for corporate policy-making processes, which was to have a profound effect on the attitudes of all employees in the company.

A transformation of corporate planning office functions

Having come to the conclusion that the existing organisation and staff of the corporate planning office were not up to the strategic task required to support his aim of changing the corporate culture, Maeda set out to bring about the transformation of the core function of this Office in July 1987. It was composed of three sub-units: a business planning unit which drew up long-term plans and proposals for new businesses; an external liaison unit responsible for liaising with external organizations including ministries and trade organizations; and most importantly, a corporate planning unit which was in charge of translating long/medium-term targets into management plans. First, Maeda appointed a vice-president to be wholly in charge of the corporate planning office. Then he replaced all ten members of the office by bringing in those with front-line experience, though the structure and the basic functions of the first two sub-units were largely left intact. The impact of the reform affected most fundamentally the corporate planning unit (CPU), transforming it into a corporate strategic staff unit. Its new briefs were:

1   To communicate rapidly the views, values and objectives of the top management to the rest of the company.

2   To act as a direct communication channel for employees' views and suggestions coming up from below.

3   To act as a consultative body for the president, reporting back to him about its views on the issues they were given, after freely deliberating and closely researching them.

Maeda's resolve to transform the corporate planning unit immediately was based on the recognition that if he were to succeed, he would have to have an effective use of its staff as a strategic human resources tool. As it existed, he could not hope to succeed. A series of changes that he wrought in the functions and organization of this unit was aimed at not only strengthening its planning function, but also improving information gathering, and processing ability, but most importantly, having it reflect the voice and thoughts of the front-line functions on those decisions made at the top.

The size of the unit was increased initially from three to eight people, all of whom were newly selected from among able middle managers who had detailed knowledge and experience of the *genba*, from the areas of overseas operations, trading, fibres and textiles, resins and plastics, production, engineering, accounting, and new businesses. One of the main criteria for selection was that the members would have gained not only an excellent grasp of the work of their respective businesses' departments, but more importantly, that they would also have an ability for self-renewal, so that they worked with a corporate point of view, rather than represented their previous departmental interests, which often happened in such a mixture. The initial rank composition of this cross-functional body was four *buchô* (general managers), three *jichô* (deputy-general managers) and one *kachô* (section manager), whose ages ranged from 40 to 52 years. The term of their appointment was, initially, two years, to avoid the formation of internal cliques, and new members were always selected from the *genba* staff. The kind of work involved at the corporate command centre close to the top management, namely, discussing, researching, planning and drawing up proposals for corporate decision matters, provided an excellent opportunity for broadening management's horizons, and for managers to appreciate the vision and philosophy of the president.

Unit members attended the twice-monthly *fukushachô-kai* (The vice-presidents' meeting) to report on, or to examine organizational themes such as the revision of management systems, and the transformation of business structure. Maeda also consciously created opportunities for members to express their views, which were backed by their *genba* experience, by requiring them to attend important meetings of each business department, and the management meeting.

Members of the unit were also required to attend the regular and cross-departmental *kakarichô* (group leader), *kachô* and *buchô* meetings where a large number of key employees from different functional areas came together to talk and disseminate the new corporate philosophy, and the vision, values and beliefs held by the president, and the strategies to achieve them. Maeda regarded the effective combination of vertical and horizontal communication, through the activities of the strategic staff unit, as one of the keys to the success of corporate change. The corporate planning unit was expanded by two more members, in 1988, representing the chemical and compound materials business. The term of appointment for all was then extended to four years. On the strength of this expansion, the corporate planning office was upgraded to become a department in 1993 and continued to play a pivotal role in the shaping of the new culture. One of its members was also the *kachô* in the president's secretariat, who coordinated the work between the two offices (Fujisawa, interview, 1997). The incumbents at the time of change were sent to the front-line functions, with a personal message from Maeda to gain a sound experience of *genba* to enhance their capability (K. Maeda, interview, 1997).

Reorganization of the corporate public relations office (*Kôhôshitsu*)

Another early and vital measure that Maeda took was the establishment, in November 1987, of the Corporate Public Relations (PR) Office, attached directly to the president. At the same time, it absorbed the in-house journal office and the corporate identity office. The aim of this reorganization was to integrate the tasks of corporate communications both within the company and to the outside, utilizing both the journal and ID concept, and allowing the president to control the activities of the corporate communications office by using it as an information nerve centre and a tool for information strategy.

Clearly the corporate PR office and the corporate planning office played the central role in corporate communications, generating ideas, carrying messages, providing important channels for two-way communications between management and employees, energizing the flow of information, and facilitating the sharing of values and vision (Nishikawa, 1995). Working directly under the president's command, members of these offices were the important channels through which to maximize the dissemination of the president's ideas and management philosophy.

Five-point guideline for individual management behaviour

In the summer of 1988, Maeda distributed a booklet called the 'Mini-Book of Guidelines for Managerial Behaviour' to all middle managers, numbering some 2,000. It was intended to increase managerial effectiveness by raising awareness about their jobs, and lists, under five headings, 25 items of short and clear guidelines, in question form, on matters ranging from their roles as leaders to the way they were expected to perform their tasks (Fujisawa, Interviews, 1997; Chiba, 1996), such as,

1   Gaining insight into reality.

2   Having a definite view of one's area of speciality, rather than a generalized and unspecified view.

3   Setting management priorities.

4   Introduction of the principle of competition.

5   'Genba-ism'.

In explaining the issuing of this booklet, Maeda stressed that it was to be used daily by all managers as a clear guide to their conduct as managers. Maeda felt that those who did not understand the principles embodied in the booklet were not fit to be managers in Toray (Nishikawa, 1995). By that time, the measures implemented earlier to bring about a change had already begun to produce effects, but the sudden expansion of activities in the company caused some confusion. Maeda thought that it was timely to review the situation and consolidate achievements so far, as well as to focus the minds of the managers on the need for constant effort at self-improvement (jijo-doryoku).

Institution of new forums

Maeda instituted several new regular meetings, early in the period of his presidency, to improve communication at the upper levels of the company management.

Buchô Konwakai (discussion meeting with departmental heads)

A channel of direct communication which Maeda developed as part of the management change, was a discussion meeting with the departmental heads, in August 1987 (Nishikawa, 1995). As he stated clearly at the beginning, the aim of that meeting was to 'achieve a better understanding of views between him and the senior middle managers, about the future of the company, and the sharing of values'. Since there were about 130 buchô, and as he wished to talk to every one of them, he met ten of them at a time, in a meeting which lasted from noon to 5 pm, at which they were encouraged to air their views thoroughly. He talked to them about his vision, his philosophy and his hopes for the future, to help them understand what his thoughts were, and for them to respond in the same way. During the following four years, he met them all twice, with a third meeting taking place in 1992. This shows the importance he placed on communication at a personal level with senior middle management, to increase mutual understanding and bring about an agreed view about the future of the company. The occasion also provided an important opportunity for the personal development of the managers.

Establishment of the *Fuku Shachô-kai* (vice-presidents' meeting)

Another innovative idea which Maeda instituted at the top of the organization, early in his presidency, that proved very crucial for the success of his presidency, was the *Fuku Shachô-kai*, a regular fortnightly meeting of the representative directors of the company which comprised the chairman, the president and the three vice-presidents. This was not a decision-making organ but acted as a feasibility study group for all new projects involving large investment, and as a nominating committee for a successor to the presidency. It was also a forum where anything could be discussed freely, and to which anyone in the post of *buchô* or its equivalent rank and above could bring any problem, presenting it on the spot. The strategic planning unit reported back and presented its proposals on specific topics that it had been asked by the president to deliberate upon; discussions also ensued, but managers and directors could come for a quick consultation and discussion to sort out their particular problems. It was a kind of emergency appeal board where problems were looked at swiftly, informally, and advice given without delay. The meeting started at 12 noon, but there was no time limit. Discussions could go on for as long as they needed to take. This meeting proved to be tremendously productive, and for the first three years, the discussion sessions regularly went on until 2 or 3 o'clock the following morning, apparently showing that Toray had had problems which required that kind of system in order to address them adequately (K. Maeda, interview, 1997). It is not difficult to imagine that Maeda's own experience of having to gatecrash the management meeting in 1984 was behind the institution of this forum. All topics brought to that meeting are still looked at exhaustively and its value is incontrovertible (K. Maeda, interview, 1997).

Toray also has the usual complement of other meetings at board level. One is *keiei kaigi* (the management meeting) which meets once every two weeks and which is for senior managing directors and above (about 11 people). Management objectives are the main area of discussion here. At *Jômukai* (executive meeting, members of the *keiei kaigi* and the managing directors), which meets once a month, basic proposals for large-scale investment for major plants, substantial changes in management objectives, and major personnel policies such as rotation, promotion and recruitment, which come from *keiei kaigi*, are further discussed and decided upon, these decisions being immediately implemented, without waiting for the next meeting of *torishimariyaku-kai* (directors' board meeting), where the important decisions are endorsed, as is required by the stipulation of commercial law.

To speak frankly at all these meetings was required of all directors. They made comments on matters outside their own territory without hesitation because Maeda encouraged them to do so. He has always regarded problems brought to these meetings as collective matters for management to discuss and resolve, not just the problems, or preserves, of a particular director or functional area. Thus, there are forums for even sensitive topics to be brought up and discussed. Maeda states that his directors do talk! (K. Maeda, interview, 1997).

The building of a formal vision

By 1990, the essential organizational framework for achieving the strategic intent of 'beat Asahi Chemical' had successfully been established, when Maeda decided to build a more comprehensive strategic vision for the company to pursue. He gave the corporate planning unit the task of coming up with an explicit vision statement (Fujisawa, 1998), and after in-depth discussions and consultation within the company on the content of the document, a long-term vision statement, AP-G2000 (Action Plan-G2000) was announced in April 1991.

Looking towards the year 2000, the *vision statement* (Toray, 1991) described the desired image of Toray and the companies of the Toray Group, in the following way:

I Image of Toray and the Toray Group companies in the year 2000

   1 A group of comprehensive chemical companies with three business domains:

      1–1: Integrated materials business
      1–2: Advanced end products business
      1–3: Human services business.

2   A corporate group with a growth superseding the nominal growth rate of the gross national product.

3   A Toray corporate group integrated through federated management.

4   A corporate group with global business activities.

5   A corporate group which plays a positive role in the protection of the global environment.

6   A corporate group which contributes to society as a good corporate citizen, with a lively and attractive culture of its own.

Further, it contained guidelines for management behaviour, and a statement on long-term business strategies.

II   Guidelines for management behaviour

1   Strengthening of the corporate constitution, and a change of attitudes: shaping a creative attitude, and strengthening a business structure.

2   Promotion of group management arrangement: demonstrating a combined strength through the promotion of group management.

3   Globalization.

4   Securing and nurturing the required human resources: shaping a personnel culture which aims to balance the needs of the individual with management requirements.

5   Strengthening of basic, and innovative research: contributing to the creation of a bright future for mankind through technological development.

6   Response to the Global environment: responding positively to move from environment maintenance to environment improvement.

7   Shaping of a new corporate culture.

III   Long-term business strategies

1   Strategic business for expansion.

2   Strategic business for nurture.

IV   Long-term business target.

To attain total group sales of ¥2 trillion by the year 2000.

The key words were globalization, group management and growth. The basic structure for carrying out these strategies was already in place. A growth of more than twofold was seen to be achievable by the end of a ten-year period, at a rate of growth above that of the GNP, at a point in time when the GNP in the previous five years had been over 5 per cent per annum.

Further strategic changes, 1991–1997

Maeda's focus for further revitalization actions centred on the lower-middle management, the *kachô* level, so that his policy of delegating authority for decision-making further down to the *kachô* (the section chiefs) level was initiated. Maeda has always maintained that the *kachô* were not mere managers, but they were the front-line executives, implying that their work was not simply in managing subordinates, but also involved their ability to make their own strategies and decisions, based on their judgement, in order to respond quickly to changes in the operating environment. In order to facilitate such a development, Toray launched two internal systems: the Toray management school, in December 1991 to nurture and develop the *kachô* as executive managers; and the ID2000 initiative, in April 1992, a company-wide movement aimed at creating a new corporate awareness (Nishikawa, 1995).

The Toray management school

The school was established in December 1991 to meet the need of Toray to develop sufficient numbers of well-trained managers to supply the group as a whole. In 1990, Toray sent out about 300 *kachô*-level middle managers to over 170 related companies, on temporary secondment, to act as their top management. With the growth of the group through diversification and internationalization, it was becoming clear that Toray needed to develop more managers to run these companies. The existing on-the-job-training and off-the-job-training methods of developing managers were no longer adequate on their own for meeting the demands of an emerging federal management. The programme was designed to take 20 selected *kachô*, and to run for five months, with participants spending one week at the training centre each month. The emphasis of the course was on the practical application of the knowledge of management learnt in the class, and assessment was centred on a series of tests, and on a group project on practical problems faced by the group companies. Upon completion, the participants were sent to the subsidiaries and affiliates, as their directors and presidents, for a period of about four years to sharpen their management skills. Some were then to return to head office for promotion. The programme is now run at the magnificent human resources development centre complex, completed in 1996, in Mishima (S. Ishizaka, interview, 1997).[7]

The ID2000 initiative

The ID2000 initiative, launched in April 1992, again aimed at revitalizing the *kachô* who, traditionally, had little authority relative to the heavy burden they had to carry, by involving them in management. The thinking behind this was that the vitality of a company would be maximized by those ideas generated spontaneously being communicated swiftly in both upward and downward directions by the lower-middle managers, rather than the normal decision making made at the top being pushed downwards or by bottom-up suggestions. The initiative was centred on the formation of 'junior boards', with a representative from each of the 66 discussion groups which had been organized by dividing about 660 *kachô* into groups of ten members.

Each discussion group was set to examine the problems related to their members, at a meeting held once a month for a whole year. Then one of the members from each group was elected to go forward to become a member of one of the six or seven junior boards, where selected topics relating to actual tasks were thoroughly examined without being constrained in any way, and the outcomes presented at the *fuku shachô-kai*. These outcomes were then directly reflected in executive policy decisions. Maeda regarded the *kachô* being positioned where they were, equally close to the top and to the bottom of the organization, as a vital link between them. He wished to encourage the development of the *kachô's* abilities for 'up-and-down' management and decision-making activities, expecting this initiative to lead to their examining the identity of the nature of their work, and to drawing out their leadership qualities (Nishikawa, 1995). In the FY 1993 Annual Report Maeda referred to this initiative being successfully and fully launched (Annual Report, 1993–1994).

Globalization strategy

Globalization is one of Toray's main growth strategies, involving other products as well as the fibres and textiles operations. Toray implemented the geographic strategy on the basis of three main considerations: cost advantages, and quality maintenance, e.g. in the synthetic fibres and textiles business in Southeast Asia; meeting local market needs, e.g. in plastic films for magnetic recording media in the US, and fibres and textiles in China and in Western and Eastern Europe; and the promotion of international cooperation, e.g. locating where Toray's presence was welcomed, as in the carbon fibre business in France, at the government's request (Seimaru, 1997). During the nine years between 1987 and 1996, Toray's overseas investment totalled more than ¥270 billion (Chiba, 1996), and contributions from overseas sales in the main business domain of fibres and textiles and of plastics, doubled (H. Maeda, interview, 1997). Thus, Toray's globalization and group management strategies are creating a synergy to propel Toray towards its vision of being a 'world class comprehensive chemical industry group'.

The New AP-G2000

In 1996, by which time a long recession had altered the major elements of the economic background to the 1991 vision statement, Toray decided that it would be necessary to re-examine the then vision statement to see if it was still appropriate to guide the direction of the future of the Toray group. Maeda set the corporate planning office the task of reviewing the vision statement in the light of Toray's current business position achieved in the previous five years, and with a forecast of the likely future management environment taken into the account (Fujisawa, 1998).[8] After deliberations lasting 12 months, the conclusion reached was that the direction in which Toray had been going was the right one despite substantial changes in the economic environment. The new AP-G2000, brought out in April 1997, announced that the 1991 vision of becoming a comprehensive chemical industry group of world scale had been realized both nominally and substantively by its ¥1 trillion consolidated sales at the end of the financial year 1996, and in so doing, had achieved their being recognized as the world's biggest synthetic fibres and textiles producer, and a pre-eminent maker of plastics and carbon fibres. It set out its future direction as being 'substantively unchanged from that of 1991', but with an emphasis on the further development of the basic aims (Toray, 1997).

The only change in the vision statement was the removal of the reference to the aimed growth rate being above the nominal growth rate of the GNP. Given the low growth of the economy in the recessionary period in the 1990s, this was sensible. There was no change in the seven subheadings in the guidelines except the addition of a 'safety and prevention of casualty' clause to an existing 'maintenance of environment' in one of the subheadings. The long-term business strategy reflected the technological developments of the early 1990s, particularly in the second domain, with the coming of the information superhighway, and the nurturing of this sector is seen as of strategic importance for the growth of new businesses in the 21st century. The timescale for the long-term business target has understandably been extended to 2010, by which time Toray envisages its group achieving at least ¥2 trillion in sales, and in so doing, the relative contribution of the second domain businesses is seen to increase.

Views on vision and visioning

In interviews conducted by the Cranfield University, it was asked how 'vision' was conceptually regarded and operationally energized. Clearly, the same question had been with Maeda from the beginning of his presidency. However, the use of the English word 'vision' caused a linguistic problem, as its import was confusing. Maeda adopted the Japanese term, 'tenbô', a wide and long distance vista, in which Toray's future image was set, a term which is not unlike the 'industry foresight' of Hamel and Prahalad (Hamel and Prahalad, 1994). According to Hiroshi Maeda, senior managing director, vision is an 'image of what a company could be', which sets the future image of a company and guides the direction the company should go, and helps it generate the strategies to get there, a 'beacon'(Burnes, 1996). However, Maeda, the president, also said that 'we must have a firm business philosophy which will provide the basis on which we could think of our future in terms of different time-scales.' (Maeda, interview, 1997)

In the scheme of visioning at Toray, these time-scales were thought of as three differing lengths of time: short term as in presenting the managers with *problems* to be solved immediately; medium term in which *issues* relating to the strategies were to be dealt with; and long term as pointing the company in the direction leading to the vision. More specifically, the short term was concerned with the budget, which set the targets in clear figures for that year, and which had to be accomplished. The medium-term thinking required the identification of issues, which had to be tackled in the space of the following three to four years in order to build up strategic advantage to achieve the *tenbô*. This had implications for resources, personnel and financial, which had to be provided, but the outcome did not need to be quantified. For example, if an issue was concerned with the inadequacy of technical ability in achieving the vision, then the technical ability had to be improved, but the provision of the means to achieve this will stretch both the ingenuity and competence of the managers. There could have been many issues, and these were kept in view as they progressed, revised if necessary. These issues did not come with numerical values. The *issues identification* emphasized the search for organizational and structural shortfalls, or competitive opportunities, and actions are initiated swiftly to deal with them.

Maeda abolished in the first year the existing practice of three-year corporate planning, which used to be largely controlled by the corporate planning unit (Nishikawa, 1995), to free management thinking from the superficial constraints of seeing the future only in the time-scale of medium-term, and of a current resources, position. 'We identify the issues in terms of our future *tenbô* and the direction of the company's future development, and adjust the medium-term strategies as we proceed. That is how we have been working under this vision concept', said Maeda (Maeda, interview, 1997).

However, Maeda warned that the majority of Japanese business leaders did not necessarily share Toray's concept of *tenbô,* and particularly the way in which it was applied in practice. The visions they held were drawn up in terms of plans and very much constrained, with numerical values and targets, and current resources limitations.

The initial vision of regaining the industry leadership was a 'given', but the means of achieving it had to be built up. The establishment of the *fuku shachô-kai*, reorganizing the corporate planning office, and the issuing of the five-point booklet, together with the measures to strengthen operational efficiency, were the bricks and mortar of advantages which built Toray's basic competitiveness. Maeda's refusal to accept that the textile industry had 'matured' and 'was declining' has echoes in Hamel and Prahalad's argument that these definitions were executives' conception of the industry, not the reality of the industry as a whole (Hamel and Prahalad, 1989), and his conviction enabled him to set the course of Toray's business in the opposite direction. Maeda's industry foresight informed him that there were emerging markets with vast growth potentials. Maeda moved into these by spearheading the expansion of offshore production, to exploit the first mover advantages into the market to build competitiveness.

When the internal systems had been revitalized and employees were completely shaken out of their apathy through the symbolic actions and actual measures that Maeda continued to take, confidence was built up, and a much more far-reaching vision was prepared. The resultant vision statement could be seen both as a declaration of intent, and as the aspiration of the management and employees of the Toray group, committed to the vision of the man who led them.

The process of the identification of issues in terms of the medium-term strategies and informed by the corporate vision at decision making is shown in this example where a large capital investment project, such as locating a major plant in a new overseas territory, was considered. Hiroshi Maeda, a senior managing director in charge of related businesses headquarters for fibres and textiles, and plastics production, explained how the projects for locating in China (and, later in the Czech Republic) were conceived in terms of globalization and group management objectives, which were very much a part of Toray's vision and a strategic choice for growth. When a new large-scale plant investment was considered, a capital depreciation period of ten years would be in the minds of senior directors, and they would try to visualize how the company's situation might be in ten years' time before deciding to invest. H. Maeda said, 'of course no one could be certain, but unless we had a vision of how it could be, we would not even begin to think about capital investment.' In order to conceive that image, the directors had to make a strenuous effort to cultivate the ability to make an informed guess about that future based on available but imperfect current information. In such a project, many people with practical ability were involved, in the earlier stages, in drawing up the framework for the future business, basing it largely on the existing resources. However, the task of finally deciding what the company's future should look like rested on the shoulders of a few people. The body to initiate this process was the *fuku shachô-kai* whose members examined and studied the pertinent factors involved in any proposal very thoroughly, in the light of the corporate vision. Once the project had been carefully deliberated upon and evaluated, its deliberation was passed to *keiei kaigi*, where the merits and demerits of the proposal were further studied and debated in the light of the overall vision, and a consensus as to whether to go with the plan or not was reached. If affirmative, then the proposal passed to the *jômukai* which examined the operational implications in great detail, identifying the issues involved in implementation, and a decision taken. It may have involved the stretching of resources beyond the then current means, but these would have to be identified as a series of medium-term issues. Those aspects of the proposal which came under the category of items requiring the approval of the *torishimariyaku-kai* (the board meeting) would be submitted to it at its next meeting, but the decisions made at the *jômukai* were set in motion for immediate action. In this way, directors had a long-term vision which drove the direction of decisions and at the same time, the corresponding operational plans to go with it. H. Maeda was convinced that it was the 'right way to do it'.

Describing the way in which a vision works, H. Maeda said, 'We keep the image in our minds at all times when we take decisions on various business matters. Keeping the picture of our company in say, ten years' time, we decide on management strategy and business policy'. Commenting on how the sharing of the vision was to be brought about, he stressed the importance of the quality and the role of leadership of the president:

> In a company of this size, the leadership of the president is absolutely crucial. He must be able to exercise his leadership at a fairly practical level, and have a management philosophy as well as an ability to manage. Another important quality he needs is the ability to win the hearts and minds of all employees, and to inspire them to focus on the shared goal. (H. Maeda, 1997)

Jaques and Clement describe the exercise of leadership account-ability in role-relationships as 'earned authority' (Jaques and Clement, 1991). Maeda, the president, also accepts the importance of the calibre of top management,

> How the company is run depends very largely on the ability and philosophical belief of the president who is at the top of the organization. I believe that a CEO must be prepared to hear everyone's views, let them discuss thoroughly matters that are important to management, and get totally involved in the process of building up of a consensus among the directors. This will ensure that the future direction of the firm will become firmly established on shared values, but the important point is that there must be constant effort on the CEO's part to create and maintain a forum at which all directors can express their views freely to the CEO. (Maeda, interview, 1997)

This was precisely what the Cranfield research found lacking in the majority of Japanese corporate boards (Kakabadse, et al., 1996). Such a forum at Toray was the *fuku shachô-kai*, which was open to all directors and to heads of departments.

Leadership

On leadership, Maeda, the president said that: 'There are many facets to leadership, but to put it simply, it is the ability of the leaders to anticipate what is coming, and the possession of the sense of balance in their judgement.'

Maeda considered that a president must have what he called an innovative sense of balance rather than a conservative one. The latter leads to judging the future of a company on an extension of what has always been the way things were. Astute managers always take an innovative balance of things. The environment in which the business operates, be it the economy, politics, society, both domestic and international, is continually evolving, and sometimes even changes drastically in unpredictable ways. The manager must change the balance between existing things and something new, in the light of what he sees coming. Good judgement is absolutely necessary. What supports good judgement is an ability to anticipate what the future has in store. This means that managers must constantly be learning, and must pool their knowledge as a team[9]. 'Those who study the present against history are wise, as Bismarck has said. The foolish learn only from their own limited experience. But there are business leaders who do not learn even from their experience.' (Maeda, interview, 1997).

Yasuhiko Fujisawa, managing director, put his definition of leadership in a slightly different way. He believed that it was a combination of an ability to anticipate what the future might bring, a strong sense of mission, and considerateness for the well-being of others in the company. A leader must be able to inspire those around him with a sense of mission and take them with him. His sense of mission would be underpinned by the vision, which in its turn is informed by his ability to anticipate the future (Fujisawa, interview, 1997). He admitted that the ability to generate trust and confidence among those whom one led was at the centre of leadership in Japan, and consideration for others helped this process. The importance of the quality of leadership is emphasized through Toray's evaluation system as the ability to inspire those below, and an incapability to do so is regarded as a fatal shortcoming in a leader.

Conclusion

It would be difficult to talk about the outstanding transformation Toray has achieved since 1987 without referring to the quality of leadership of the President, Katsunosuke Maeda. His seemingly unorthodox and sometimes drastic policies may not have endeared him to those who bore the brunt of change. However, he was unwavering in his resolve to pursue the vision he established, and this has driven the changes the company needed to move successfully towards that goal.

Toray is now committed to building further competitiveness through the synergy of globalization and group management strategies under the new AP-G2000, which gives them an ability to deal with future difficulties through the organic integration of the worldwide member companies. But the increasing complexity of managing a large group of far flung companies holds many issues for Toray to face, some, like that of globalized personnel management,[10] are already clear and others as yet unseen. However, Maeda is confident that the group will be steered successfully towards that *tenbô* under the leadership of his chosen successor, Katsuhiko Hirai, the first president with a non-science and engineering background for 30 years (Maeda, interview, 1997).

Notes

1. In Dempsey, 1997, and Maeda, interview, 1997.
2. Only Toray and Kurare were permitted access to nylon and vinylon industries during the Second World War by MITI's predecessor, Shôkô-shô. Toray also entered the polyester market, in 1957, together with Teijin in cooperation with each other, chosing a common trade mark of Tetolon, and jointly controlling the market. When the demand for synthetic fibres expanded, MITI permitted first-movers only to enlarge their plants, to avoid excess competition. Toray greatly benefited from these government policies (Suzuki, 1995).
3. 'Mae' and 'katsu' are the first character of both Maeda's surname and personal names in Japanese.
4. Chiba, 1996. This sounded unreasonably optimistic and rather incautious to his colleagues.
5. This section is based largely on Chiba, 1996.
6. Some became teachers in major universities, others presidents of listed companies. Many of those who changed their jobs during the 'bubble' years were grateful for the greater opportunities they had in finding an alternative job.
7. This information was given to the author while visiting the company in June 1997.
8. This was given in a letter from him in February 1998.
9. What has been happening under Maeda has the echoes of Senge's concept of learning organization (Senge, 1992).
10. Opening the way to key posts at Toray headquarters for the indigenous CEOs

of the foreign subsidiaries has long been Maeda's concern. The recent assignments of Rhone-Poulenc top management to the headquarters certainly indicates that this has been put into practice, in order to strengthen the organic integration of the group companies (The *Nikkei Weekly*, 16 February 1998)

References

Burnes, B. (1996), *Managing Change: A Strategic Approach to Organizational Development and Renewal*, 2nd Edition, Pitman, London.

Chiba, A. (1996), Tôre fukkatsu ni miru 'sakabari keiei' no gokui (The Ultimate Essence of the 'Management against the Trend' seen in the Revival of Toray), *Keieijuku*, October, pp. 116–121.

Dempsey, E. (1997), 'Toray Industries: How the World's Largest Textile Manufacturer Meets the Complicated Global Challenge', *ITS Textile Leader*, January, pp. 30–41.

Fujisawa, Y. (1998), a private letter sent to the author, January.

Hamel, G. and Prahalad, C.K. (1989), 'Strategic Intent' *Harvard Business Review*, May–June, pp. 63–76.

Hamel, G. and Prahalad, C.K. (1994), *Competing for the Future*, Harvard Business School Press, Cambridge, MA.

Hasegawa, H. (1997), Keiei o kataru – Tôre Shachô, Maeda Katsunosuke-shi (Talking about Management – by Katsunosuke Maeda, President of Toray), *Nikkei Sangyô Shinbun*, 26 May, p. 23.

Ishizaka, S. (1996), 'Management Development in Toray – Now and in the Future', *The Journal of Management Development*, Vol. 15, No. 8, pp. 38–46.

Ishizaka, S. (1997), an interview by the author at the Human Resources Development Centre in Mishima.

Jaques, E. and Clement, S.D. (1991), *Executive Leadership*, Blackwell Business, Oxford.

Kakabadse, A.P., Okazaki-Ward, L.I. and Myers, A. (1996), *Japanese Business Leaders*, Thomson International Business Press, London.

Kanno, K. (1998), 'Fibre Maker Aims for Top in Polyester Film', *The Nikkei Weekly*, 16 February, p. 7.

Kôhôshitsu, (1997), *Pîpuru* (People), Toray Industries Inc., May.

Ministry of Finance (1986–1996), *Yûka shôken hôkokusho – Tôre Kabushiki Kaisha* (Reports on Company Stocks and Activities – Toray Industries Inc), Ministry of Finance.

Nikkei Business (1997), Henshûchô intabyû – Maeda Katsunosuke-shi, Tôre Shachô: 'Fukakachi tsuke Ajia ni taikô – ryûtsû kaikaku sureba mada tatakaeru (Chief Editor interview – Katsunosuke Maeda, President of Toray, 'Compete with Asian Countries by Adding Value – We Can Still Compete Through Changing the Distribution System'), *Nikkei Business*, 17 March, pp. 60–63.

Okazaki-Ward, L.I. (1997), A Collection of unpublished interviews with K. Maeda, H. Maeda and Y. Fujisawa, *Cranfield University*. References from these are shown as 'K. Maeda, interview, 1997, 'H. Maeda, interview, 1997', and 'Fujisawa, interview, 1997', respectively.

Seimaru, K. (1997) Maeda Katsunosuke – Kokusaiteki 'renbô keiei' o mezasu (Katsunosuke Maeda – Aiming at International 'Federal Management'), *Chûô Kôrôn*, June, pp. 192–201.

Senge, P.M. (1992), *The Fifth Discipline*, Century Business, London.

Suzuki, T. (1995), 'Toray Corporation: Seeking First-mover Advantage', in Yuzawa, T. *Japanese Business School – The Evolution of a Strategy*, Routledge, London, pp. 81–93.

Toray Industries Inc., Annual Reports, from 1986 to 1996.

Toray Industries Inc., (1991), *AP-G2000, Chôki Bijon* (AP-G2000, A Long-Term Vision Statement), Toray Industries Inc., April.

Toray Industries Inc., (1997), *Shin AP-G2000, Shin Chôki Bijon* (New AP-G2000, A New Long-Term Vision Statement), Toray Industries Inc., April.

Yoshida, H. (1996), Batteki no kenkyû – Tôre Maeda Katsunosuke ni nukareta 14-nin no senpai yakuin no yukue (A Study on Fast-Track Promotion – Where the 14 Senior Directors Went after They were Passed Over by Katsunosuke Maeda at Toray), *Kieiejuku*, May, pp. 42–45.

CHAPTER NINE

A vision of learning

A.L. Buley

Where There is no Vision the People Perish. (Proverbs XXIX verse 18)

And the Lord answered me and said, – write the vision and make it plain upon tables, that he may run that readeth it. (Habakkuk, II verse 2)

One of the recurring themes of those studies of successful companies which comprise so much of the substance of the strategic management literature is that 'excellent companies' have invariably been founded, often by one man, on the basis of a very clear vision of what it is destined to become and a set of principles which laid out, with unerring foresight, the sure path for the fulfilment of its destiny. Moreover for those organizations which did not have the benefit of such auspicious origins, 'vision' is apparently an equally necessary requirement in those who are given the responsibility for masterminding their subsequent promotion to the premier league.

If this visionary quality is indeed an essential requirement of successful strategic management, it raises the rather important question as to what it actually comprises, whether it is something that can be learned and, if so, how it can be developed, at least in those who are destined to those levels of influence at which it would appear to be such a critical factor for organizational survival.

In some cases, the founding father's vision is frequently represented in such a way as to appear almost as an act of 'hubris' – a commitment to a project which at first sight seems so disproportionate to the current reality of what any 'rational and objective observer' might then have seemed possible as to pose a question about the sanity of the individual in question.

The implication is that these were men (so far they have almost invariably been men) possessed of a combination of intellectual insight and intuitive capacity.

A similar commitment was demonstrated in 1945 by two Japanese entrepreneurs, Masuru Ibuka and Akio Morita. They had the vision of building a company that would enable engineers to feel the joy of technological innovation and to apply technology in ways that would serve the needs and aspirations of post-war Japanese society. After many trials and tribulations, they brought to market the first transistorized pocket radio, the Trinitron television, the Walkman personal stereo and a whole host of other products which, through the miracle of 'miniaturization', have helped to transform lifestyles not just in Japan, but across the world. Initially, they named their company 'Tokyo Tsushin Kyogo' ('Tokyo Telecommunications Engineering Corporation'). In the late 1950s (when it was still a small company almost unknown outside Japan), it took the costly step of changing its name to The Sony Corporation, because it was more 'easily pronounceable in foreign lands'.

In the search for the Holy Grail of business success, this mixture of foresight and principle has assumed magical properties without which no self-respecting company should be caught unawares. The consequence has been a worldwide vision industry which has left some more than a little disillusioned and others querying the fundamental validity of the concept.

In a recent piece in the *Financial Times*, the journalist Lucy Kellaway delivered a timely note of scepticism when she wrote 'the very idea of visions – and missions and value statements and all the rest of it – has always made me feel uncomfortable. The jargon is repulsive and the idea of distilling a complex pragmatic world of business into a few sentences has always seemed a peculiar thing for anyone to want to do.' (Kellaway, 1997)

The trigger for this observation was an article by Professor Charles Schwenk (Schwenk, 1997) in which he argues that a powerful vision can actually do damage to an organization. In his view, by creating and communicating a clear vision, and by creating conditions which require his 'followers' to commit themselves to that vision, a leader is in danger of imposing a uniformity of thinking and of stifling healthy debate which can ultimately have dire consequences. Quoting Hayek's *'The Road to Serfdom'* (Hayek, 1944), he compares a strong vision thrust down the throats of a workforce as akin to the worst excesses of totalitarian regimes. Imposed values, he argues, destroy dissent and discussion which are essential to creative decision making: 'for this reason strong leaders are not to be trusted. What we want is weaker leadership.'

Another writer who comes to a similar conclusion, by a different route, is Ralph Stacey (Stacey, 1992), who bases his argument on chaos theory. Stacey sees effective organizations as 'spontaneously self-organizing systems operating within the boundaries between total order and total randomness'. This 'area of bounded instability' is technically known as 'chaos'. In this view, strategic success depends on whether, at any given moment, the conditions exist to enable largely unpredictable situations to be effectively exploited as they arise.

Basically, Stacey is saying that the long-term future is unknowable.[1] Therefore any sense that long-term outcomes are controllable is an illusion and any idea of individuals or organizations *purposefully striving* towards a long-term vision is also an illusion. Instead, he argues that strategic management can only be about one thing – creating those conditions of bounded instability which allow new strategies to emerge as a spontaneous response to the dynamic interaction between the external forces of change and internal processes of learning and political control – which together legitimize initiative and determine the allocation of resources.

The role of top management is therefore to deal with *current issues which have long-term consequences*. Any attempt by top management to exercise control over the longer-term destiny of the organization, other than in these ways, will be counterproductive because they will undermine and constrain the very conditions which are the source of fresh opportunity.[2]

The 'post-modernist' school of organization theory approaches these ideas from yet another perspective based on the notion of organizations as being no more (or perhaps one should say *no less*) than a dynamic set of transactions based on relationships between individuals, the resultant of which is a restlessly evolving process of change. From this perspective, the organization is an (ambiguously defined[3]) arena within which multiple motives and aspirations (i.e. personal visions) exist and where as many 'agendas' are being acted out as there are organizational actors and relationships between them.

Because each individual has his or her own way of interpreting the world, any attempt to impose a common vision will, at best, result in the collective acceptance of the lowest common denominator of these individual world views and, at worst, result in human beings being treated as mere cogs in a totalitarian machine, which is both dehumanizing and, in the longer term, counter-productive.

From none of these perspectives does the notion of vision and values[4] emerge with credibility or credit.

At first sight, these views equate to the sort of heresy that brought the full weight of the Inquisition upon the head of Galileo when he supported the Copernican theory that the earth revolves around the sun. They sound like abstract theorizing and contravene the received wisdom communicated with increasing fervour by successive waves of highly articulate and respected management prophets such as Tom Peters and Bob Waterman. Initially[5] this school of thought seemed to downplay the importance of individually motivated action in favour of the imposition of a superordinate set of 'vision and values' designed to channel the behaviour of all its members to within a single agenda and towards demanding goals. One of the mechanisms for achieving this was 'empowerment'.[6] This they argue, is the hallmark of 'high performing organizations' and the starting point for any significant 'organizational transformation'.[7] Organizations need visions and they need visionary leaders to proclaim them.

For most of us, this message does have considerable face validity. Surely, it is strong visionary leadership which, to adopt the phrase of Peters and Waterman, 'yields extraordinary performance from otherwise ordinary people'. What was Churchill, arguably the greatest leader of the 20th century, doing in his wartime speeches if not communicating a clear vision and appealing to a set of values when he talked about the British Empire's 'finest hour'; likewise President Kennedy[8] when he promised to put a man on the moon (*and bring him back again* – an important detail that), and Martin Luther King, who 'had a dream'. Did not Henry the Fifth make a bit of name for himself as a leader when he addressed the troops before Agincourt? So Shakespeare would have us believe.

What could be clearer or more authoritative than the two Old Testament quotations which stand at the head of this chapter. The parallel with modern times is perhaps not overcontrived, for the Old Testament chronicles the history of an emerging nation afflicted by great uncertainty, internal dissent and the breakdown of authority. Does that sound familiar?

Turning back to the realities of modern business organizations, it is not difficult to accept the basic idea which underpins the rhetoric of vision and values. On its own, the goal of profitability, or its latter-day surrogate, shareholder value, provides little in the way of strategic direction for a company and even less as a concept to inspire the wholehearted commitment of the organization's members. For both these reasons, companies need a more precise idea of their purpose to guide strategy, to provide unity among disparate personal motivations and ultimately give meaning to the existence of the organization.

Over the last decade, there can be few long-established organizations for which the world has not become infinitely more complex, fluid and unpredictable. Competitive forces have threatened to overwhelm even such dominant businesses as IBM. Many more have been transformed out of recognition while some have failed to survive at all.

In such circumstances, for many working in those organizations, the future has appeared, not merely highly unpredictable but *totally unknowable*. Under these circumstances all the old rules go out of the window and all bets are cancelled. Ambiguity and uncertainty are the recurring reality with which we all have to come to terms.

The immediate human response to ambiguity is to attempt to reduce it by seeking a new source of certainty. It is in this climate that the charismatic leader is particularly welcomed – the messiah destined to restore the fortunes of the chosen. Frequently the leader is an outsider, untainted by the errors of the previous regime and with some manifest source of wisdom or expertise to reinforce his credibility. Continuing the Old Testament theme, Moses was a leader who was able to meet such challenges in exactly this way, not least because of the unique advantage of his direct access to the ultimately well-informed and influential Mentor who provided him with a perfectly scripted set of vision and values.

So we are faced with a paradox. There is one school of thought which argues that uncertainty, ambiguity and internal dissent (which some might even describe as chaos) are, not merely uncomfortable, but positively dysfunctional and for which the remedy is strong leadership (based on a clear vision) and conformity to a prescribed text.

The alternative, less fashionable, view argues an exactly opposite case – that because the future is unknowable, and because human beings are human, we must learn not merely to tolerate uncertainty but positively to exploit it. We do this by allowing, even positively encouraging, ambiguity in the interpretation of meaning, diversity of thought and eccentricity[9] of behaviour and by exercising what in the conventional sense is termed weak leadership. By allowing 'a thousand flowers to bloom' we increase the likelihood of innovation, of flexibility and speed of response and of sound objective judgement in the making of crucially important decisions. The role of top management is both to nurture and to channel this creativity in ways which from their, albeit limited, perspective appear to have the most favourable longer-term consequences.

Surely both points of view cannot be correct. Where does that leave us with regard to the questions which were posed at the beginning of this chapter?

Two of the most influential writers on strategic management in recent years have been the duo, Gary Hamel and C.K. Prahalad (1994).

They do seem to believe in the importance of vision as a prediction of a future state. They see this as an 'assumption base' which enables managers to answer three critical questions. First 'what new types of customer benefit should the organization be seeking to provide in 5, 10 or 15 years? Second, what new competencies will be needed (to be developed or acquired) in order to offer those benefits to customers? Third, how should the organization seek to reconfigure its interface with customers in order to be able to deliver those benefits?

They argue that no company can survive, let alone thrive, without a well-articulated point of view about tomorrow's opportunities and challenges. At the same time they distinguish between such well-considered prescience and those constructed visions 'that are as grandiose as they are poorly conceived'. They are critical of companies that seem to prefer rhetoric to action. Like Lucy Kellaway therefore, they see 'vision' as devalued terminology because it has been used, all too often, as no more than 'window dressing for the CEO's own ego-driven acquisition binge' supported by a set of rather empty straplines and catch phrases which often have little foundation, either in current organizational reality or in any concerted attempt to create such a reality. For this reason they prefer to use the term 'foresight' or more specifically 'industry foresight'.

What these two thinkers particularly believe in is something they call 'Strategic Intent' and with which they associate the notion of 'stretch' (Hamel and Prahalad, 1994). In adopting this phrase, they are apparently distinguishing between 'vision as destination' and 'vision as destiny'. In their view

> strategic intent must be a goal that commands the respect and allegiance of every employee. The destination must not only be different, it must also be worthwhile ... strategic intent is as much about the creation of meaning for employees as it is about the establishment of direction (ibid.).

But the key premise upon which Hamel and Pralahad base their thesis, that the long-term future is *not* totally unknowable, has to be questioned. It is possible, they assert, for managers to read the future. Unfortunately, they provide only the sketchiest advice on how this may be achieved. This seems a great pity as there must be a lot of people who would like to know more about how to manage this particular trick.

Arguably, all companies which enjoyed even a brief period of success were able to exploit an idea which fitted an opportunity which was then transformed into reality through acts of leadership. But as organizations grow, leadership becomes more diffuse. All individual leaders, no matter how charismatic or 'visionary', eventually die and all great ideas eventually become obsolete. One of the distinguishing features of the business era we have now entered is that the rate of obsolescence of great ideas has increased dramatically and is still increasing. And as great ideas become obsolete, so do the formerly great organizations which were founded upon them. Many of the companies which were household names and whose stock was most energetically sought only 30 years ago no longer exist. New technology has replaced their traditional products and processes, more dynamic competitors have introduced new ways of finding, serving and retaining customers. Yet some organizations, despite encountering similar setbacks, have weathered these storms and continue to retain their dominant positions in their chosen sectors.

Another duo of American writers, James Collins and James Porras (1994) published an in-depth study of 18, nearly all American, such companies. They called them 'Visionary Companies'. These are companies which have prospered over long periods of time, through multiple product life cycles and multiple generations of active leaders. As it happens, they do include IBM, Ford and Sony but not Federal Express or Apple Computers whose early successes are also ascribed to visionary founders. Each was made the subject of a comparative historical study (over several decades) with another less consistently successful, but nevertheless well-regarded and profitable, company operating in the same industry sector. In most cases, therefore, the comparator company was a direct competitor with the visionary company in question and had been for many years.

Collins and Porras (1994) point out that the visionary companies do not have perfect unblemished records – most of those in their sample have, at some point in their histories, faced major crises, in some cases even near bankruptcy, subsequently to recover. They all demonstrate an extraordinary ability to bounce back from adversity. Their record in creating shareholder value over a period of several decades is significantly superior to the comparator companies, even more so in relation to the general run of stock market performance.

The research goes back to the early years of each of these companies and demonstrates that the visionary companies share with each other a number of characteristics which are not shared by the comparator companies. Four are of particular relevance to this chapter.

The first is that, contrary to popular myth, the early years of these companies were not unduly successful, unlike say Apple Computers and Federal Express (or for that matter of Netscape or Peoples Express). Indeed there was a significant tendency for them to take off relatively slowly and more painfully in relation to their, ultimately less successful, competitors. For some, such as Sony, 3M and even IBM (or rather CTR), the early years were a real struggle characterized by a series of successive market failures.

Secondly, these companies have been remarkably consistent in pursuing a policy of promotion from within, at all levels, including the appointment of successive generations of chief executives who were long-term employees of the organization. Thirdly, they have a significant tendency to invest much more heavily than their comparator companies in training and development for all categories of employee.

Fourthly, despite the doubts expressed by Charles Schwenk (Schwenk, 1997), these companies do exhibit some of the characteristics of cults. They make very heavy demands on their employees, both in terms of the goals they are expected to achieve, individually and collectively, and in the extent to which they are required to 'buy into' certain characteristic norms of outlook and behaviour. These, in the mythology of the organization, are linked to the strong beliefs of the founding father(s) and are seen as central to the companies' continuing success. These value-based norms have become essential criteria in the initial selection and subsequent retention of individuals within the organization. Those who do not buy in, soon leave either from their own choice or because they are required to. Surprisingly, however, there seems to be absolutely no commonality in these espoused values. What works for one company is distinctly different from what works for another, unless of course, the different words disguise more fundamental issues of outlook and behaviour which they do all hold in common.

Interestingly, there is no evidence to suggest that these companies are any more successful than any others at planning the future. Indeed their success seems to lie much more in their capacity for enlightened opportunism – 'to be able to respond to the moment'. This supports the long held and well articulated arguments of thinkers such as Henry Mintzberg (Mintzberg, 1994) and, for that matter Stacey's chaos model.

In a recent article (1997), Jules Goddard points out that much of what has been researched and written on how to create successful organizations (i.e. on strategic management) is primarily a description of 'successfulness' rather than a prescription for success. It clearly and comprehensively describes how successful organizations character-istically behave (thereby providing all sorts of models for others to emulate) but has relatively little to say on how the successful organization got to behave like that in the first place and therefore how others could do so also (other than appoint a visionary leader with a good track record). It also tends to be light on how, over an extended period of time, these qualities are able to be transmitted from one generation of managers to the next.

He quotes a leader article in the *Economist* magazine, apparently designed to 'bring businessmen back to basics'. He quotes the article as proposing six questions which, it asserts, good managements should keep permanently at the top of their agenda. Rather like the famous aphorism about the three secrets of successful retailing ('location, location and location'), it suggests that three of these six should be the repeated mantra 'How is our product?'

While acknowledging the self-evident truth of these observations about the importance of successfully differentiating product, Goddard points out that that they are not terribly helpful because 'sustained success relies upon a deep-seated competence to produce an endless stream of strongly branded products that work'.

He points out that the prime responsibility of management is 'continually nurturing and exploiting this competence through investment in skills, processes and systems'. 'If the latter are mundane' he suggests, 'the company is unlikely to create products, services and brands that are other than mundane themselves.' 'The continual stream of great products and services from highly visionary companies stems from them being outstanding organizations, not the other way around.'

Conclusions – the nature of vision

Where then does this lead us and what conclusions can we reach about the nature of this much used and abused term, 'vision'. I believe it has four rather different interpretations. All are important but before we get too excited about the notion, we need to be very clear about how they differ and why they may or may not be relevant.

Vision as focus

Despite their rather more ambitious language, Hamel and Prahalad's notion of industry foresight seems to equate with Stacey's (1992) view of strategic management as 'identifying and focusing on current events which have longer-term consequences'. To do this requires a diligent monitoring of trends in the wider environment, scenario planning, conducting surveys and blue skies R&D, brainstorming and sharing information (especially the latter). Surely, this is not so much about anticipating the future as reading the best available form book before placing your bets on a horse.

Many would regard this as a reasonable definition of what strategic planning should be about. It is continuous, based on monitoring incremental change, involves regular discussion and debate and, as pointed out by Arie de Geus (1988), is primarily a process of learning. As

Goddard so rightly points out, this requires highly developed and effective organizational systems and processes and depends on the micro-inputs of many people rather than relying on the special expertise of a few. It is therefore a feature of visionary companies rather than of visionary individuals.

Vision as competence

Nevertheless, individual managers and executives do, through their role in the organization's political processes, ultimately have to exercise judgement[10] about how to interpret the present in order to commit resources for the future.

This requires a quality of conceptual and analytic thinking which is also sometimes termed 'Vision' (sometimes also known as the 'Helicopter Quality') It is about the ability to think holistically, to distil meaning from ambiguity and to handle increasing levels of complexity by thinking in successively higher levels of abstraction.[11] It requires an ability to exercise both imagination and logic about issues which do have significant longer-term consequences and ultimately to have the confidence to make decisions. There is a lot of evidence that, unlike some other competencies which can be learned and expanded throughout life, these intellectual qualities are largely determined by the age of about 20 and that they are a (if not the) key limiting factor in determining an individual's long-term potential for senior management. A former head of recruitment for Shell has estimated that only about 2.0 per cent of the graduates who apply to Shell worldwide for employment possess these qualities to an extent which, even when other factors are favourable, would enable them to reach one of the higher levels of senior management in that company. For the highest level, the percentage is no more than 0.05 per cent.

If you want this sort of vision, and you surely do, then look to the way you select your young entrants and subsequently develop them through the provision of a combination of rich and varied experience coupled with numerous opportunities to reflect upon it and to draw lessons from it.

Vision as destination

'Vision as destination' implies the ability to 'envision' and describe a future world with such brilliance and clarity that others will be compelled to follow the creator of the vision in order to inhabit the promised land.

It has all the characteristics of myth and, like most myths, it has some basis in substance but, in reality, is rather rare. The reason it is rare is not because people are not capable of having such dreams nor even because unforeseen circumstances prevent them from being realized (although that is often the case) but because, on those occasions when the promised land is attained, it frequently proves inadequate to build and sustain a community there.

Even if the dream is realized for a time, the chances of it being repeated by the same individual seem vanishingly small. In recent history, Steve Jobs, one of the founders of Apple Computers, probably came closest but it appears that in the end others have hijacked his dream and fashioned it in different colours.

Vision as destiny

On the other hand, 'vision as destiny' is real. The vision lies not in 'the world that awaits us' but 'the sort of people we are and the sort of purpose for which we exist'. Moreover the purpose is not distinct from the values – it is a direct consequence of them. It implies not the creation of an end state, or even a series of end-states, so much as an avowed, mutually beneficial and open-ended relationship with the world at large.

Collins and Porras (1994) provide strong evidence to show that, despite the sinister undertones and the concerns expressed about them, the existence of an almost 'cult-like' set of strong core values is highly correlated with significant and lasting organizational success. As in the case of the early days of Sony, the values are the reason for the organization's existence rather than, as they are often presented, the means to an end. The message is clear, 'we exist for a purpose which is to harness technology in the service of the Japanese people – we will be successful because we are the people we are. We are not yet clear how, but we will succeed in our purpose.'

'Vision as destiny' is a very different way of thinking from 'vision as destination'. It was the essence of Churchill's leadership. He believed it was the destiny of the British people to win the war. He didn't know how, where or when. He just believed it – and because he believed it, so did the British people. Or could it have been the other way round? The answer is academic. The important thing is that Churchill succeeded in mobilizing the energy and courage of the British people to overcome disasters and setbacks until (with a good deal of outside help!) the war was won.

The powerful message of Collins and Porras's (1994) recent research is that, in the visionary companies, the core values they identified have been articulated at an early stage of the organization's history. This is the critical role of the founding fathers, who strongly believed that the sort of behaviour represented by the values they espoused would bring success as its own reward[12].

If you believe that 'these sort of people have a destiny to be successful', you go to some lengths to develop a core of people who share your values. In the early days, everyone learns from the failures while rejoicing in the successes. By their own behaviour and enthusiasms, as the organization begins to grow, this critical group of people transmits its values to others, many of whom will have been attracted to the organization by its ethos as well as its growing success. Those who join 'by accident' will either become believers or leave.

Over time, the values become part of the 'genetic code' of the organization. Because of the promotion from within policy, new generations of CEOs reinforce the values in their behaviour and in the messages they convey. The values become an integral part of the selection, reward and promotion mechanisms of the organization. The people who prosper do so, not because they are sycophants but because there is a natural fit between their abilities, their values and the sort of behaviour which brings success in that particular organization.

There are two possible objections to this scenario. The first is that there seems no particular reason why so many different sets of values, reflecting the particular beliefs of a number of rather different individuals, should all be so effective as the driving force for exceptional achievement. The second is the objection posed by Charles Schwenk; namely, that the creation of such a strongly value-driven culture inevitably creates an inflexible, self-absorbed, even totalitarian community and encourages 'group-think'. This surely is the death knell for successful innovation and realistic and objective decision making.

Schwenk is surely correct – this is one highly probable outcome and no doubt accounts for many promising organizations which failed to prosper – including perhaps Apple Computers. It is also the reason why so many so-called culture change programmes are unsuccessful. Attempting to impose a set of values on an organization is about as crude, and doomed to failure, as trying to conduct brain surgery with a pneumatic drill.

So why are these dire consequences not observed in Collins and Porras's visionary companies? Their research shows that there is one value which every one of the organizations have in common – though interestingly it is not classified as a value. This is the value of personal development and organizational learning.

One of the characteristics of the visionary companies identified by Collins and Porras is that of high aspiration. They call it 'setting Big Hairy Aspirational Goals'. But they note that the goals are continually evolving; things never stand still. People and teams (and the whole organization) are continually seeking new challenges and being held accountable for achieving them. This can only happen if individuals are continually learning and developing themselves. Otherwise it could not work. So everyone is encouraged to develop and be successful in an organization for which they already feel a natural affinity. That is highly motivating and a recipe for continuing success.

A characteristic of these organizations is that they were not all that successful in their years. They had failures. The best way to overcome failure is to get together as a team, think about what you did wrong, challenge your assumptions, devise a new scheme and try again – and again – and again. You learn to learn not only individually but collectively. All the visionary companies recognize *the value of learning*. This is why they invest highly in the training and development of all their people.

This provides the answer to the remaining question: Why have the values continued to remain relevant over all these years? That was, of course, the visionary genius of the founding fathers. They, no doubt, had their own preconceptions of what it takes to be successful in their particular chosen field and their values reflect that as well as their own personalities and ethical beliefs. So they expressed their values as the basic blueprint for the people and the behaviour that fitted the sort of business they wanted to create.

But their values are not constraining – they are enabling. While they remain powerful guides to 'the way we do things around here', the early struggles created a climate of collective learning and sharing which acted as a catalyst for continual development. So it became possible for the values to be continually revisited and reinterpreted in ways that remained not only true to the spirit but were also relevant in a modern world. This was what IBM seems to have lost sight of for a time.

So it appears that visionary companies are sustained, not by a vision of the future but by a vision of the past – a sense of purpose and principles of behaviour laid down by their founding fathers. But it appears they all share one value in common. Whether explicit or not (interestingly there is not a single reference to it in the index of Collins and Porras's book), the most fundamental characteristic of the visionary companies seems to be a commitment to the value of learning, and the whole point about learning is that it is about creating the future.

So far this chapter is open to exactly the criticism highlighted earlier. It is a description of successfulness rather than a prescription for how to become successful – other than to have been founded by someone with shrewd judgement and a strong set of personal values and to have struggled somewhat in the early years. This is not helpful for the senior management of an already corporate organization seeking to improve.

Vision and the value of learning

Because the future is largely unknowable, we cannot set precise long-term goals nor can we lay out the strategies for achieving them in terms of predictable options and logically determined outcomes. Strategic management therefore has to be conceived as something akin to a process of enlightened opportunism. Strategic success depends on whether at any given moment the conditions exist to enable largely unpredictable situations to be effectively exploited as they arise. Those conditions will be a function of the various components of organizational design, (see Figure 9.1) providing the link between some broadly defined concept of 'strategic intent'[13] (to adopt Hamel and Prahalad's (1994) term) and behavioural outcomes whose overall collective result is organizational performance.

In this scenario, strategic management has three key roles. The first is to give very careful consideration to the definition and quantification of the organization's strategic intent. The second is to make some extremely difficult decisions by giving or withholding support for initiatives and proposals which could have critical significance for the long-term (and hence unknowable) future of the business.

The third and in many ways the most important is to think and debate very long and hard about the sort of behaviour which is most likely to deliver the required level of performance. That has two implications. The first is spending a great deal of time debating and

FIGURE 9.1   The critical link

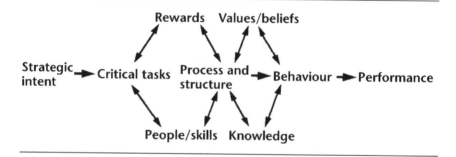

deciding the sort of people who should be recruited, promoted and developed into key jobs in the organization and ensuring that an equivalent amount of time and brainpower is devoted to exactly those issues at every subsequent level.

A key part of the process is to ensure that job holders are prepared for their roles, through first-class training and development including rich and varied experience, given full authority to carry them out and held accountable for their results. Included within this remit should be the criteria for selection and development and retention of young entrants.

The other key issue is to ensure that learning is seen as the key value of the organization. One way of doing this will be to ensure that programmes and processes are in place to bring together people regularly from all parts of the organization to discuss issues and share ideas and then act upon them.

The most effective way of doing that will be for top management to participate in as many of those activities as they can and to spend a great deal of their time listening.

In this way over time (about ten years), the purpose and values of the organization will gradually become apparent, shaped by the type of people who have achieved success and influence. This might be a good time to write them down and publish them.

Notes

1. Not an entirely original idea. The Greek philosopher Heraclitus was of a similar view about 2500 years ago. However, Chaos Theory is based on the mathematics of non-linear systems from which the notion of the 'butterfly's wing effect' derives. Stacey is saying that the future is unknowable because random events in the environment create totally unpredictable interactions with business organizations which are themselves non-linear feedback systems.
2. According to Stacey's analysis, managing the shorter-term future is a different matter. Project plans and budgets, monitoring and control systems and all the panoply of periodic planning and review cycles operate within a timeframe within which linear feedback conditions still apply. Two quite distinct approaches (and mind-sets) are therefore needed for dealing with different time horizons within the same organization. The point at which predictability breaks down (i.e. the system becomes 'non-linear') may well vary from industry to industry, although probably not by much.
3. 'Ambiguously defined' in the sense that, because of the complex network of relationships of which organizations are comprised, it is virtually impossible

to distinguish clearly between relationships that are internal and those that are external. Indeed the extreme post-modernist position (which will not be developed in this chapter) is that organizations are no more than the figment of a particular ('modernist') way of thinking and that they should not be conceived as discrete entities at all.

4. More recently, under the influence of Peter Senge who talks about 'Building a Shared Vision' (1990), the messages have become more subtle and more realistic.

5. The school of thought referred to as the Excellence Movement was as much initiated by *In Search of Excellence* (1982).

6. In the process, a new irregular verb seems to have been introduced into the English language: 'I control, you empower, they are empowered'.

7. These are themselves phrases which risk becoming part of the litany of repulsive jargon which Kellaway scorns.

8. Interestingly, the recently released 'Presidential Tapes' have given support to the view that Kennedy's finest hour as a leader was at the time of the Cuban Missile Crisis when (having learned painful lessons from the Bay of Pigs fiasco) he consciously exercised 'weak leadership'. In other words, during the long discussions about how to handle the crisis, he avoided adopting a clear position, encouraged all points of view to be aired and challenged those who based their arguments on dogma and rhetoric rather than logic and imagination.

9. In the sense of attitudes, motives and behaviours which depart from established norms.

10. Defined by Gillian Stamp in a memorable phrase as 'What you do when you don't know what to do' (Stamp and Stamp, 1993).

11. A quality which sounds remarkably similar to Peter Senge's 'Fifth Discipline' (Senge, 1990).

12. Churchill was relying on values which were the legacy of Empire; unfortunately, he failed to appreciate that the British people's interpretation of those values was changing and that they had a different view of the end state from him which was why they rejected him as a leader in 1945.

13. Strategic intent defines the chosen arenas in which the company intends to operate (a key decision or top management) and setting ambitious but realistic goals within the further limits of the predictable future.

References

Collins, J.C. and Porras, J.I. (1994), *Built to Last: Successful Habits of Visionary Companies*, Harper Business, New York.

Geus, A. de (1988), 'Planning as Learning' *Harvard Business Review*, Vol. 69, March–April, pp. 70–74.

Gleick, J. (1987), *Chaos, Making a New Science*, Heinemann, Portsmouth, NH.

Goddard, J. (1997), 'The Architecture of Core Competence', *Business Strategy Review*, Vol. 8, No. 1, pp. 43–52.

Hamel, G. and Prahalad, C.K. (1994), *Competing for the Future*, Harvard Business School Press, Boston, MA.

Hayek, F.A. (1944), *The Road to Serfdom*, Routledge and Kegan Paul, London.

Kellaway, L. (1997), 'Beware: Vision and Values Can Damage Your Company', *Financial Times*, 15 September.

Mintzberg, H. (1994), *The Rise and Fall of Strategic Planning*, Prentice Hall International, Hemel Hempstead.

Peters, T.J. and Waterman, R.H. (1982), *In Search of Excellence*, Harper and Row, New York.

Schwenk, C.R. (1997), 'The Case for "Weaker" Leadership', *Business Strategy Review*, Vol. 8, No. 1, pp. 4–9.

Senge, P.M. (1990), *The Fifth Discipline*, Doubleday, New York.

Stacey, R.D. (1992), *Managing the Unknowable; Strategic Boundaries between Order and Chaos in Organisations*, Jossey Bass, San Francisco.

Stamp, G. and Stamp, C. (1993), 'Well-being at Work: Aligning Purposes, People, Strategies and Structure', *International Journal of Career Management*, Vol. 5, No. 3.

CHAPTER TEN

Limits to visioning

Frédéric Nortier and Nello Bernard Abramovici

Today's organizations are, more than ever, dynamic systems facing the contrasting forces of the global environment. World-wide markets, aggressive competitors, confrontation with different norms and legislation, discovery of different cultural needs and habits, are all factors that illustrate an increasing interaction with external realities. In so doing, they induce stronger organizational openness which, de facto, creates a need for not only a higher level of relationships with other systems, and for an ongoing flux of information and knowledge to integrate, but also leads to a higher level of unpredictability, incertitude, instability, and the prospect of continuously facing the unknown. This situation represents a critical paradox for every senior executive in charge of leading an organization towards future success: the complexity factor fosters the desire to be in control, to structure the environment and to predict the future, while this same environment is becoming increasingly unpredictable and unstable.

Such circumstances strongly question the validity of any visioning process. Too many so-called visions are well-designed, well-structured, with formal descriptions of a very precise nature relating to the desired state of the organization in the future. A three- to five-page mission statement, presented as an organizational vision, may be an important intellectual or conceptual contribution to strategic management. But as such, it can only be something which remains external to people, and, therefore, have a limited impact on their motivations, their actions or their contributions. Is it still possible, then, to call it a 'vision'?

In 1995, Jeffrey Abrahams collected 301 corporate mission statements from a number of America's top companies. Many are presented as visions, but it appears that few really are. Some of them offer an eight-page long statement of commitments which are so complete and detailed that they can neither be grasped by the individual, nor interpreted in creative ways by people. Such statements are too self-

and internally focused, overstructured, overpredictive, and are likely to generate little action and result in the avoidance of change. Visions stated in such a way can easily give the impression that situations within these organizations have become the only reference and that no external environment can influence them. Such beliefs lead to organizational closure, as they are of little value to the organization. Moreover, they are dangerous, since such notions strongly reduce the ability of the organization to adapt or to evolve outside the mission statement.

In contrast, other statements provide a one-sentence or one-paragraph description of how the organization desires to approach the future. These are closer to what are considered to be effective visions in the long term: less descriptive, less prescriptive, more global, more inspiring. The statement of Aztech Controls Corporation is a good illustration of this second category of vision (Jeffrey Abrahams, pp. 92–93):

Vision statement

To be recognized by our customers, vendors, and employees as the industry leader.

Mission Statement

To exceed our goals by embracing the changes in technology, and distribution that results in growth and reinvestment.

Guiding principles

- Integrity is the foundation of our business.

- Anticipate and create new ways to add value.

- Teamwork is vital throughout the company.

- Quality is what the customer states it is.

Action, decision making, customer service, work organization, goal setting and management practices are considered as deeply influenced and focused through such a vision. This example shows how a vision can influence current action and behaviour, by defining an organizational ambition, by setting the direction, by providing certain desirable behaviours and goals, without trying to predict any definitive future.

An effective vision has to be open to unpredictable events, not overly detailed, and not focused on specific outcomes. An effective vision provides a perspective, an ambition of how people as the human system involved in a company want to operate in philosopohical terms, in terms of decision making, in terms of serving customers, in approaching the environment, in dealing with people, in measuring success, or adding value to the global society. Vision gives a simple but powerful insight into what an organization would like to be, how to function and to express itself as a complex living system.

A vision should not be fixed. It is recognized that visions can be powerful and motivational because of their inspiring and stimulating impact on people. A vision has to be open to other possibilities (individual and collective), which may remain unknown whilst it is being created. A vision should provide new perspectives, not a reduction of them. To some extent, a vision provides an existential answer to the following question: 'What kind of organization do we want to be, or do we want to become?' in much the same way as an individual would try to address the question: 'What kind of person or human being do I want to be in five years' time?'. By so doing, the individual is setting a target, but not the precise way in which to reach it.

In order to avoid a one-shot vision, and to provide effective conditions in which to create a vision, there are several limits or pitfalls that senior executives need to avoid.

Giving a vision for all, not for an elite

To be effective, a vision cannot remain within a group of a 'happy few' senior executives. To generate new enthusiasm, new shared energy, a vision has to become a collective driver. The visioning process usually starts with the CEO, the managing director, or the management team. They all play a key role in such a process, and it is primarily their responsibility to provide future direction for the organization.

Although visions emanate from or require the approval of the top management team, one danger exists with the fact that the top team holds such exclusive responsibility. The management team is usually the first group to elaborate on and experiment with the vision. However, the group that created the vision may be the only one to benefit. An effective visioning process usually generates a good team spirit and interpersonal dynamic among people when the vision is being moulded and expressed. People tend to describe the stage of the sequence as being uniquely emotional, insightful and creative. Often, there is a tendency to try to preserve this moment, and to avoid the risk of losing the dynamic once the group decides to open up and share it with the rest of the organization.

The management team of the IT department of a French public health care institution experienced an intense visioning process which allowed it to create a vision of the kind of department the team wanted it to be in three years, vis-à-vis the internal clients. The members also agreed on the core values to be developed within the management team that should be displayed within the department. This greatly increased team spirit, the effectiveness of their teamwork, and the quality of the decision-making process. It allowed the building of new relationships among the team members on both a professional and personal level, to improve global effectiveness of their management practices, and to lead their department to real success in a fast changing, complex and uncertain environment, for three years. But during this period, only they were aware of the vision. The 'credo' was 'Let's act our vision, not talk *the vision!*'

Little by little, the team's members became isolated from the rest of the department. Frustration grew among their direct reports, who had the feeling that their management team was too self-centred and kept things secret, was unwilling to share issues that could be impactful and helpful to the rest of the department. What was initially intended to improve management effectiveness became counterproductive. The management team sensed these feelings – the inability to lead the whole group and failure to share the vision – but was afraid of losing the management team dynamic if they started to discuss the vision freely with all others in the department!

This is a classical example. By falling into this trap, a management team experiences a strong feeling of belonging which, in the end, focuses more on maintaining the current situation than on what can be built in the future. This is reinforced by a frequent reaction: once the vision is clear for a management team, it becomes so obvious to its members that they neither see, nor realize that the rest of the organization is still lacking a future perspective.

The emergence of a new dynamic is an essential step in the visioning process, but is only a step. Taking the risk to set aside an effective but limited dynamic, in order to allow a new and more collective one to emerge, is another step, but a critical one. Any management team that delays in taking this risk, will progressively cut itself off from the rest of the organization and experience a tangible limit to the visioning process.

Visioning allows a company to move ahead in an unfolding environment by providing meaningful and certain guidelines for an emerging self-organization.

As stated already, to create a vision, a group ambition shared by six or eight people, with only a few guidelines, leads to a complex human system.

One can easily imagine that a corporate vision created for a company of several thousands of people, could lead to such a level of complexity that no computer could cope with it. Any attempt to control and predict the future with a visioning process is an illusion and will not generate an effective visioning dynamic. It can become a stimulating intellectual exercise, it can be reassuring, it can provide strategic planning, it may help to set up a control system, but it will not be a vision!

Executives should bear in mind that the visioning process should always be distinguished from the final sentence, paragraph or statement which will come out of the process. One of the limits to visioning is to rely only on the final product, the sentence expressing the vision, and to forget to use and display the process in the organization. Top teams who start to share on the 'beautiful statement' they have created, are leading the visioning process to a dead end! To be successful, top teams will have to find a way to display, simultaneously, the statement and the process. The combination of these two elements, and a high level of consistency between them, will lead to effective visioning. Visioning and the vision should always be addressed together.

Visioning is similar to an entrepreneurial process. The entrepreneur who decides to create a company, has a conception of the kind of organization he/she wants to achieve. This is the starting point to an organizational experience. The entrepreneur's vision must provide space and freedom for those who will join the company. Everyone will need to identify that one's personal contribution is possible, even though he/she was not involved in the initial definition of the company's vision.

Expanding access to the vision, spreading the vision throughout the company, allowing, progressively, the vision to become alive at every level of the organization, permits the vision to exist beyond those who have created it. An organization is a living system where not everyone can play a part in the initial creation of the vision. However, the visioning process should allow people to join in during that process. The process needs to be flexible so that people have the possibility of appropriating the vision into their function, and in personal ways. A vision which does not provide such an extension to others, is little more than a simple intention or a simple dream.

Providing open inspiration, not futurism

Visioning should not mean presenting a description of the future, even though it will allow people to recognize a way to relate to the environment. Any too detailed vision reduces the possibility of identifying the personal contribution they could make to the fulfilment of the vision. Visioning is powerful and effective when it fosters imagination, creativeness, self-contribution, openness in the future, and new personal and professional options.

Any attempt to describe the future, in terms of specific mission, roles, contributions, products and services, impact on the market, organizational rules and systems, means adopting a predictable and deterministic approach if not demonstrating an omnipotent attitude. It is denying the environment, the complexity of today's and tomorrow's economical and social worlds, the existence of all other complex living organizations, and it is denying the existence of human beings and their ability to self-organise for the organization's sake.

A vision must inspire and challenge every individual in the organization. It must allow personal ways to link the vision to one's job, to open up different perspectives, and to stimulate finding out how it will influence every function in the organization.

The kind of energy and the kind of self-organization generated by an effective vision is quite similar to what can be observed in a flock of birds flying in the evening light, like starlings in the fall. A flock of starlings has a global scope, which continuously changes, but which remains a flock. Each bird flies as part of the flock. Each bird seems confident in the overall group because it 'knows' that each bird plays its part in the main aim to create a flock. The exact form of the flock is not decided, nor could be, but the idea of having a global shape is there. Each bird experiences that its action is contributing to something larger and bigger, and that this is the best way to reach the common goal. This analogy is limited, but interesting, because it illustrates how visioning provides freedom, improvisation and autonomy. Imagine if greater forces were to decide precisely what each bird should do, and where to do it . . . it would be the best way to make the flock impossible! It is also a pleasant example to consider. In observing birds flying at twilight one has a strong feeling and sense that these birds gain pleasure in moving together!

The flock of birds example illustrates how a living system can organize itself in order to achieve a common goal or common purpose. Self-organization is a key factor for the success of a vision, since the vision itself does not provide the 'how' to achieve it. There is a famous training exercise that illustrates how a self-organizing pattern can emerge effectively in a group by providing some group rules or guidelines. Three guidelines are given to the group:

1   Select, mentally, two persons in the group.

2   Position yourself at an equidistant point from the two.

3   Maintain the equidistant position while people move around.

If each member of the group applies these 'guiding principles', a group pattern will soon emerge, but how is totally unpredictable. As in visioning, the guidelines are clear, and represent a common agreement on something to achieve or to aim for, but the final result and how to get there, remains unknown. The overall shape or figure cannot be predicted, but the spirit or the idea of a shape can be stimulated by the definition of a meaning, or by guidelines. No one can predict who will choose whom. No one can predict where people will stand in the room. No one can predict how the different equidistant positions will be influenced by the relationships and movements within the group. Most people tend to believe that this exercise can lead only to a static figure or pattern after some minutes. But in most situations, the emerging pattern is a dynamic one, which keeps the group in endless motion. The group will soon experiment with new situations and define, with autonomy, new guidelines such as different ways to position the equidistant point, or to reproduce attractive lines in the movement. The group will also recognize that it needs additional rules to be able to maintain and monitor the previous one.

Similar processes can be observed in the way visions are achieved. An effective vision will release a personal and individual response from each member of the organization, which will be in harmony with the responses of others. It is the release of an individual response driven by a collective issue. In so being, people will feel comfortable with it, despite, or because of, the autonomy level: each knows that his/her response, idea, action fits with the global organizational response, idea and purpose.

The kind, and the amount of information that people need in order to act and contribute effectively to a vision, varies greatly from one person to another. There is a well-known metaphor about three young fellows in the Middle Ages, who were travelling around 'Old Europe' to discover and to learn about the art of architecture. One day, while they were walking in the English countryside, they came to a little town where hundreds of people were very busy on a large building site next to the town. All the different types of craftsmen were represented. The young travellers walked about the place, curious about what was going on there and wondering if they could find an opportunity to get a job as apprentices. They came to a place where a mason was engrossed in his art. Curious, one the three fellows asked: 'What are you doing, master mason?' 'I am building a beautiful wall. I need someone to help me if one of you wants to learn my art.' One of the three fellows was interested in learning to build walls, so he took the job and said farewell to his friends. These two walked on until they came across another mason doing exactly the same thing as the two previous masons. 'What are you doing, master mason?' The man looked at them and answered, embracing the whole place with his arms to include the whole building site: 'I am building a cathedral! I need assistants to help you if you want to learn my art.' The fellows found that building a cathedral was a far more exciting job than simply sculpting a stone or building a wall, so they took the job.

In this metaphor, each youth ends up sculpting stones. Only one chooses to work for the first master mason because the other two could understand the purpose in doing that task. The first young man concentrated on the individual stone he was carving and was happy and motivated by these being used in the building of walls. He sculpted stones, which he found a hard and less than exciting a task, until he could see how each stone fitted and contributed to the wall he was building. The other two youths also agreed to sculpt stone, but they found their motivation in thinking how each stone contributed to a most important and beautiful cathedral.

Sometimes it is important for people to be able to focus on their current and short-term contribution. Sometimes, 'building a wall' is necessary in order for progress and for defining meaning to guide one's action. Sometimes, 'building a cathedral' may become the key collective driver in engaging in an important, long-term process. In the Middle Ages, each cathedral master builder knew that his vision was the key motivational driver to start building a cathedral. They had a vision of what the cathedral should look like, and they knew that it would be accomplished, though fully aware that the end result could be different from their vision because of unpredictable matters involving architecture, politics, financing and craftwork. They were also aware that by the time the cathedral was finished they could well be dead! When Antonio Gaudí created the Sagrada Familia in his mind, it was a revolutionary vision for the late 19th century, of a cathedral for the city of Barcelona. However, one hundred years later, the power of his vision is still real. It still provides a strong collective driver for the Catholic Church, architects, craftsmen and bankers. The vision of the cathedral is even now evolving, new materials are being used, as are new colours and new building technologies. The people now working on the project never met Gaudí, and will probably never see the cathedral finished, since the most optimistic plans forecast completion in about the year 2050! But Gaudí's vision is still operating.

Being process-driven, not deadline-driven

It takes time for a vision to influence organizational patterns such as decision making, professional behaviours, cross-departmental inter-actions, organizational beliefs, power structures, and customer service. A vision is something very personal, but not individual.

An effective vision strongly impacts on people's inner being. This could almost be described as an intimate impact, the nature of which will vary from one person to another. It is a key factor in effective visioning.

Once a vision has been created by a management team, there is too often a tendency to expect that others will quickly be committed to the vision, and to make it theirs. This is a dangerous mistake for management teams to make, since they might start enacting the vision and taking it for granted, whereas the rest of the organization may not yet have developed an intimate commitment to it. Each group in an organization has different priorities, different paces of activity and specific time frame perspectives. Pacing the impact of a visioning process in respect of each level of the organization, and of each group's specific timeframe perspective, is another key factor in effectiveness.

Creating vision for a future concrete world, not a virtual one

Some leaders tend to jump from vision to vision. Visionary leaders and teams have an ability to project themselves into the future. However, there can arise a dangerous mental bias, by which a future perception is progressively considered to be a current one, or something already achieved. When such an issue is not considered, the vision becomes virtual. Visioning should not be an avoidance of the present, but an ambition to take note of the present in order to reach a new organizational level.

Visioning must strike a balance between projection in time and proximity to current environment. The deadline by which a vision should materialize is difficult to define. It has to be far ahead to become a vision driver, but if it is too far ahead, it will no longer be seen to be a vision. Too long term visions are unlikely to generate commitment because people are not able to project themselves. A regional director of a major French insurance company, once had a real vision of what the sector would be like in the year 2040! He was strongly committed to his vision, and it was an effective driver for him. However, it failed to become an organizational driver because his employees could not buy into this vision. People considered it to be too abstract, a kind of dream, and totally disconnected from their reality. Some even had difficulties in identifying with such a future perspective, since they considered that they might no longer be in the organization by that time. With such a time span, it was impossible for the great majority of them to feel involved as organizational contributors.

To be effective, a vision requires enough flexibility for people to find practical involvement in, and consequences for, their personal contribution to the fulfilment of the vision. Everyone involved in a vision needs to see and feel how he or she will influence the context in making the vision happen. A vision which does not stimulate people in their present job and contribution has little chance of being achieved, and will most likely be quickly forgotten.

Conclusion

Visioning is not a managerial recipe; it cannot be applied as a technology, by following instructions. However, despite the various limits described above, it is an essential component of the executive's job. Visioning is, by essence, a typically human process. It is the expression of a human characteristic, which cannot be replaced by any computer system, nor be ignored when thinking about organizational effectiveness.

Effective visioning is the result of a mix of 'Rational – Emotional – Impulsive' dimensions. It is the specific way of addressing these three dimensions together. In today's organizations, it is evident that these three dimensions are usually considered contradictory. The current dominant model is still based exclusively on the rational dimension. Despite all the criticism of Taylor's model, or of the military's, they still deeply influence the executive's mind. Even the word 'organization' is an illustration of the 'rational' dimension. As a result, it is frequently observed that one or two of these human dimensions are preferred to certain others. Taking into account only one or two of them cannot be enough or be effective, even in the mid-term.

Visioning is the unique process that allows links between one's mind, heart and gut! Effective visioning is the unique result of combining these factors, and a specific way of taking all three of them into account. Of course, it is based on the assumption that a CEO, managing director or management team, is able to be in contact with these three and willing to use them. It would seem that this is seldom the case, and probably why real visions are rare.

Because of the increasing complexity of today's organization, visioning will become a key competitive advantage. The strength of a vision, based on a consistent mind–heart–gut integration, is a key factor in individual success. The same applies for a group, or a human system. It provides meaning and existential purpose, which are deep human needs.

Reference

Abraham, J. (1995) *The Mission Statement Book: 301 Corporate Mission Statements from America's Top Companies*, Ten Speed Press, Canada.

Index

3 5282 00469 1195